Thank you. By b[illegible] [illegible]ervice customer you are helping save the world's remaining rhinos.

The CRASH *of* RHINOS

Rhino Ray

RAY DEARLOVE

www.rhinoray.com.au

www.rhinoray.com.au

ISBN 978-0-6487578-0-1 (print)
ISBN 978-0-6487578-1-8 (digital)

Printed in Australia by McPherson's Printing Group
Cover design by briobooks.com.au

FSC
www.fsc.org
MIX
Paper from
responsible sources
FSC® C011613

The paper this book is printed on is in accordance with the standards of the Forest Stewardship Council®. The FSC® promotes environmentally responsible, socially beneficial and economically viable management of the world's forests.

CONTENTS

FOREWORD

With my African heritage, I am deeply concerned about the threats to endangered species by poachers. As an example, on average, three rhinos are killed every day for their horns which are believed by some people to have mystical powers to cure anything from the common cold to cancer. The reality is that rhino horn is made of keratin, a protein found in human hair and fingernails.

I cannot conceive of a world without rhinos and a few years ago, Ray kindly invited me to sit on a panel discussing the rhino crisis at the launch of The Australian Rhino Project. Sadly, since that date, more than 6000 rhinos have been slaughtered for their horns. I am very happy to support any efforts to save rhinos from extinction in the wild. I have observed Ray working tirelessly to play his part and *The Crash of Rhinos* is a bittersweet account of his journey. As in my sport, situations such as this require tenacity and resilience and Ray's innovative approach provides hope for the remaining rhinos on our planet.

George Gregan AM
Former captain of the Australian Wallabies

I have known Ray for several years and have watched with interest his tireless work to help prevent the extinction of rhinos in the wild.

Rhinos face so many challenges including loss of habitat, human encroachment into their lands and the might of the international crime syndicates who create havoc with poaching for their horns. People like Ray Dearlove with their passion and resilience are making a difference and their work is so important.

The Crash of Rhinos shows us just how much one person can achieve. I hope that it inspires and encourages you to take action to help the world's remaining rhinos.

Jane Goodall, PhD, DBE
Founder, the Jane Goodall Institute & United Nations Messenger of Peace

"YOU CAN SEE RHINOS AROUND

EVERY CORNER"

I had requested a meeting with the South African Minister for the Environment, Edna Molewa, in late 2014 to brief her about my plan to relocate rhinos from South Africa to Australia and establish a breeding herd as an insurance policy in the event of extinction in the wild, a project I had named The Australian Rhino Project (TARP). The meeting was facilitated by the Australian Minister for the Environment, Greg Hunt, who had proven to be a strong supporter of the project.

The meeting had an interesting start. I was waiting outside the Sydney Olympic Park boardroom when the door opened and Wendy Black, Greg Hunt's Chief of Staff, saw me and gave me a wink. Shortly before 10am, Minister Molewa and her large entourage walked up the stairs to the boardroom. I stood up to introduce myself and at the same time, the boardroom door opened and there was Minister Hunt. He saw me, came over and said, *"Ah Ray, good to see you. By chance I've just met with the head of the WWF, Carter Roberts, and I was telling him about your wonderful project."*

Minister Molewa was standing by quietly and I asked her if she had met Minister Hunt, she said she hadn't, so I said to Greg, *"I'd like to introduce you to Minister Molewa."* Both seemed pleased with the introduction. I felt like Henry Kissinger.

Minister Molewa had responsibility for the wellbeing of rhinos and other endangered species and it was critical that she had a clear understanding of what I was trying to to achieve. I hoped to gain her support for the plan. Her first question was not an unreasonable one: Why did I think that Australia was safe from rhino poachers? My answers had been well researched and practiced and I explained that, as an island, Australia has robust border controls; there is little comparable poverty or corruption in Australia; there is no history of poaching in the country and, because of the size of Australia, there is no community pressure on wildlife areas. Furthermore, if there were to be just one poaching incident, there would be an uproar – led by the media. The Australian media is not to be meddled with.

I was stunned when Minister Molewa responded, *"But Ray, you can see rhinos around every corner in the Kruger Park."*

Then, and still today, South Africa was losing three rhinos a day to poaching, mainly in the Kruger National Park. A total of 1004 rhinos had been slaughtered the year before and the monthly kill rate had jumped to over 100 in 2014. Could the minister be serious? With a value of approximately US$23 billion per annum, illegal wildlife trafficking is the fourth most lucrative global crime after drugs, humans and weaponry. The international crime syndicates, mostly Asia-based, considered rhino poaching low-risk but with extraordinarily high returns.

I was the sole representative of TARP at the meeting while the minister brought along eleven members of her support staff. There was not enough room at the boardroom table so some had to find seats along the wall.

As the minister dropped this bombshell, I glanced at the others for any reaction to her provocative statement. There was none – everyone had their eyes down gazing intently at their notes. My mind was racing, the retort was so unexpected. Was she trying to be amusing and this was just a throwaway line? I didn't think so. Was she trivialising the issue? Perhaps. Was she in denial? Perhaps. Or was she asserting that she was in complete control of the situation and the global focus on rhino poaching in South

Africa was unreasonable, misinformed and unwelcome, and the last thing that she needed was help from outside, particularly from Australia? I felt it was a reckless and unnecessary comment and it troubled me.

Having lectured me for the first twenty-five minutes of the meeting, the minister finally heard me out but made

The author with the late Edna Molewa, South African Minister of Water and Environmental Affairs

it clear that, while my plan certainly had merit, there was a comprehensive strategy in play in South Africa to counter the poaching crisis and that all of these strategies needed to be tested before considering any offshore or ex-situ solution such as TARP.

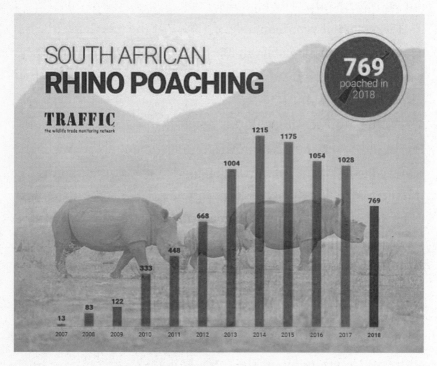

Source: South African Department of Environmental
Affairs, Forestry & Fisheries

It is worth noting that the total number of rhinos poached in South Africa had increased from 13 in 2007 to peak at 1,215 in 2014 and has marginally reduced each year since. These numbers are jaw-dropping and unsustainable. The South African authorities, for reasons best known to themselves, no longer publish regular poaching statistics. Why hide the true situation? If the official numbers are not made public, people will make up their own numbers. My personal view has always been that the official statistics are understated by up to 20 per cent simply because where the rhinos roam, the authorities don't find all the carcasses – the Kruger Park is a vast area, about the size of Israel or Wales and, it is also sparsely populated, so the number of dead rhinos since 2007 is more likely to be closer to 9,500 in total.

This dire situation persists despite millions of dollars being thrown at the anti-poaching onslaught – conservative estimates are more than R600 million (US$45 million) and yet the poaching numbers remain stubbornly high. One could argue that the reason for the recent decline in the reported numbers is because the few remaining rhinos are that much more difficult to find.

Corruption is rife at every level of government in the countries of Africa and Asia involved in rhino poaching. Further, human lives are at stake. The poachers are ruthless, as evidenced by the near fatal stabbing attack on Dave Powrie and his wife in 2015; Dave is the warden of one of South Africa's best-known game reserves.

The conversation with Minister Molewa threw some light on why I was having so much difficulty with South African National Parks (SANParks) and other South African Government agencies in my attempts to source rhinos for the translocation program. I realised that TARP was going to be a very tough road to travel. I also sensed some resentment that it was Australia, rather than other countries, offering to assist.

With approximately 4,000 rhinos killed since the minister and I met, I very much doubt it's possible to see many rhinos around any corner. Tellingly, in a statement from July 2018, she said that strategies to keep rhinos safe from poaching now included translocation alternatives. What a difference a few years and 4,000 rhino carcasses make.

If anything, Minister Molewa's glib comments steeled my resolve to help prevent the extinction of this iconic species by bringing them to Australia.

A FEW WILD IDEAS TO

PROTECT OUR WILDLIFE

I spent thirty-three years of my life selling IT solutions in South Africa, Europe, Australia and Asia, and by my standards I had a successful career. Those who know me could never accuse me of being overly technical. The success I had in my sales career was almost entirely due to relationships. I worked really hard on building and nurturing such relationships, never more so than when we arrived in Australia.

With no money, no friends, leaving South Africa was tough. Margie and I had really good jobs in South Africa, great friends and a wonderful, if false, lifestyle. Arriving in Australia with a young family, a container of furniture and not much else, I determined there and then that I would focus on building relationships and a network in Australia, if not just for Margie and me, but for our children Paul, Kevin and Hayley. I did not regard this as a burden, I like people and I like meeting new people. My time as General Manager at Sydney University Rugby Club certainly gave me a head start. It is the epitome of a high-quality networking organisation.

I was born in Pietersburg in South Africa in the days when driving in the countryside, you would see kudu, impala, giraffe and, if you were really fortunate, a leopard. The Kruger National Park was three hours away and since the closest beach was about twelve hours away, we took all of our holidays in this paradise of wild animals.

My parents could not afford a car, so we would all squeeze into their good friends Frank and Phyllis Locke's vehicle and set off for the park. My earliest memories are of camping at Punda Maria or Pafuri with my sister and my parents; camp fires, communal toilets and animals calling in the night. I can still recall the awe and shock of meeting an elephant on one of the gravel roads near Shingwedzi. Fortunately, Frank maintained control of his car despite plenty of advice from the back seat. More than sixty years later, my love for wild animals, and the Kruger National Park, is undiminished and somehow, I managed visits to one or another game reserve every year until we emigrated to Australia in 1987.

Around 2009, news started to emerge about the threat of poaching in Southern Africa. Until this time, the region had been spared the onslaught on the rest of the continent's rhinos and elephants.

Well before TARP was established, as I thought about the perils of endangered species and how the whole poaching issue was spiralling out of control, I had what I thought was a great idea and called the CEO of the World Wildlife Fund, Jim Leape, at the Switzerland headquarters. I was connected with the Chief Operating Officer, who was quite encouraging and suggested that I write to Jim and outline my proposal.

"I am South African born and now live in Australia. Growing up, I was fortunate enough to be taken to the Kruger Park by my parents on an annual basis. Wildlife and conservation have always been extremely important to me and my family. As you know, the poaching situation with a number of species is dire, with elephants and rhinos of particular concern, and I'm sure front of mind for the WWF.

Here in Australia, and I am sure across the rest of the world, there is an endless stream of advertisements that feature the 'African Big Five' and other endangered animals such as tigers and cheetahs.

If your product is 'fast', the cheetah is featured in the advertisement; if your product is 'strong', the rhino or elephant are featured or, if your product depicts stealth, it is tigers or leopards and so on. The question is, how can we harness this global interest in wildlife and direct some proceeds of using their images for marketing purposes into endangered species conservation?

My proposal is that each global Fortune 500 CEO be approached with a request that, should their company wish to feature any such endangered species in their advertising (and they should be encouraged to do so), that company would pay a nominal 'commission or fee' to the WWF for the use of that image. My sense is that the commercial world has changed and continues to change and executives are much more aware and concerned about public perception of their products or services than ever before.

These companies may well ask 'What's in it for me?' and there are many answers to that question, including ensuring that such animals are not confined to zoos in the future; being seen as good corporate citizens as well as demonstrating good faith in humanity. In terms of cost to these organisations it would be miniscule. In terms of benefits and the goodwill which would be generated, these are infinite. So many people want to contribute but don't know how to go about it. They want to ensure that their children and their children's children will experience the magic of animals in the wild as opposed to seeing some sad creatures in a zoo.

In return, these global organisations would be permitted to use the WWF Panda logo as a certification. This would add enormous credibility to their advertising campaigns – the Panda logo is an extremely powerful brand. The competitive nature of business is such that if just one organisation signs up, others will rapidly follow."

I really thought that this proposal was exciting, had merit and was worthy of discussion and a trial, but the response that I received from Suds, Head of WWF Communications, was disappointing. Jim asked him to review my suggestion and while Suds agreed that WWF was in a position to drive change, the company's strategy aimed at encouraging businesses to tackle climate change. WWF worked with companies to transform the way they do business and influence markets, bringing together investors, consumers and political leaders to work through complex issues, but his view was licensing on corporate advertising would not fit with their "current business engagement strategy."

I saw this as a pretty poor response and felt that Jim Leape/Suds had not given my idea a great deal of thought; it was a potential winner for all parties. That was the end of the conversation, but in truth, the proposal is even more valid today than it was four years ago. Perhaps a WWF executive might read this book and have a light-bulb moment.

A young rhino greets the day. (Photo credit: Shannon Wild)

Undeterred, a few months later, I reached out to Pfizer Corporation, the manufacturers of Viagra, with what I thought was another absolute cracker of an idea to curb the usage of rhino horn in Asian countries. Throughout my career, I had come to realise that if you want something to happen, you start at the top of the tree and I wrote to Ian Read, CEO of Pfizer International in New

York, requesting his support for what might be called a "left-field" proposition. I explained who I was and briefed him about the three rhinos being killed each and every day by poachers for their horns which are believed to have magical powers, including curing cancer and also improving sexual performance. I stressed that there was no clinical evidence to support any such claims, but that the demand for horn was actually on the increase because of the increased affluence of the Vietnamese and the Chinese – the biggest users of rhino horn. *"I passionately believe that rhinos must be available to the world in the wild, not only in zoos."*

I then outlined my proposal that we work with his team at Pfizer on a campaign which basically said, "Viagra works. Rhino horn doesn't".

As I said to Ian, this may seem simplistic, but the message was crystal clear and I concluded by saying, *"This is not a frivolous exercise, we cannot allow the oldest mammal on our planet to become extinct on our watch".*

Soon after, I received a response from Ms Oonagh Puglisi, Director, Corporate Responsibility, Pfizer Foundation, who was asked by Ian Read to respond and she said that, unfortunately, Pfizer were not in a position to extend support. Their strategy was *"to improve access to quality health care for underserved populations and their current focus was directing support towards non-communicable diseases, healthy aging and cardiovascular disease prevention."*

She had shared my proposed campaign slogan with their Viagra commercial team, but they were unable to provide endorsement to the idea, saying that, *"Viagra is a prescription-only medicine indicated for the treatment of erectile dysfunction in men."*

Well, not surprisingly, I didn't think that was a particularly helpful response; they had missed the point. I wasn't requesting support. I wrote back asking if we could have a telephone hook-up to discuss the proposal. Her response took quite a while, but eventually Ms Puglisi wrote back, saying that the idea was not a fit for funding from Pfizer and that they focus on the areas where they believe they can make the greatest difference and have focused on health care.

I hate being patronised and, in this instance, I really felt I was being patted away to extra cover. I wasn't asking for funding but was strongly of the view that wildlife trade is a global issue and will only be solved when the world realises that. So back I went. I had spent most of my life working for global American companies and was very familiar with the bureaucracy these organisations seem to breed. I wrote that while their decision was disappointing and I did understand their position, the world had to do something about educating the users of rhino horn and that a powerful message from a global leader in pharmaceuticals, such as Pfizer, that they were wasting their money and pushing an iconic animal into extinction was not only a positive message but a critical one. I concluded by reminding Ms Puglisi that solving this crisis was a global responsibility.

The dogs bark, but the caravan moves on.

By this time, I was pretty fired up and, unperturbed, I decided to approach Eli Lilly, the makers of Cialis – the competitor to Viagra. I wrote a similar letter to Ms Becky Morison, General Manager of Eli Lilly Australia, and received a response basically saying that they could not participate. I figured that I had nothing to lose and phoned Ms Morison. She turned out to be a terrific, sympathetic and passionate person who really wanted to help, but whose hands were tied by the constraints of her firm. She was kind enough to drop me a line after our conversation.

"Gosh Ray . . . as much as I love your initiative, I need to be transparent that submitting a request might not be a good use of time. I would not want you to take the time to complete and submit the application, when you likely have options with a closer fit."

So here we are, several years later and more than 5,000 rhinos dead in the interim, I still think it is a really good idea. Good friend, Julie Furlong, owner of the Design+Marketing Agency, pointed out that what I should have done was to include some potent imagery of a limp and droopy rhino horn. This may have made more of an impact.

Onwards and upwards.

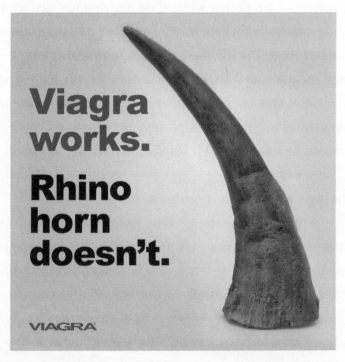

Graphic by Julie Furlong of D+M Pty Limited

In May 2013, my wife Margie and I were attending a wedding on the beautiful Hamilton Island in the Australian Whitsundays when I received an SMS from an unknown South African number. It turned out to be from Humphrey McAllister, with whom I had worked many years before at IBM in Johannesburg. Humph was deeply concerned about the plight of the rhino population in South Africa and, being a direct kind of guy, asked me to establish a breeding herd in Australia. Humph moved fast and followed up with a well-thought-out note reasoning why I should give this a go and why Australia seemed ideally suited as a destination.

"It will need movers and shakers like you to get things going, Ray." Thanks, Humph.

With the full support of my family, I decided to give it a go. My first visit to the famous Kruger Park had been when I was just four years old. I loved it and have loved it ever since. In addition, I had "sort of" retired but didn't really have the appetite to play golf five days a week or to spend my remaining years sitting in front of a computer swapping silly jokes with my retired friends. So why not, but where to start?

I called Glenn Phillips, CEO of the Kruger Park, for some "off the record" advice. He said that they were looking at all possible options and were currently moving rhinos to undisclosed "safe" havens in other parts of the country. He agreed that the situation was critical and their ability to fight the poaching scourge in such a vast area with limited resources was near impossible. He added that my type of solution could be one of the options in the tool box.

Being the eternal optimist, I took Glenn's advice as positive and my first phone call was to longtime friend Allan Davies. Allan and I met when our sons were at The King's School in Sydney, and we had been on rugby tours to France and New Zealand for Rugby World Cup tournaments. Why did I phone Allan? Demonstrating just how naïve I was, I knew that he and Lyn owned a large property in the Hunter Valley, north of Sydney, and quoting another Aussie mate: "*Ray thought he'd have a few rhinos running around the back paddock of Allan's place.*" Well not quite, but in truth not that far off.

The Australian Rhino Project was born on 1st June 2013. A relatively simple idea that was to become immensely complex and far-reaching. Margie and I met Allan and Lyn at the Boatshed Restaurant on spectacular Balmoral Beach. Allan's first reaction to my plan was one of uncontrolled mirth but once this had subsided, he looked at his wife Lyn and said "We're in." Allan is a fairly serious individual and also very conservative. How conservative, I was yet to find out. However, being the man of action that he can be if he believes in something, by the end of that day he had set up a meeting with the University of Sydney Veterinary School to discuss my proposal.

The Vet Faculty moved equally quickly and within a week Allan and I were sitting across the desk from Professor David Emery and Jackie Dalton. There are people one meets in life who immediately display their intellect and wisdom – David was one of these. David has a seriously impressive resume holding the title of Professor of Veterinary Parasitology at the University of Sydney. He had visited Africa on several occasions and clearly understood what we were trying to achieve and why. From that moment he was on our side. He made some enquiries from a friend in the Department of Agriculture who responded that the animals to be imported had to first spend a year in quarantine in *"an approved country/zoo or wildlife park"*. The ground rules were therefore very clear, although over time, they were cleverly manipulated by the Department of Agriculture to make compliance exceptionally difficult, if not impossible.

David alerted us by saying that we would fail unless we engaged with Taronga Zoo. This came as a shock to me – it wasn't something that I had considered at all. While I do understand the need for zoos, I do not like them at all. The sight of an animal, such as a lion, in a cage is a complete anathema to me.

The Taronga Conservation Society Australia, to give its full title, is a NSW state-owned zoo with two campuses, one in the beautiful surrounds of Mosman in Sydney where, as the story goes, the giraffes have the best view of the Opera House and Harbour Bridge. The second campus is outside a country town, Dubbo, about five hours west of Sydney, known as the Western Plains Zoo. Like Taronga, it is a special place. It is set on 300 hectares and is much more a safari park than a traditional zoo.

Throughout the journey thus far, I felt that the day would come when someone would sit across the table, pat me on the knee and say, *"Ray, this is a great idea and we admire your creativity and passion, but, sorry, old chap, it just won't work."* Was this about to happen when we met the Taronga management? Allan and I braced ourselves for what we expected to be a polite rebuff. But as Mark Twain said, *"The secret of getting ahead is getting started."*

My heart sank when David had said that we had to engage Taronga. Bringing rhinos from South Africa to live in an Australian zoo was never the objective. Allan, a man of the land, felt exactly the same way. Hence, it was with a very low level of expectation that we arranged a meeting with Cameron Kerr, Chief Executive of Taronga at his lovely office in Mosman.

Well, what a pleasant surprise for both of us. Unbeknown to us, Cam had long held the desire of doing something for the conservation of rhinos in Australia. After a lengthy and lively conversation, Cam gave us his in-principle support for two reasons – obviously conservation, but also to introduce some genetic diversity to the rhinos at Western Plains. He also provided us with a brief history of Taronga's long association with rhinos, having acquired its first black rhino way back in 1938. The decline of wild rhino populations spurred the organisation's former CEO, Dr John Kelly, to make a commitment to rhino conservation by becoming a founding member of the International Rhinoceros Foundation (IRF) in 1991. The IRF's principal objectives include support for in situ conservation projects for all species of rhinoceros and the development of captive breeding programs.

All of the world's five rhino species are on the verge of extinction and Taronga focuses on three species: the southern black rhino (critically endangered); southern white rhino (threatened), both from Africa, and the greater one-horned rhino from India and Nepal (vulnerable). When we met in 2014, Western Plains was home to twelve black and five southern white rhinos.

Initiatives to establish a captive breeding program at Western Plains began in 1990 with negotiations between the IRF and the Zimbabwean Government and eventually one male and seven female wild-caught black rhinos from the Zambezi Valley arrived in late 1992, imported under a Memorandum of Understanding (MOU) with the Government of Zimbabwe. This translocation was fully funded by the late Kerry Packer.

Prior to their arrival in Australia, the rhinos were quarantined on the Cocos Islands in the Indian Ocean for two months. A further four males were imported from the US in 1994 and breeding began in that year.

White rhinos have been at Taronga since 1980, when three animals were received from Europe. Over a period of twenty years, six calves were born, four of which died. In 1999 an Australasian region plan was initiated to acquire more rhinos and "target managing" them in more natural social groups of a male with multiple females since no successful breeding had occurred for the past ten years.

What really interested me was that in 2003 Taronga received two male and three female white rhinos from the Kruger Park. All these rhinos were wild-caught and then managed through the Australian authorities' prescribed pre-export quarantine facility in Kruger. Two of the females went to Monarto Safari Park in South Australia and the remainder to Western Plains. All of the costs were met by the two zoos. Since then each of the three imported females had birthed a number of calves. I was encouraged by the success of the previous precedents of importing rhinos to Australia thus giving me confidence that my plan could actually work.

We all agreed that to advance the project we needed to conduct a formal feasibility study, looking at vital logistical issues such as biosecurity; the regulatory hurdles that would be posed from government; possible timelines; and the funding challenges with a view to making a "go or no go" decision. Our unanimous view was that if we were to proceed with our plan, we would do it properly.

Cam Kerr's contribution was to provide a skilled resource from Taronga to lead the study and he made sure that we understood that we would be required to pay full market rates for such a resource. This came as a bit of a surprise that Taronga insisted that we pay commercial rates – full freight – for the costs of their nominated leader of a feasibility study. I thought at the time *"Is this really a partnership, aren't we all trying to achieve the same goal?"* Cam knew that we had no money but costed the resource at approximately $30,000 – a lot of money in anyone's language. Thank goodness Allan Davies, and not for the last time, undertook to chip in and cover this cost. With the benefit of hindsight, perhaps this was a tactic by Cam to scare us off. I was subsequently told that he is regularly approached with grand schemes to save this, that or another species and, not knowing us at all, he placed us in the high-risk category.

Cam was rightly very proud of the success of the breeding program at Taronga and we left the meeting with his tentative support and a clear understanding that Taronga was completely risk-averse. I also had the distinct feeling that Cam was pretty certain that he would not see us again – that this plan would prove to be all too hard and we would give up.

I undertook to prepare a discussion paper outlining the scope of a feasibility study and as I wrote, I surprised myself as to how clear my vision was. This was so important, since the study would make or break the project.

THE FEASIBILITY STUDY

By this time, I was even more committed to bring the rhinos to Australia and all the early signs suggested that it could be done. I was excited and while feasibility studies can be used to justify already decided projects, others are genuine forensic evaluations of the likely success or failure of a concept. Ours definitely fell into the latter category.

Considering the importance of this study to the whole project, it is worth noting some key components of the scoping document.

I highlighted the horrific slaughter of rhinos by poachers with the result that rhinos were now officially extinct in most African countries and in steep decline in South Africa. More than 2000 rhinos had been killed in South Africa since 2010 and the kill-rate was spiralling with three a day being killed.

I explained that a core group of people had been established to assess the feasibility of enabling a controlled breeding program in Australia for both southern white and southern black rhinos. This program would build on the work already done by Taronga and would result in the establishment of a stable herd or "crash" of both species in Australia.

The document outlined the scope and content of a feasibility study to import two male southern black and white and four female southern black and white rhinos to form the nucleus of the breeding program.

It was expected that the study would investigate, in detail, issues that would include, the regulatory requirements in Australia and South Africa; estimated lead-times to prepare the necessary documentation and obtain approvals; quarantine requirements; travel logistics and potential sources of rhinos; an ideal environment for their location including ecological requirements; risk assessment; modelling to determine the population requirements for a genetically and demographically stable stand-alone population; a detailed project plan; potential security issues and mitigation strategies and detailed cost estimates.

Ideally the plan would clearly demonstrate that the project could succeed and would detail all potential obstacles, estimated costs and potential timelines to achieve the objectives.

The study would be staffed by a current employee of Taronga and ideally could be assisted by University of Sydney Veterinary Science undergraduates.

In terms of resourcing the study, I was deeply concerned. How would we do this? I had the will but neither the knowledge nor the experience to be a part of the team and we had no financial capability of paying anyone.

Several years before, as General Manager of the Sydney University Rugby Club, I had initiated a research project with the university's Economics Faculty (later to become the Business School) which was resourced by a group of students who produced some excellent work. I wondered whether the Business School would, once again, be willing to participate in this study. Being a strong believer in the "you don't ask, you don't get" school of opportunities, I called Dr Kristine Dery who headed the Business School Work and Organisational Studies group and asked if she would like to be involved.

Just recently I had a note from Kristine which read, *"I remember so clearly receiving that first call from you, 'I want to bring a breeding herd of rhino to Australia, do you think your students would be interested in such a research project?'. It was not a call you expect as a program director!! I wondered how it would all work and I think my superiors at the time thought I was crazy to engage with this project. How wrong they were!*

The students loved it, I loved it and ultimately the university benefited in so many ways. You remain one of my inspirations. You remind me daily that the impossible can be possible with passion, endurance and sheer bloody-mindedness! You also remind me that being a leader is never easy and the road is often rocky but you just keep moving and bit by bit you inch forward. You remain an inspiration and I will always be grateful for that crazy phone call three years ago."

With a silent prayer, Kristine gave us the go-ahead. I knew there was a fair degree of scepticism and nervousness on her behalf, but she really gave the project impetus and gravitas. I met with Dr Betina Szkudlarek – appointed by Kristine as the project leader – and we were ready to go. From that day on, the relationship between TARP and the University of Sydney Business School was absolutely outstanding.

Nick Boyle, a Taronga curator, was appointed as Project Manager for the study; the costings were agreed and, once again, Allan Davies kindly covered the costs. (Without Allan's financial support, the Australian Rhino Project would have struggled to get off the ground.) The Business School appointed five Masters of Management students to the team, two of whom were Australian, the other three from Singapore, China and Israel respectively – an eclectic bunch.

I vividly remember my first meeting with the five very smart and enthusiastic students. I had planned to give them a brief on what we wanted to achieve. I launched into the poaching problem. One of my favourite expressions at that time was "Don't let the Big Five become the Big Four". I noticed the blank looks on the students' faces. I gently asked if anyone knew which animals made up the "Big Five". One hand went up, somewhat tentatively, "*Tiger?*" There are no tigers in Africa, I said. "*Hippo?*" was the next guess. Not a bad response but not correct. Then came "*Cheetah?*" I decided to limit their embarrassment and told them that the "Big Five" are lion, elephant, buffalo, leopard and rhinoceros. (The term "Big Five" has nothing to do with the size of the animals, but was coined by big-game hunters and refers to the five most difficult and dangerous animals to hunt on foot in Africa. Subsequently the term was adopted by safari tour operators for marketing purposes and it is now the Holy Grail for every tourist to Africa.)

I cannot speak highly enough of the students. Superbly led by Kate Morison, the team of Justin Tsang, Rikki Stewart, Shay Koren and Zhiwen Weng went to extraordinary lengths to ensure that the study covered every conceivable requirement, piece of legislation, potential obstacle and also every possible opportunity. This report will stand the test of time. Since the biggest users of rhino horn were from China and Vietnam, I was especially pleased that the team included two young men of Chinese origin. The team displayed maturity and sensitivity way beyond their years, their average age being just twenty-two. They also understood the urgency of the project and were sensitive to the fact that we were short on money and every additional day would cost us financially.

The team employed a formal project management approach and Kristine and Betina were tough but fair mentors. It was a learning experience for all of us and, as Kristine said, the students seemed to relish the challenges. Each Thursday they would turn up to Taronga Zoo to work on the study and when I arranged for them to spend a night at Western Plains Zoo, they were the envy of the entire cohort (including some of the teaching staff).

It was around this time that I came up with the name, "The Australian Rhino Project". I was determined not to have anything that included the word "save". I wanted something understated. Whatever we managed to achieve, it would not be the "saving" of the species. The name stuck.

While doing some research one of the students came across an article about global supermodel Elle MacPherson promoting anti-aging creams that contained rhino horn. Well, you can imagine the international uproar after she advocated the use of a banned Chinese medicine made from rhino horn.

The WWF reacted immediately with a reminder that rhino poaching was at a 15-year high, driven by the demand for rhino horn products and the Humane Society International emphasised the group's condemnation of rhinoceros poaching, particularly for their use in beauty products, and characterised Elle's actions as reprehensible.

Elle rapidly backed away from her comments, saying that she has *"never knowingly consumed or encouraged the use or consumption of any products which contain material derived from endangered species"*. She added that she regrets *"any distress or offence that her banter with an interviewer might have caused."*

A few years later, I reached out to Elle's New York-based agent, Glenn "GG" Gulino, Esq. as he refers to himself, and who sounded like a poor man's Jerry Maguire, but he was less than helpful. I'd like to think that Elle might have supported our goals.

Another contribution from the students was the design of our logo, which I loved.

Our steering committee played a strong role in the development of the study and, in days to come, most of these people would form the nucleus of the inaugural Board of Directors of The Australian Rhino Project.

By November 2013, the feasibility study document was complete and Nick Boyle presented the findings to the steering committee. It was a quality piece of work which concluded that the plan to import 80 rhinos to Australia, to establish a breeding herd in the event of extinction of the species in the wild, was feasible. Nick left us in no doubt that this was going to be a really tough assignment.

I was reminded of a comment by my son Paul, who coached a junior rugby side which was about to commence their first game of "contact". . . in other words, tackling, "We *will soon see who is here to play rugby or only turn up for the lollies at the end of the match."*

My excitement was building and I wondered if I could build a team which would have the passion and endurance to see this project through.

THE SOFT LAUNCH

In 1983, Margie and I bought into a wildlife development in the Timbavati area bordering the Kruger Park. Margie is an Aussie, but spent fifteen happy years in South Africa. Sharalumi was a favourite weekend destination for Pretoria and Johannesburg people, mostly couples. It was renamed Ingwelala – where the leopard sleeps – and I was elected to the founding Board of Directors. We spent long hours discussing how to turn a fairly wild party resort into a nature conservation area solely for a different type of wildlife.

In Sydney, once school fees were out of the way, we tried to get at least a week at Ingwelala each year. In September 2013 I took advantage of the trip to gauge the South Africans' appetite for exporting rhinos to Australia. By this time, I had concluded that this project had four critical components and from here on in, I constantly referred to the "four pillars": governance; the approval of the Australian government; the approval of the South African government and fundraising.

My first port of call in South Africa was to Dr Markus Hofmeyr, Chief Scientist and Head of Veterinary Services for SANParks. Without any shadow of a doubt, Markus is one of the most impressive men I have ever met. He is a man who has dedicated his life to conservation and his reputation for working with animals such as rhinos and wild dogs is internationally recognised. Unfortunately for Markus, the rhino poaching crisis had dwarfed almost all of his other responsibilities.

Markus had participated in the previous translocation of rhinos from the Kruger Park to Western Plains Zoo in 2003 and, with this precedent, I felt confident that obtaining the South African approval for my plan would be something of a formality. Markus was gracious and listened intently as I outlined the plan. He was interested and supportive of any attempts to protect South Africa's rhinos but made it clear that this would not be a simple exercise and would almost certainly require the South African Government's approval. Markus then wrote a note of introduction to Dr Mike Knight, Chairperson of The IUCN (International Union for Conservation of Nature) African Rhino Specialist Group: *"Ray is trying to establish a semi-free-range herd of white rhino in Australia with the long-term objective to serve as source for re-introduction back to Africa (if needed) and short-term to act as alternative sanctuary for rhino out of Africa."*

Markus asked if Mike and Dr Hector Magome, Managing Executive of Conservation Services for SANParks, could meet with him and me in Skukuza the following week. We met, it was purely a meet and greet, but I was quite happy since I had managed to sow the seeds of my plan to these three key stakeholders.

Margie and I then travelled to Klerksdorp, 320 kilometres west of Johannesburg, to meet John Hume, the largest private rhino breeder in the world. I wanted to meet John as a potential source of rhinos. At the time he had 937 rhinos on his farm – his goal was to have enough rhinos to produce 200 rhino calves a year. In talking to John, I had no doubt that he would achieve this goal. I couldn't decide whether he was a conservationist or an opportunistic entrepreneur – or both.

Within weeks of returning to Australia, there was a press release from SANParks, "*We aim to reduce rhino poaching by 20 per cent a year. The war against poaching is not yet won, but we can reduce the figure.*" So said Major General Johan Jooste, head of the Kruger Park anti-poaching team, explaining that the vast two-million-hectare Kruger Park had experienced the largest number of killings. The remaining rhinos in the Kruger Park were estimated to number between 8,500 and 9,500. "*The war against poaching cannot be won in the bush, the law needs to take its course as well when it comes to prosecuting the syndicates,*" he said.

Jooste said he would like to see increased co-operation between South Africa and Mozambique, which had limited laws against poaching, making it a breeding ground for those who slipped through the porous 360-kilometre border with South Africa. With the benefit of hindsight, this statement is revealing. Clearly, the scale of the poaching onslaught on the Kruger Park rhino population was seriously underestimated. At that time, Kruger had "*between 8,500 and 9,500 rhinos*"; these "official" numbers would fluctuate wildly in the next five years.

In November 2013, the TARP steering committee accepted the recommendations of the feasibility report and agreed that we should proceed with phase one of the project, being governance, registering the organisation and so on.

I had promised the five students that, once the study was completed, I would arrange an event where they could present their findings. I was very much aware that each of these students would soon be seeking employment and I planned to invite some senior executives to the event where the students could have their day in the sun. I felt that was the least that I could do for them.

A breakfast seemed to be the best vehicle for this and I approached the Classic Safari Company who had supported me for years with fundraising activities and asked if they would sponsor the event. Principals Julie McIntosh and Sarah Hoyland were happy to do so and asked how many people I expected. I said that I would be happy if thirty to forty people turned up. I spoke to Mark Burns and Karyn Primmer, General Manager and Deputy GM respectively of the Sydney Westin Hotel and asked them to do a special deal for me. I had arranged major fundraising lunches at the Westin for years and Mark and Karyn were keen to help.

I then approached George Gregan, Cliff Rosenberg and Adam Spencer to form a panel to discuss the rhino situation at the breakfast. Former Wallaby captain Gregan was born in Zambia and has a great love of wildlife while Cliff was CEO of LinkedIn for Australia and New Zealand, is South African born and gets back to the game parks as often as he can – he is also a world-class photographer. Adam Spencer is one of the smartest and amusing men on the planet. He and I had worked together on events for years. All three were delighted to accept the invitation. I later asked Matt

George Gregan AM, Cliff Rosenberg,
Matt Fuller, Adam Spencer at the
launch. (Photo credit: Julia Salnicki)

Fuller, General Manager of Taronga Western Plains Zoo, to join the panel. As a rugby man, he was over the moon to sit alongside George Gregan.

From the outset, I had wanted to document the journey of The Australian Rhino Project. This was not a case of vanity, but I felt that, if we got this right, it would be one of the great conservation stories in recent times. Sure, animals are moved around the world every week, but this was a sincere attempt to try and save a species from becoming extinct in the wild, by moving the animals to a safer place.

The first opportunity to film what we were trying to achieve arose at this breakfast. I approached Taronga to fund the filming and they declined, I then asked the Business School and in no time at all Deputy Dean Professor John Shields, had agreed to cover the cost of filming the morning's proceedings – this was one of many times that John stepped in to help. Needless to say, the students were very excited and prepared hard for the event. As 12 December approached, so the interest in the event increased and we eventually landed up with 150 attendees. Full credit must be given to Julie and Sarah, who watched the numbers and their sponsorship dollars grow and grow. I like to think that the event was excellent exposure for The Classic Safari Company since both Julie and Sarah are wonderful supporters, lovely people and ardent conservationists.

There was an electric atmosphere in the room and the students and leader Nick Boyle, did an outstanding job in presenting the feasibility study findings. Many tears were shed when Shay Koren delivered the "Imagine You Are a Rhino" segment.

Adam Spencer was masterful in leading the panel discussion and brought the house down when he asked Matt how these massive animals were "encouraged" to mate, was it soft music and dimmed lights? Matt almost choked.

Allan Davies and I were overwhelmed by the response from the attendees at the breakfast. We realised we were not alone and that the project had touched a nerve with so many people. After the formalities were over, I was approached by a number of people offering their help. Amongst these were Bob Tucker, who offered the ANZ Bank's assistance (we landed up banking with ANZ and it has been a very good partnership); Godfrey Abraham, a retired senior executive who was very well connected in Sydney's eastern suburbs; and Mark Stanbridge, a partner at the global legal firm Ashurst. Without Ashurst, this project would not have been as successful as it was. I had worked with Barbara Buttery when she was Marketing Executive at AMP Capital and she is one of the most organised people you could ever meet; Barbara also introduced David Humphreys. David, a highly experienced lawyer, was to become one of the rocks of TARP when it came to governance and secretarial matters and an additional bonus was that Susan, David's wife, is also a lawyer, so we scored two for one. Susan is also a highly accomplished photographer who became our official photographer.

Suzy Devery and Vanna Seang produced a world-class video

clip showing the highlights of the breakfast, which we used extensively in our subsequent marketing. The breakfast was far more successful than we could have hoped although the truth of the matter is that we didn't have much to launch other than a good idea and a great deal of excitement and enthusiasm.

Now we needed to deliver.

WHAT THE FUSS IS ALL ABOUT

Why does the world have rhino fever?

To quote from a letter written to me by the late Dr Ian Player, a true rhino warrior. *"In this 21st century it would be unforgivable if we who are custodians of the wildlife that many people have spent their lives saving, allowed the same situation that developed in the 20th century to happen again, but I regret to say that the current lack of politicians and bureaucrats are not taking to heart one of the most urgent tasks affecting this generation".*

I had written to Ian, bemoaning the lack of urgency with bureaucrats in both Australia and South Africa with regard to getting traction for the TARP initiative.

In early 2017, the South African Department of Environmental Affairs (SADEA) stated that a recent *"rhino survey recorded that 6,649 to 7,830 white rhinos lived in Kruger Park and that this total was significantly lower than the 8,365 to 9,337 in 2015."* The KNP rhino population had decreased more than 25 per cent in just one year. There is a strong body of expert opinion that says that the "tipping point", where the rhino kill rate exceeds the rhino birth rate, has already been reached. The spiral to extinction is swift once this occurs.

'We're on the brink of extinction and you have a headache?'

Illustration credit: Bernard Cookson

Even assuming that of the rhino population of the KNP, 30 per cent are breeding females (about 2,400); that a calf is born every three years from each female and that all newborns reach adulthood, that would result in these 2,400 females producing 800 rhinos a year. In this case, the birth rate oscillates at around 11 per cent, compared to a mortality rate of 26.5 per cent through poaching, which is unsustainable for the survival of a species.

From these calculations, based on media numbers, it suggests a loss of around 1,600 rhinos just in KNP in 2016, against an official figure of 1,054 rhinos throughout South Africa.

These words from General Johan Jooste perfectly sum up the situation in South Africa today, "*We are fighting a war. These rhinos in Kruger are the most valuable cache of environmental assets in the world. Rhino horn is more valuable than gold, cocaine or platinum. Gram for gram, it's the most expensive commodity on the planet. This problem will not go away. Supply meets demand in Africa. Poaching of rhino is a low-risk criminal activity, it requires few logistics and is relatively easy. A poacher can easily carry a set of horns between six and nine kilograms and he can ultimately earn millions of Rand.*"

When you have the key components of greed, poverty, high unemployment, corrupt governments that are unwilling or incapable of acting, a valuable commodity based on generations of cultural usage, an endless supply of people willing to risk their lives for gain and international syndicates right in the middle of the action, you have the perfect storm which will inevitably result in the extinction of a species in the wild. A single bull rhino carrying eight kilograms of horn might buy a new life for a Mozambican poacher who slips over the border into Kruger.

In 1960 there were more than 9,000 black rhinos in Kenya's Tsavo National Park. Poachers killed every single one of them. By 1980, Africa's population of more than 100,000 black rhino had plummeted to less than 15,000.

"*It's a blatant disregard for international law,*" says Karl Ammann, an investigative wildlife filmmaker, "*The criminal syndicates seem to have decided a long time ago that they can run circles around the international conservation establishment and there will be little repercussion from governments.*"

Black market rhino horn sells for up to US$60,000 per

kilogram, and in the last decade alone more than a quarter of the world rhino population has been killed in South Africa, home to 90 per cent of the remaining animals. An average-sized horn could sell for upwards of US$400,000 per kilogram on the black market in Asia.

The cold statistics tell the story; almost 8,000 rhinos killed in the past decade. The numbers are jaw-dropping. If you make the assumption of one horn per rhino, an average weight of six kilograms per horn and a conservative black-market price of US$60,000 per kilogram, that equates to US$2.8 billion that has changed hands in this period. Is it any wonder that the international crime syndicates are so deeply entrenched in the rhino horn poaching "industry"? CITES estimates illegal wildlife trade to be worth US$23 billion a year, making it the fourth biggest illicit international activity after guns, drugs and human trafficking.

The cruelty of the kill is heartbreaking. Man is capable of unspeakable cruelty. I wrote this poem, in the middle of the night, whilst flying from Perth to Johannesburg. *Cry the Beloved Country* was the title of Alan Paton's prescient novel of 1948.

I titled the poem, "For the Rhino":

See them stand
Side by side
Mum's super large horns. His just starting to grow
Both so proud

See them run
The oldest mammals on the planet
Majestic, powerful and free

See them stop
Sniffing, staring
Uncertain and nervous

Hear the shot
See her fall
Trembling, shuddering

Hear the saw. Feel the pain.
Ruthless, cruel, greedy humans

Hear his cries
His mother's face a bloody mess
All alone
Mother and child. No reunion
Cry the Beloved Country

As mentioned earlier, South Africa is home to more than 90 percent of the rhinos left on earth, down from several hundred thousand across Africa before the 1800s, when the European imprint on the land intensified.

There are five rhino species: Indian, Javan, Sumatran, the black and the white rhino, of which there are two subspecies, northern and southern.

These five species are spread across two continents; the white rhino, with approximately 8,000 remaining; the black, with less than 2,500; the greater one-horned; the Sumatran and the Javan.

The Sumatran Rhino. (Photo Credit: Charles
W. Hardin, Wikimedia Commons)

At the turn of the 20th century, the four subspecies of black rhinoceros, numbering about a million in all, thrived in the savan-
nahs of Africa. Today, that number has plunged to less than 2,500
– a figure that does not include one single Western black rhino, a
subspecies now presumed extinct after the last animal was sighted
in 2006.

Like the western black rhinoceros, the Vietnamese rhino was
hunted to extinction. The very last of the subspecies, a female,
died in 2009 in the jungle in southwest Vietnam. Her skeleton was
found a year later, her horn crudely hacked off and a bullet lodged
in a foreleg. A poacher had used a semi-automatic weapon to shoot
her. The rhino had survived the shooting and had fled, injured,
through the dense jungle. She eventually died, perhaps months

later, near a grove of towering bamboo. *"The gunshot did kill the rhino,"* Ed Newcomer, a US Fish and Wildlife Service agent, told the BBC. *"It just took a long time to do it."* Newcomer was part of the team that investigated the rhino's death.

On visiting the site where the Vietnamese rhino breathed her last, ending the lineage of an entire subspecies, Newcomer described being "incredibly" moved. This rhino was a subspecies of the Javan rhino, now regarded as one of the most endangered mammals on earth. Of the three subspecies of Javan rhino, only one still exists. Fewer than 60 individuals survive on planet earth, all of them in Ujung Kulon National Park in Java, Indonesia.

A Javan Vietnamese rhino in London Zoo in the 19th Century. (Photo Credit: T. Dixon/ZSL)

The northern white rhino once ranged over areas of Uganda, South Sudan, the Central African Republic and the Democratic Republic of the Congo. Around 2,000 survived in the wild in 1960, but widespread poaching brought about a sharp decline in numbers. By the 1980s the northern white had reached critically endangered status, and despite conservationists' best efforts numbers continued to decline. By 2010 no northern whites were known to exist in the wild.

A slaughtered South-Western black rhino.
(Photo Credit: Getty Images)

The world's last three northern white rhinos were moved from the Czech Republic to the Ol Pejeta Conservancy in Kenya, where they are kept under constant armed guard. At the time of writing, only two remain, both females. Sudan, the last male northern white rhino died in March 2018 at the age of 45. Only Najin, Sudan's 30-year-old daughter and Fatu, aged 20, the daughter of Najin, remain. It is the end of the line. The subspecies is doomed to extinction.

Most of the world knows that the rhino species is threatened, but the status of these particular animals is in another league. They are the last two, both females. The northern white, which once roamed Africa in its thousands, is now extinct. On our watch.

The Northern White Rhino. (Photo Credit: Adobe Stock)

The horn of a rhinoceros is the world's most valuable appendage in an exotic marketplace that values nature's oddities, such as elephant ivory, tiger penis, lion bones and giraffe tail. Unlike the horns of many species, including cattle, rhino horn is not made of bone. It is made of keratin, a protein also found in human hair and fingernails, and if you trim a rhino's horn, it grows back within two years.

An international group of scientists are attempting the seemingly impossible – to rescue the northern white rhino from the jaws of extinction. They plan to remove the last eggs from the two female northern whites and by using advanced reproductive techniques, including stem cell technology and IVF, create embryos that could be carried to term by surrogate rhino mothers. The northern white could then be restored to its former glory. The procedure would be a world first.

It is an audacious plan – and a controversial one. Many

conservation experts believe the resources being used to create northern white embryos would be better spent on saving other rhino species by providing them with protection in the wild. Why try to restore the species if the cause of its extinction has still not been tackled, they ask? Others say that taking a hi-tech approach to species preservation could lull the conservation movement into thinking it would always be able to fall back on science to help reproduce a species once it gets into trouble.

These points are rejected by the project scientists. *"Unless we act now, the northern white rhino will go extinct"* said one of the project's leading scientists, Professor Thomas Hildebrandt, of the Leibniz Institute for Wildlife Research in Berlin. *"There are only three or four rhinoceros from Borneo left in captivity and none known in the wild. We could use this technology to rescue them as well."*

The booming illegal trade in horn supplies mostly Vietnam and China, where rhino horn is often ground to a powder and ingested as a treatment for everything from cancer to sea snake bites and hangovers. It is also used to (supposedly) improve men's sexual performance.

The shadowy collusion of South Africa with Mozambique, Laos and Vietnam is satiating Asia's great thirst for illegally trafficked wildlife. Despite public announcements, displays for the media and signed MOUs, these countries are doing little to combat the criminal networks involved in the flood of wildlife products out of Africa. The four countries have become a nexus of an international criminal network that rivals drugs, arms and human trafficking in both scale and profitability.

A slaughtered black rhino.

As Dr Sam Ferreira, Large Mammal Ecologist in the Kruger National Park, says in the article 'Combating Rhino Horn Trafficking: The Need to Disrupt Criminal Networks' authored with Timothy Haas, "*The combination of governance failures and the attractiveness of wildlife trafficking facilitate organized crime entering the illegal supply chain – with attendant increases in poaching. Because organized crime syndicates control middlemen, once these syndicates add wildlife trafficking to their roster of illegal activities, they tend to monopolize that trade. Then, any attempt to conduct legal trade in a wildlife product is jeopardised. This is because either the syndicate itself will purchase such legally harvested wildlife products with the intention of reselling them; or will lower their own prices for the product. Such temporary or permanent price reductions are not difficult for criminal syndicates due to their diversified business model that tolerates a wide range of profit margins, low overheads and large cash reserves. Either way, price conscious consumers will see little reason to purchase legal as opposed to illegally harvested products.*"

Organised criminal syndicates once hired Vietnamese nationals with no hunting experience to hunt rhino to illegally procure rhino horn – a practice known as 'pseudo-hunting'. This was eventually stopped but the flow of rhino horn from South Africa continues unabated.

The budget for the SA Department of Environmental Affairs to protect rhinos represented less than 1 per cent of total government expenditure in the financial year 2015–16. This leaves wildlife enforcement agencies woefully underfunded and allows law-enforcement officials to easily become corrupted.

Corruption in South Africa is currently the main obstacle in effective enforcement relating to wildlife crime. In a February 2018 Department of Environment report, a total of 502 alleged rhino poachers and 16 alleged traffickers were arrested the previous year – a decrease in arrests by 162 from the 2016 high of 680, although the number of rhinos poached remained roughly the same. Worryingly, of those arrested, 21 were police officers, environmental monitors, SANDF members and Correctional Services officials.

In 2018, 39 complete rhino horns and 75 pieces of horn were stolen from a safe in the Mpumalanga Province Government office. Most believe that this was an inside job.

Corruption seems to be endemic in parts of Africa and South Africa is no exception, This corruption seems to extend to the highest level in South Africa. Early in 2017, Al Jazeera's Investigative Unit uncovered evidence of high-level political connections to rhino poaching suggesting that Minister of State Security David Mahlobo, who runs the country's intelligence services, was implicated in trafficking rhino horn. Said Jeff Radebe, a senior adviser to President Zuma, "*Cabinet noted the allegations in an Al Jazeera documentary against Minister of State Security, Mr David Mahlobo, and the South African Police Services are investigating the allegations.*"

There has been no further word on this.

Mozambique is a major conduit for wildlife products coming from South Africa. The Mozambican authorities are notoriously ineffectual in enforcing legislation, which has proved inadequate anyway.

As quoted by Adam Cruise in his article, 'Wildlife Trafficking: The sordid Southern African-South East Asian connection', "'*In Vietnam,*' says Karl Ammann, '*they seem to be happy to seize a container every now and then, get the international media attention, then hand it back to the importer. Vietnamese nationals are the most commonly arrested Asian nationals related to wildlife trafficking in Mozambique and South Africa*'."

Julian Rademeyer, author of the best-selling book *Killing for Profit* best sums up the situation, "*Again and again efforts to target syndicates are hamstrung by corruption, governments that are unwilling or incapable of acting, a lack of information-sharing and approaches to tackling crime that wrongly emphasise arrests and seizures over targeted investigations and convictions as a barometer of success.*"

Although selling rhino horn is illegal internationally, in South Africa, if you have a permit, you can cut off a rhino's horn and sell it but only within the country.

What really troubles me is that there is now a whole industry around rhino conservation – many people do not necessarily want the rhino poaching crisis to abate since so many of them are dependent on the "cause" for their own employment and gain and, sadly, they go on wanting their salaries and the prestige attached to their efforts.

The world has rhino fever. The plight of the rhino has caused intense global interest in the poaching of this iconic species which, according to the experts, has been on Earth for ten million years or more. It is therefore critically important to have current and accurate information and statistics of the remaining rhinos and also poaching statistics and yet, the Department of Environment now publishes rhino poaching statistics approximately twice a year.

A total of 93 per cent of the global population of white rhinos reside in South Africa. White rhinos occur in various landscapes. Four National Parks protect approximately 57 per cent, 36 Provincial Reserves 20 per cent and about 400 Private Reserves 24 per cent of South Africa's white rhinos.

While the focus to date has been on the Kruger Park, rhino poaching has recently shown a dramatic increase elsewhere in South Africa, notably KwaZulu-Natal (KZN), where at least 159 rhinos were killed in 2016, compared to 104 during the same period in 2015, and in 2014 the kill number was 22. As the number of rhinos killed in Kruger reduces, so it increases in other parts of the country. The poachers simply change focus and location. Cedric Coetzee, head of rhino protection in the KZN park, comments that while it might take poachers days to track a rhino in Kruger, the high density of animals in KZN meant they might only spend two to three hours there before finding and killing a rhino and escaping with its horns.

May and June 2017 were dreadful months for rhinos in KZN Park, with twenty-three rhinos killed in two weeks. It is believed the rhinos were killed during the full moon period, known as "poachers' moon".

In January 2018, Environment Minister Molewa disclosed that while the overall number of rhinos poached had declined slightly from 1,054 in 2016 to 1,028 in 2017, there had been a corresponding increase in numbers in KZN, the Northern Cape, Mpumalanga, Free State and North West provinces.

She revealed that 404 rhinos were poached in the Kruger Park in 2017, down on the 662 poached in 2016. Again, no surprises there, as there are fewer rhinos to poach in Kruger and as the security net is tightened, poachers will strike easier targets and come up with new ways and methods to process horn and smuggle it out of the country. Just like drugs in sport, the baddies are always at least one step ahead of the authorities.

Zimbabwe and Namibia have been hit hard as well, feeling the effects of the shifting poaching operations. Official poaching statistics released by the Namibian environment ministry showed that rhino poaching declined in 2016 while elephant poaching doubled as compared to 2015. In total, 216 black and white rhinos have been killed over the past four years, while 266 elephants have been poached since 2013.

Another worrying statistic is the revelation that conviction rates for poachers are agonisingly low despite an increase of arrests for the year and an often-positive spin by the South African Environment Minister.

For the whole of 2016, anti-poaching officials made 281 arrests in the Kruger Park. Once arrested, poachers are taken to the Skukuza Magistrate's Court, which has become severely overloaded. State Prosecutor Isbet Erwee is on record saying: "*Arrests and convictions do not seem to scare off poachers. This is a crime of greed, the kingpins pay a lot, and the poaching business has become a fashionable one. Although many suspects are killed during contacts or end up losing limbs, the lure of money is stronger than the fear of death."*

Let me repeat that, *"the lure of money is stronger than the fear of death."* It seems that the world accepts that life is cheap in Africa, but surely this is a root cause of this whole international poaching crisis. As Doctor Jane Goodall says, we need to educate the masses to give them hope so that they do not take what some seem to think is the easy way out – by risking their lives.

If you've grown up in destitution and poverty, one successful poaching expedition will change your life. It's the powerful social force at play. The communities adjacent to the game parks don't own the park, it has never been theirs, so, with some justification, they may ask: *"What do I get from that park? A few of my community work there, but most of us, what do we get?"* (Major General Johan Jooste, SANParks)

Tourism is critical to South Africa, with one in twenty people employed in the sector. In the 2018 financial year, tourism contributed US$30 billion to the economy, representing almost 9 per cent of all economic activity, generating 1.5 million jobs or 9.2 per cent of total employment. Of the 17 million tourists, approximately 7.1 million visited South African national parks, generating approximately US$300 million in revenue. Most come to see the wildlife and the holy grail of the Big Five.

In early 2016, I had a long letter from Malcolm Homer, an ex-South African now living in Queensland. He headed his letter "Who will they blame?" and wrote, *"I read about your laudable rhino project and wonder if I could be of assistance.*

Some years ago, a man by the name of Elie Wiesel, a holocaust survivor and Nobel Peace prize-winner, gave a speech to President Clinton and guests at the White House entitled, 'The Peril of Indifference.' The speech has been acknowledged as one of the great speeches of the last century. Elie argued that America under Roosevelt knew about the Holocaust and the horror going on in the concentration camps but did nothing. They were indifferent which begged the question 'who was to blame?'

I know that many organisations and individuals are involved in initiatives to save the rhino, only recently Warren Buffet gave the Kruger anti-rhino poaching unit A$31 million. Wonderful. The question of course is whose responsibility is it to save the animals? Is it purely an African responsibility or is it that of a wider audience? If rhino become extinct in the next couple of decades who will be blamed. The poachers? The wider audience? Both? But then Ray you know the answer that is why your project has been created and unlike President Roosevelt you and your colleagues are not 'indifferent' to the problem. You recognise that the solution does indeed belong to a wider audience. I salute you."

I was deeply moved by Malcolm's comments and, if anything, they strengthened my resolve to do whatever I could to help save this iconic species. The more people and organisations that shone a light on the issue, the better.

BUILDING A BOARD OF
DIRECTORS

I was rapidly realising that however hard and long I worked, I could not do this on my own. Time was one thing, experience and expertise were a whole different matter and so, immediately after the launch breakfast I started to build a Board of Directors. While this was a statutory requirement, I was also keen to have a powerful support network of partners, ambassadors and technical experts.

The board would include representatives of the three major stakeholders (Taronga, University of Sydney Veterinary and Business Schools) plus a treasurer, a secretary and legal counsel. With fundraising being such a critical component, Godfrey Abraham was a key man. The only other person that I really wanted was Shaun Smith. He was my designated successor.

The first ever Board of Directors of The Australian Rhino Project comprised Ray Dearlove, Chairman; Allan Davies, Deputy Chair; Mark Stanbridge, Legal Counsel; George Raffan, Treasurer; Godfrey Abraham, Fundraising; Dr Kristine Dery, Business School Representative; Professor Rosanne Taylor, Veterinary Faculty Representative; Simon Duffy, Taronga Representative and David Humphreys, Secretary

I was really proud of this board, I had hand-picked each member based on their skill-set, experience, passion and energy. I took a great deal of pleasure in presenting profiles of each for inclusion on the website. My view, at the time, was that a largish board was required since there was so much to do. What really pleased me was the sense of excitement with each director – they couldn't wait to get cracking.

The board would meet every month in Sydney, kindly hosted by either Allan or Mark in their CBD offices. Meetings were formal affairs. We had an excellent governance protocol which we all took very seriously and in the first six months a great deal of time was devoted to making sure that we were compliant in every way. Mark did an exceptional job for us here and he had access to some outstanding young talent in his firm with people like Tanja Maley, Leslie De Bruyn, Chelsea Parker, Hetty Downer and Justin Steele.

I had met Peter, universally known as Pod, McLoughlin at the launch breakfast and he and I hit it off immediately. He pledged to assist me as much as he could, given that he commuted from Sydney to Melbourne every week in his role of Marketing Director for Carlton United Breweries. Throughout 2014, we built up a good relationship and then one day he told me that the prostate cancer that he had previously fought off was back and that he would be resigning his job to tackle this awful disease. He would be at home in Sydney and, in his always positive way, said that this would give him more time to devote to the rhino project. Pod and I worked together very closely for most of 2015 and everyone benefitted from this. Pod is extremely bright and spent many years on the board of South African Breweries, one of the largest companies in the world. I involved him as much as I could and he became a de facto member of the board. He sees things so clearly and is able to break down what seem to be very complex issues into manageable chunks. His knowledge and experience certainly strengthened our board. While he was very supportive of me, he measured everything by asking, "*Is it good for the rhino*?" My philosophy exactly. A thoughtful and considerate man, he thought of everyone else even in his dark days when the cancer caused him grief.

About a year later Pod returned to work, initially as a consultant to Coca Cola Amatil and then quickly rising to the position of Managing Director. Sadly, Pod passed away in 2018 – a wonderful man who was universally popular and is missed by all.

The JBWere team of Donna Gulbin and Shamal Dass were amongst our biggest supporters, who stuck with me through thick and thin and unfailingly invited me to their philanthropic events, meetings and presentations. It was at their invitation that I met Professor Warren McFarlan, Professor Emeritus at Harvard Business School. Through their and David Knowles' efforts, I was invited to attend a private session with Warren, and

Mark Stanbridge and I attended. As a brief, we were given some excellent guidance by Donna:

"Explain that you are brand new and need help with governance. You have a clear mission, passion for the cause, access to smart people and through this a starting point for fundraising but need support on the organisational level. Also, what is the role of the board in fundraising. Have your mission statement with you to speak about developing it". Donna whispered that Warren was very enthusiastic about the meeting, which gave me a real buzz.

Both the private and general meetings with Warren were exceptional. In my thank you, I wrote, *"Professor McFarlan is an exceptional teacher/entertainer/presenter, I just could not believe his energy, stamina and humour."* I asked Warren to sign his seminal book, *Joining a Non-Profit Board*, and to my delight, he wrote *"Best wishes for the most interesting non-profit I have ever seen."* High praise indeed from a man who has spent a lifetime working with not-for-profit boards.

In Warren's presentation, he repeatedly used the phrase, "give, get or get off" – in other words, donate, get others to donate or find something else to do. Warren was very strong on this, saying that too many people joined not-for-profit boards for all the wrong reasons, such as ego or perceived glory. He stressed that there is no glory on serving on such boards, it is bloody hard work and if you're not suited for it, accept it and move on.

At the time, and since, it made me think about the make-up of our board, who were invited because of the skills that I thought were required including experience, passion, energy and trust. As Ernest Hemingway said, *"The best way to find out if you can trust somebody is to trust them."*

It is said that there are three types of people; those who make things happen, those who watch things happening and those who say, "What happened?" We were all determined to be in the first category.

Mark Stanbridge is a partner in the global law firm, Ashurst, he is a very busy man with wide responsibilities.

Godfrey Abraham is a delightful man who had a successful business career in South Africa. A man with a big heart who is very well connected with the large expatriate community in the eastern suburbs of Sydney – a significant target for us in terms of fundraising. Sadly, Godfrey has also passed away – a generous, caring man until the end.

David Humphreys is a lawyer with serious qualifications. A quiet, gentle man, David was the ideal board secretary, honest, efficient, with a sharp sense of humour.

Dr Kristine Dery is one of the most delightful people you will ever meet. As the board representative for the University of Sydney Business School, Kristine brought a serious intellect to our board. Unfortunately, through outside issues, Kristine resigned and now works with the Massachusetts Institute of Technology in Boston.

Professor David Raubenheimer was the board representative for the Veterinary Faculty. I felt we never fully utilised David's considerable skills. Much of this was due to the fact that I championed the Scientific Advisory Board and others did not necessarily share my views about the value being presented to us on a plate.

George Raffan is an accountant and a family friend. He and I were at school together in Johannesburg and he brought vast experience, integrity, knowledge and loyalty to our board. He is conservative by nature and was an ideal foil for me. His jousts with

Mark Stanbridge were truly epic (and occasionally quite amusing). The accountant and the lawyer.

Simon Duffy was the Taronga representative on our board and he fulfilled this role to perfection. Simon is wise beyond his years and made a massive contribution with his conservation knowledge and experience. In time, Simon will be seen as a significant contributor to conservation in Australia.

Before Shaun Smith joined us, he chaired the NSW chapter of Nicholas Duncan's Save the Rhino organisation. Shaun had boundless energy and passion and he and I had several discussions about him succeeding me. He would have been ideal and would have brought so much to the role. Sadly, Shaun passed away from pancreatic cancer. He was a wonderful man and I miss him.

With Kristine's resignation, John Shields recommended Professor Leanne Piggott as her replacement. Leanne made an immediate impact. Well-travelled, highly intelligent and the only woman on the board, Leanne would listen intently and then speak with deep sincerity and understanding. I valued her contribution, loyalty and friendship and I was really disappointed when she left Sydney University and our board to take up an executive position with the University of NSW. She was not replaced.

Matt Fuller replaced Simon on the board as the Taronga representative and Paul White was appointed by Allan to handle the media and marketing portfolios.

I met Lindi-May Lochner at one of Hein Vogel's Southern Crossings networking events and, soon after, recommended her as a replacement for the retiring George Raffan. Her skills and cheerful personality were welcomed with open arms and to this day she is performing strongly in this role.

While not on the board, Sarah Dennis was the only paid employee on a part-time basis. She was very good at social media.

Our board, probably like many others, had strengths and weaknesses. What we achieved in such a short time was remarkable. Different people contributed differently. Some people had the project front of mind, but while others didn't that was probably due to time pressures. The best measuring stick was, as Pod so often asked, *"Is it good for the rhino?"*

As the board evolved and everything became more and more complex, most of the tasks fell into my lap. I really didn't mind since I was driven to succeed and sensed that we had a window of opportunity and I was determined to take advantage of it. Most board members had serious full-time jobs and were happy to follow my lead.

During my sales career, I had benefitted greatly from what I termed Advisory Boards. Some of these were more formal than others, but the basic concept was to have access to a group of people who were enthusiastic about or committed to the project and, through their skills and networks, who would add value to the board and thus to the project. Theirs was an honorary role and they could be called upon to help in whichever direction we needed assistance. For example, Wallabies captain George Gregan's name would open doors; author Tony Park would speak at boardroom lunches; Chris Hibbard was an important person in the Australian government approval process; Barbara Buttery could make a difference in networking; LinkedIn CEO Cliff Rosenberg could guide us in terms of social media; SANParks Chief Scientist Markus Hofmeyr could make or break this project.

I envisioned this group meeting once a quarter in a less formal environment, maybe a cocktail party, but they had the "honour" of being closely involved and hence, hopefully, felt some obligation to contribute. Other targets included Claire Pryce of Greenpeace and the CEO of The Classic Safari Company, Julie McIntosh.

Some people invited were simply rock stars. Dereck Joubert is the driving force behind the move of the 100 rhinos from South Africa to Botswana. He is a legend in wildlife and wanted to be informally involved.

I felt that we needed more "gravitas" and sought out several people who I thought could add credibility to our fledgling organisation. I invited all of the following to become patrons of TARP: John Rendall of Christian the Lion fame, Dr Jane Goodall DBE, Dr Ian Player, former Springbok rugby captain Francois Pienaar and Elle MacPherson.

You may be thinking, what on earth was Ray smoking, thinking that he would get such luminaries? Well, one way or the other, I contacted every one of these people. All except Elle agreed.

I decided to approach world leaders to make them aware of what I was trying to achieve – making a difference by helping to save a species from potential extinction. I wrote letters, similar to the one below to President Obama, to Sir David Attenborough, Hillary Clinton, Prince Constantijn of the Netherlands, Princes Charles and William, Prime Minister David Cameron and Sir Richard Branson.

I also wrote to the president of Vietnam and also Xi Jinping, President of the People's Republic of China. I even had my letters translated into Vietnamese and Mandarin.

18 January 2014
The President of the United States
The White House
1600 Pennsylvania Avenue NW
Washington, DC 20500

Dear President Obama,

I am writing to you to seek your support for The Australian Rhino Project. Last year, I was contacted by some people in South Africa who were desperately concerned about the scale of poaching of rhinoceros in Africa in general and in South Africa in particular. Their suggestion was that I try and set up a breeding herd of black and white rhinos in Australia as an "Insurance Population" in case of the extinction of the species.

I am South African born and have lived in Australia for many years and I decided to take up the challenge. I have established The Australian Rhino Project in partnership with Taronga Zoo and both the Veterinary Faculty and Business School of the University of Sydney.

As you would expect, this is a massive undertaking and our plan is to initially import up to thirty rhinos (a mix of white and black, males and females) into Australia to build on Taronga's existing rhino population. The Project has the support of the South African authorities, with whom I am in constant communication, and they have privately told me that, in an ideal world, they would like us to have a herd of 500 rhinos. The greater plan is to establish a large, secure breeding herd within Australia, most likely in Western Australia. We have identified the land and the owner of the land is very keen to be involved.

The Project has the blessing of Dr Ian Player and also Lucia van der Post, daughter of Sir Laurens van der Post, who has kindly offered to write an article for the Financial Times *in support of the Project. We have built significant momentum across the world, but equally, we know that we have a long way to go and we would welcome your support, in whatever form that might take. The situation is dire and there is certainly urgency from our point of view and I would like to invite you to be a patron of The Australian Rhino Project.*

Thank you for considering this request.
Ray Dearlove
Founder
The Australian Rhino Project

The letter to President Xi Jinping:

致
中华人民共和国国家主席 习近平先生阁下
尊敬的主席先生：
　　我叫雷尔迪洛夫 (Ray Dearlove)。我出生在南非，在澳洲生活多年，是澳洲犀牛保育项目 (The Australian Rhino Project) 的创办人，我与悉尼塔龙加动物园 (Taronga Zoo)、悉尼大学 (University of Sydney) 商学院和兽医系合作成立了该项目。我希望通过该项目来缓解南非犀牛遭当地非法捕猎而濒临灭绝的情况。
　　我此次来信目的是希望您能支持我们的澳洲犀牛保育项目。该项目始于二零一三年六月，当时一群关注犀牛情况的南非野生动物保护者向我求助，原因是他们发现有人在非洲大量非法捕猎犀牛而导致牠们的数量急剧下降，严重影响当地生态环境，南非的情况尤为严重，当地犀牛数量急速减少，长久下去将导致犀牛这一珍贵野生物种濒临灭绝。当地人民建议我在澳洲为黑白种犀牛建立一个繁殖群，利用他们作为主要的繁殖品种对犀牛进行重点保护。

南非政府也参与了此项目，并给予大力支持。通过双方的紧密合作，该项目已经取得一定进展。现阶段，我们计划将三十头犀牛从南非运往悉尼塔龙加动物园 (Taronga Zoo) 进行保育工作，以确保他们得到有效的看护。

这项目得到了各界的广泛支持，对此我深感荣幸。尤为值得一提的是恩普莱博士 (Dr. Ian Player) 和劳伦斯·范德普斯特爵士 (Sir Laurens van der Post) 的女儿露西娅·范德普斯特女士 (Lucia van der Post)，她为此在《金融时报》上撰写了文章来宣传并推广了这个项目。对于我们全人类共享的生态圈来说，犀牛保育计划迫在眉睫，任重道远。中国作为一个世界大国，在国际舞台上有著举足轻重的地位和影响力，这个项目若能获得您的理解与支持，必定能够取得长足的进展。我们在此不胜荣幸的邀请您成为此项目的赞助者。

如蒙俯允，至深感铭。

政安

澳洲犀牛保育项目创办人
雷尔迪洛夫
二零一四年二月二十日

Despite being the eternal optimist, I didn't expect many or even any replies, but I'm delighted to say that Princes Charles and William responded, as did Sir David Attenborough, David Cameron and Sir Richard Branson.

With regard to the presidents of China and Vietnam, I didn't expect anything and I wasn't disappointed, but what the hell – you don't ask, you don't get.

Stephanie Gilmore, Tim Jarvis AM, Andy Fell, Anne Moore, Rachel Ward AM and John Platten were all co-opted during the life of the project. Every single one of them made a solid contribution, for which I am most grateful.

As I travelled this rocky road, it became clear to me that the next generation would need to fix the mess that my generation has created. I decided to establish a chapter of younger supporters and the Young Australians for Rhinos was born. At various events and meetings, I marvelled at these young people's enthusiasm, energy and active support for what I was trying to achieve.

Their responsibilities included the recruitment of members, organising events, fundraising, acting as a lobby group and an ideas incubator and, finally and importantly, to have some fun. The only qualifying criterion was that members had to be forty years of age or less. To me, everyone under forty is young.

What was in it for them? It was a networking forum and I invited three members at a time to our board meetings as a mentoring opportunity. I arranged for a dedicated portal on our website. It was expected that they would meet every six weeks or so. It is my firm belief that it is their generation that will change the world; that they will not tolerate entrenched "customs" such as using rhino horn for curing cancer, preventing or curing hangovers or enhancing sexual performance. Essentially, they will make the world a better place.

In my invitation, I quoted 22-year-old Alex Weng Zhiwen who lives in China and who was part of the feasibility study team, *"Thank you for this project, the invaluable experience working with you deeply changed my understanding of human responsibility. I sincerely wish that Australian Rhino Project will not only save rhinos, but also further change the way people think in terms of their capability and responsibility to actively protect the world."*

Alex's words reminded me of one of my favourite quotes, from T.E. Lawrence. *"All men dream, but not equally. Those who dream by night in the dusty recesses of their minds wake up in the day to find it was vanity, but the dreamers of the day are dangerous men, for they may act their dreams with open eyes, to make it possible."*

I asked Bob Tucker, a senior executive with ANZ Bank and a strong supporter, if the bank would host a function to launch the Young Rhinos program and I invited Cliff Rosenberg, CEO of LinkedIn, ANZ to give a presentation on the use of social media and how the Young Rhinos could exploit its power. With the attractions of a world expert on social media as well as free beer and snacks, the evening could only succeed, with more than 50 attendees. Cliff gave an insightful talk about the advantages and pitfalls of social media.

The original Young Rhinos executive committee was led by Vincent Stander, supported by Claire Pryce, Neil Raffan, Chelsea Parker, Hayley Dearlove, Hetty Downer, Kate Morison, Dane Squance, Gabriel Raubenheimer, Stan Mastrantonis, Cass O'Brien, Ross Simon and Sandy Field. It was a strong group which was subsequently joined by Danielle Fryday, Keighley Bell, Belle

Lamond and Ciara Halliday. Everyone enthusiastically updated their LinkedIn profiles as a result of Cliff's guidance.

This team made a real difference to the workings of the project and every one of them was a quality individual determined to make a difference. They organised film nights and they formed the support core of major events. For me, their finest hour was the Sydney fundraising dinner. With 650 people attending, we needed a lot of support and they all stepped up smartly kitted out in their white TARP shirts.

They were a special group of young adults and I would like to think that each received some benefit from being a part of TARP. We certainly did.

At the launch breakfast, the Veterinary Faculty Dean, Professor Rosanne Taylor was particularly moved and asked if it would be possible to have some of the faculty's leading scientists in reproduction, genetics, nutrition and health contribute to the project. She said, *"While Taronga has great vets, we are able to underpin the excellent practice with outstanding science, by leaders in the field – a collaboration with some of our best"*.

This was really exciting and the timing perfect. During the feasibility study, I had become keenly aware that we were totally reliant on Taronga for veterinary and scientific advice and this made me somewhat uneasy. Simon Duffy and Nick Boyle were both good executives, but at the end of the day, quite understandably, they would always put Taronga first. But I felt we also needed to have impartial advice and direction. We had no scientific or technical expertise on the board and Rosanne's suggestion resonated strongly with me and thus the Scientific Advisory Board (SAB) was born.

Rosanne recommended Professor David Raubenheimer to represent the faculty on our board. David had just been recruited to head up a major nutritional thrust at the university and was known internationally as an inspirational leading nutritional researcher with expertise in wildlife nutritional strategies. He had past experience with rhinos, with most of his diverse research work in wildlife undertaken in the field. He was a South African who would bring the necessary passion to this project that also speaks to national pride and commitment to conservation of heritage.

What a coup for us.

What was a little more concerning was Rosanne's thoughtful comment that she hoped that there would be space, scope and a welcome for their nutrition, reproduction, genetics and health researchers to be involved *now that it's a zoo led project,* adding that her team had much to contribute in research led expertise. I understood Rosanne's concern and I shared it. In my own mind I questioned Rosanne's use of the words, *a zoo led project,* as this was neither true nor the perception that I wanted but I concluded that perhaps I was being a little over-sensitive.

As an aside, Channel Seven TV presenter, Simon Reeve introduced me to Grant Weyer, a South African who had spent time in several African game reserves. Grant's area of academic expertise was veterinary epidemiology, where most of his work had focused on rabies and foot and mouth disease. Grant is a highly intelligent and passionate conservationist who provided me with invaluable advice. In Australia, he is chairman and CEO of SmartVet Pty Ltd, which develops, manufactures, commercialises and markets veterinary medicines and vaccines.

I briefed Grant on what we were trying to achieve and he

commented that Taronga's influence on the project naturally came from a zoo mindset that might make generating zoo outcomes inevitable. He believed strongly that a zoo-based thought process was the antithesis of the approach required to generate a viable outcome for our rhinos. In his experience in wildlife projects, the zoo mindset posed almost as big a threat to truly viable conservation outcomes as poachers themselves. Grant apologised for being so blunt, but said that he had some battle scars and felt an obligation to send up a flare to hopefully help others avoid making some of the same mistakes that he had. Well, I wasn't sure what to make of these comments so kept them to myself although his views certainly kept me alert.

David Raubenheimer moved fast, inviting highly qualified scientists and academics to join, all experts in their fields. Professor Kathy Belov – conservation geneticist; Professor Alex Chaves – animal nutrition and rumen microbiology; Dr Simon de Graaf – reproduction of domestic and wildlife animals; Dr Jaime Gongora – immunogenetics, retrovirology and diversity of wildlife; Dr Catherine Herbert – reproductive and genetic management of free-living and captive wildlife populations; Dr Gabriel Machovsky-Capuska – nutritional ecology; Dr David Phalen – infectious, nutritional, and toxological diseases of wildlife; Sean Coogan – wildlife biologist and ecologist; Dr Derek Spielman – wildlife pathology, diseases and ecology and epidemiology; Professor Bill Pritchard – from the School of Geosciences; associate Professor Roslyn Bathgate – reproduction in domestic and wild animals.

David and I agreed that Taronga Zoo was a vital cog in this wheel and Dr Benn Bryant, veterinarian at Western Plains Zoo, became involved. I was very pleased that he did, Benn is a no-nonsense professional who has zero tolerance for political games. His view mirrored mine – it was always about the rhinos.

This truly was the Dream Team. Within this group, there was world-class skill and expertise. I would argue that this cadre of professionals was as good as, if not better than, any other similar conservation group in the world. These people were handpicked from one of the finest academic and research institutions on the planet.

With a powerful Board of Directors, an experienced Advisory Board, a highly skilled technical Scientific Advisory Board and a team of the younger generation on our side, we were well placed and poised to tackle the complex task of bringing the rhinos to the safe haven of Australia.

CORRUPTION,

THE AFRICAN DISEASE

The scourge of corruption is not limited to South Africa.

In January 2018, it was reported by Al Jazeera that Grace, the wife of ousted Zimbabwe president, Robert Mugabe, had been placed at the very top of a criminal enterprise that poached and poisoned hundreds of elephants and rhino in Zimbabwe. Investigations into ivory and rhino horn poaching led and directed by the former first lady have intensified. It is alleged that Grace Mugabe and a number of close associates, including a Chinese associate, were part of a ring of organised crime also responsible for several tusks that are said to have disappeared from ivory stock piles, when ivory was carved at factories in Harare before export permits were forged. The investigations are ongoing.

Grace Mugabe, wife of the late Robert Mugabe. (Photo Credit: Photo by Khuluma Afrika)

As Lord Acton said, *"Power corrupts, absolute power corrupts absolutely"*.

Zimbabwe is home to the world's fourth largest black rhino population after South Africa, Namibia and Kenya. Those responsible for the disappearance of 56 rhino horns worth $3 million from a government strong-room were never identified. Organised gangs of poachers slaughtered nearly one-quarter of the country's rhinos between 2007 and 2009.

In Namibia the debate about hunting black rhino continues ferociously. In the 1980's, Zambia boasted a healthy rhino population of around 12,000 but less than twenty years later the animal was declared extinct due to rampant poaching.

Tanzania has its own problems. President Kikwete recently sacked four government ministers following accusations of abuses committed by security forces during a huge operation against wildlife poaching. The dismissals came after reports of arbitrary murder, rape, torture and extortion of innocent civilians by members of the anti-poaching crackdown dubbed "Operation Destroy". *"The anti-poaching operation had good intentions, but the reported murders, rapes and brutality are totally unacceptable,"* he said. Investors have long complained that graft is one of the main reasons for the high cost of doing business in Tanzania and a new wave of poaching is now threatening elephant and rhino populations in East Africa's second-largest economy, which is the epicentre of Africa's elephant poaching crisis. Government census figures suggest that the number of elephants in the country fell from 109,000 in 2009 to 40,000 in 2014. That's 69,000 slaughtered in just five years.

A recent report revealed that Chinese-led criminal gangs conspire with corrupt Tanzanian officials to traffic huge amounts of ivory, while even diplomatic visits by high-level Chinese Government delegations have been used to smuggle ivory. In December 2013, an official visit by a Chinese naval task force to Dar es Salaam spurred a major surge in business for ivory traders, with one dealer making a cool US$50,000 from sales to Chinese naval personnel. In addition, a Chinese national was caught trying to enter the port with 81 illegal tusks intended for two Chinese naval officers. Earlier that year, the visit of a large official delegation accompanying Chinese President Xi Jinping to Tanzania created a boom in illegal ivory sales and caused local prices to double.

Tanzania is the largest source of poached ivory in the world and China the largest importer of smuggled tusks. Tanzania's world famous Selous Reserve has seen its elephant population plunge by 67 per cent in just four years, from 38,975 animals to just 13,084. Based on available evidence, Tanzania has lost more elephants to poaching than any other country. As far back as 2006, Environmental Investigation Agency (EIA) investigators were told that some Chinese embassy staff were major buyers of ivory. An official of Tanzania's wildlife department offered to sell the investigators tusks from the government's ivory storeroom and to put them in touch with a dealer who could provide ivory from the Selous Reserve. EIA Director Mary Rice said: "*The future of*

Tanzania's elephants is extremely precarious. The ivory trade must be disrupted at all levels of criminality, the entire prosecution chain needs to be systemically restructured, corruption rooted out and all stakeholders, including communities exploited by the criminal syndicates and those on the front lines of enforcement, given unequivocal support. All trade in ivory, including all domestic sales, must be resolutely banned in China." Everyone agrees but nobody does anything to make it happen.

Then there is Mozambique where, in 2013, fifteen rhinos were shot in the Great Limpopo Transfrontier Park area, which also covers South Africa and Zimbabwe. They were thought to be the last of an estimated 300 rhinos that roamed through the special conservation area when it was established as "the world's greatest animal kingdom" in a treaty signed by presidents Mandela, Mugabe and Chissano in 2002.

There is a possible game changer. An estimated 20 billion barrels of natural gas was recently found off the Mozambique coast, making the country an emerging giant in natural gas. 85 trillion cubic feet of natural gas was found in the Rovuma basin, which has been described as "one of the largest global gas finds in years."

Mozambique sits seventh on the table of poorest countries in the world. This discovery could add $39 billion dollars to its economy by 2035.

If, and it is a very big if, the government of Mozambique were to build an economic and social model whereby the whole population benefits from this wealth, the need for crimes such as poaching may well dissipate.

Sources with first-hand knowledge of smuggling routes point to transnational rhino horn and ivory syndicates that have been shipping hunting rifles to cross-border and domestic poaching kingpins via Maputo in Mozambique. This is big business and everyone is out to make a buck.

Increasingly in South Africa, evidence continues to surface of underpaid law enforcement officers and park rangers who have been corrupted by gang bosses and middle-men with offers of financial gain. Early in 2016, five suspected poachers were arrested as they coolly tried to enter the Kruger Park at one of the main gates. The suspects included a member of the South African police force.

In Kenya, the government's move to build roads in remote areas is a doubled-edged sword. It has made it easier for poachers to reach the animals and transport their loot. There had been almost no poaching around Amboseli Game Reserve for 30 years before a Chinese company got the contract to build a 120km highway just north of the park. A recent International Fund for Animal Welfare (IFAW) report says the growing number of Chinese nationals on the African continent may have a direct influence on increased poaching. *An increasing number of Chinese nationals (workers, businessmen and visitors) are reaching every corner of Africa – and a rising number are implicated in illicit ivory trade.*

The first ever legal auction of rhino horn was held in South Africa in September 2017. It was reported that one notorious trader in the black-market of endangered animals was none other than North Korean leader Kim Jong Un. It came to light that North Korean officials in Southern Africa have a huge appetite for the region's endangered species. They've been involved in illegal poaching and selling of rhino horns in the area for decades, and the business appears to have grown dramatically since Kim Jong Un succeeded his father as Supreme Leader in 2011. One major seizure occurred in October 2012, when a North Korean diplomat named Kim Jong Guk was caught by Mozambican customs officials as he tried to smuggle around 130 pieces of ivory out of the country. In 2014, a report by the Washington-based Committee for Human Rights in North Korea accused North Korean diplomats of earning hard currency for its nuclear and missile programs through illicit trading of wildlife.

Another finding on the illicit trade, published a year ago by the Geneva-based Global Initiative Against Transnational Organised Crime, showed that North Korean diplomats have been implicated in more than half of the cases of illegal trading of rhinoceros horns and elephant tusks involving embassy officials stationed in Africa since 1989. Of the 29 seizures of contraband horns and tusks in the period, 16 have involved North Koreans. The highest profile cases occurred after Kim took office. In May 2015, Pak Chol Jun, the political counsellor at the North Korean embassy in Pretoria, was arrested in Mozambique alongside a so-called martial arts teacher, Kim Jong Su, in possession of close to $100,000 in cash and 4.5 kilos of rhino horn. Both men were later released after posting $30,000 bail. On returning to Pretoria, Pak, the second highest ranking North Korean representative in Southern Africa was expelled. Recently, United Press International reported that North Koreans regularly travel to Mozambique to acquire horns. As a South Korean embassy source told UPI, the horns are then transported to China where they are sold on the black market.

Stories abound that the North Korean embassy in Pretoria is *actively involved in smuggling ivory and rhino horn.* There are allegations that the North Korean embassy in Ethiopia's capital, Addis Ababa, is being used as a transit point for the smuggling of illicit wildlife products to China, with officials in the embassy using their diplomatic status to act as couriers. The totalitarian state expects its diplomats to *"earn enough money to supplement their paltry salaries and be able to make sizeable financial contributions to the central government in Pyongyang."* according to the Global Initiative report. *"It is likely that many more cases of diplomatic involvement in the illicit trade have gone undetected and unreported,"* wrote Julian Rademeyer, the author of the report.

This graphic, with thanks to TRAFFIC, clearly demonstrates the scale of the poaching issue. With so many countries involved and so much money at stake, what will change to prevent the extinction of not only rhinos, but also elephants, lions, pangolins and other iconic African wildlife species? All roads lead to Asia.

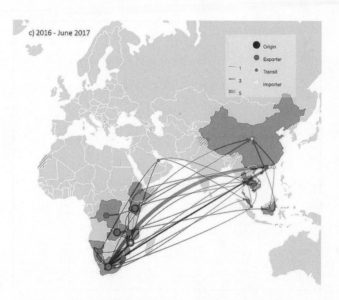

Known trafficking routes for illegal rhino horn originating in Africa, 2016–June 2017: *Pendants, Powder and Pathways* report (TRAFFIC).

Some people see the statement, *"the world has rhino fever"* as alarmist. To them, I say, thank goodness, because the rhino crisis has shone a very sharp spotlight on international crime syndicates and the poaching of animals globally.

To be in a situation where less than fifty years ago, hundreds of thousands of rhinos roamed freely across several continents, to where the numbers are now counted in their thousands and the animals are extinct in most of Africa north of the Zambezi River, is a severe indictment on humankind. The time was right for TARP to get cracking. When the buying stops, the killing stops.

CONVERTING AN IDEA

INTO A STRATEGY

Walt Disney said, "If you can dream it, you can do it". Now that the feasibility study had been approved, it was time to build upon an idea and develop a plan. We had solid momentum and all parties were supportive, but they looked to me to build that plan. I was champing at the bit.

Our original goal was to import eighty rhinos over four years, commencing in 2016, to build on the existing rhino populations at the Taronga Western Plains Zoo and Monarto Safari Park as well as having a stable herd of rhinos located on a large and secure property in outback Australia.

How was the number of eighty derived? I simply worked backwards from an arbitrary goal of 120 rhinos and assumed standard birth and mortality rates over an eight-year period.

The late Dr Ian Player was a wonderful mentor and source of inspiration as he wrote to me, "*It is impossible to overemphasise the importance of having a decent white and black rhino population surviving in Australia, particularly as the habitat in certain parts of Australia, thanks to the African exotic introductions, is just made for the rhino.*" My base assumption was that the translocated rhinos would always remain the property of the source and once the situation stabilised in Africa, it was our intention to repatriate the rhinos or their progeny to Africa.

After the highly successful launch breakfast, we met with Taronga. Everyone was satisfied that the study had provided a solid foundation for proceeding and there was now a need to formalise the various relationships. At the meeting in January 2014, we agreed to the following priorities:

- Craft an MOU between TARP and Taronga, the Business School and the Veterinary Faculty
- Submit a proposal to the Australian government
- Register the company, build the constitution and apply for Donor Gift Recipient tax status
- Build a website and communication strategy.

These were the building blocks of my "four pillars" being governance, the approval of the Australian government; the approval of the South African government and fundraising.

At this meeting, we were introduced to representatives of the Zoo and Aquarium Association (ZAA), who were to become an integral and vital part of the project. I had met Dr Andrea

Reiss, the Veterinary Officer for ZAA, at the breakfast and was impressed with her knowledge and calm approach to any and all matters that came up – and there would be plenty of those in future years. We also met Andrea's superior, Chris Hibbard. He and Andrea had already commenced discussions with their colleagues at the Department of Agriculture, Forestry and Fisheries (AUSDAFF) and advised that the department was sympathetic to our plan, but we would need to develop an actual business plan. Then came the sting in the tail: we would have to pay for Andrea's time on a "cost recovery" basis which, he assured me, was a "very reasonable rate" and would I please arrange to send ZAA a cheque for $5,000?

Well, that was all very fine, but there were two fairly important obstacles from our side. We didn't have any money and, just as with the feasibility study, was this really a reasonable request considering that we were partnering with ZAA and were planning a revolutionary approach to help save a species, from which ZAA would unquestionably benefit? Not having much choice, we bit our collective lips and, once again thanks to Allan Davies' Family Foundation, we sent the $5,000. No free lunches here.

During the discussions we were hit with another lightning bolt when we were told there was only one quarantine space and that only two rhinos could be added to the existing facilities at Western Plains. This was a major, major issue for us – we had assumed, in fact been told, that Western Plains had the quarantine capacity to meet our plans and Allan and I were surprised and less than impressed.

In April 2014, I kicked off the Australian government approval campaign by writing to Dr Andrew Cupit, Assistant Secretary,

Animal Biosecurity at AUSDAFF. It was a long, but important communication which requested the department's support for importing rhinos from South Africa as an emergency measure to safeguard these species against the imminent threat of extinction. I gave details of the poaching issue and the seemingly insatiable demand from Vietnam and China for horn. I explained that TARP had been set up "to ensure the survival of the species" by maintaining a viable population of rhinos well out of the danger zone. I mentioned that we had been working closely with Taronga, ZAA and the Veterinary School to develop plans to import the rhino from the Kruger Park to Western Plains and that these animals, saved from likely poaching in their native land, would supplement the existing rhinos in Australian zoos, increase genetic diversity and help to safeguard these species from the threat of extinction.

I mentioned that the plan had received in-principle support from the South African authorities who were prepared to consider every viable alternative to save the rhino and that they considered the TARP project as but one alternative in a variety of possible strategies to combat the poaching. I asked that the Australian Government undertake the necessary review of the 1999 South African rhino import conditions so that importation of rhino from South Africa could occur as soon as possible. I included details of ZAA's support and Taronga's three-year partnership agreement with us.

A month later I had a response from Andrew Cupit. It was way better than any of us could have hoped for. Andrew agreed to a review of the importation policy and assigned it a high priority. He specified that the review would be limited to animals sourced from Kruger Park and imported as part of the Australian Rhino

Project. At a meeting in Andrew's office in Canberra, I noted his "Top Priorities" list on his whiteboard. Half in jest, I suggested that the next time it would be good to have TARP on the list. Sure enough, the next time we met, there it was on the whiteboard.

Andrew detailed the import policy designed to manage the biosecurity risks and animal welfare issues associated with the importation and handling of wild animal species, noting that the animals must be resident in an approved, licensed or registered zoo or wildlife park in the exporting country since birth or for at least 12 months immediately before export. He went on to say it was likely that an AUSDAFF officer would need to undertake a site visit to inspect the pre-export quarantine facilities and stipulated that we would need to meet these costs. Andrew concluded the note by saying, *"I look forward to a continued close working relationship with you for the prioritisation of import access requests."*

I was over the moon, we all were and, with the benefit of hindsight, I have always felt that had Dr Andrew Cupit and Dr Jill Millan of the Biosecurity Branch of the Department of Agriculture continued to have carriage of this project, the rhinos would by now be grazing peacefully in a paddock in Australia. They both had a "can-do" attitude.

For the time being, we were ecstatic. Pillars one, two and three were on solid ground.

FIGHTING POACHERS WITH TECHNOLOGY

If there was no poaching there would be no crisis for endangered species. In developing our translocation plans there was no way that the poaching issue could be ignored. I believed then and believe still that the demand for rhino horn will never be satisfied and I also knew there were very few opportunities for me or the board to influence that demand. We could, however, assist with anti-poaching solutions on the supply side. I would happily disband the Australian Rhino Project if the demand for rhino horn went away.

In 2013, I was introduced to Dave Weidner by Dr Ian Player. Dave has a rich history of success, mainly at US software organisations and Ian was confident that he would support us financially. Dave co-founded Four Winds Interactive, which has a symbiotic relationship with Wildlife Protection Solutions (WPS), a not-for-profit, which Dave also conceived. With these two organisations Dave is now able to bring his entrepreneurial nature, high-tech background and resources and love of animals together in service to wildlife conservation.

I asked Dave if he would be willing to donate to the project. Understandably, he was cautious in his response and suggested that, as a first step, I visited the WPS Research Facility in South Africa where I duly met with some of Dave's team, Executive Director Eric Schmidt and Head Ranger Brendon Schmikl.

Over the years, I had been exposed to a number of anti-poaching concepts, projects and systems but once I reviewed the WPS system, I was convinced that it was, at that time, best of breed. Rather than the traditional silos of information that most organisations, large or small, have to deal with, the WPS system integrated several sources of information and presented them in a simple dashboard interface for the user. More than thirty years in IT certainly helped me here and I looked forward to seeing a demonstration of the system.

Dave had put his money where his mouth was and had signed a long-term lease for a 10,000-hectare property in the Waterberg area and had bought ten white rhinos as his contribution to conservation. Despite the fact that the newly built research facility had almost been washed away by a flooding river the week I got there it was obvious this was a serious venture that Dave was funding.

I returned to Sydney very impressed with what I had seen of the WPS system and determined to assist Dave in getting some traction. I offered to arrange meetings with senior people in Southern Africa involved in protecting rhinos in an effort to spread the awareness and potential implementation of his system. Dave is a pretty dry guy, but he enthusiastically agreed and I set up meetings with John Hume, the biggest private rhino owner in the world; Major General Johan Jooste, head of anti-poaching for SANParks; Dave Powrie, General Manager of the world famous Sabi Sands Game Reserve and the Honourable Tshekedi Khama, Botswana Minister for the Environment (and brother of the President, Ian Khama).

Through my relationships I was able to arrange meetings with people at the top of the rhino conservation field. but I knew I was taking a risk since I didn't know Dave Weidner at all. He probably felt the same way about me. When I finally met him, he was not at all what I expected. He is a quiet and thoughtful man and, in my view, almost spiritual. I now understood why he got on so well with Ian Player, whom he held in the highest regard.

Our first stop was at John Hume's farm, a couple of hours west of Johannesburg. I had met John a few times and found him to be an amusing but also an intense man. Raised in Zimbabwe, John made his money building holiday resorts. He is wealthy by any standards and that wealth excludes the value of the six tonnes of rhino horn that he has stashed away in bank vaults in and around Johannesburg. John claims to be a conservationist and who am I to argue, but I will say that he is equally an entrepreneur and also a very clever businessman. At the time of our visit, we estimated that, at current black-market prices, John's rhino horn stocks would be worth about US$100 million.

After the introductions, John took us on a tour of his 700-hectare farm, housing almost 1,000 rhinos. It is a pretty desolate place.

Make no mistake, I love rhinos, but to see every rhino without a horn was disturbing, even heartbreaking although the horns do regrow. And then John dehorns them again. John's strong view was that by dehorning his rhinos, poachers would not be interested. Sadly, he was wrong and he had recently lost a number of rhinos to poachers. Furthermore, in the previous few months, he had lost more than 40 rhinos to a virus which he suspected was clostridium. He had sent blood samples all over the world to try and establish the cause of death, without any firm result. One possible reason, offered by a SANParks veterinarian surgeon, was that it resulted from such a large number of rhinos being kept in close proximity to each other. Taronga Zoo had a similar problem in 2015 when they lost four white rhinos in one go. Those deaths were never fully explained either.

John's goal was to have sufficient rhinos to produce 200 births each year. He was very open with us and spent a lot of time going through the comprehensive data he maintains on each rhino. What is crystal clear is that he is deeply concerned about the safety of his rhinos. His security system costs him approximately US$3 million a year. He has to be a key player in any discussions about rhinos since he owns up to twenty per cent of the world's remaining animals. Some would say, obviously, that he is also a passionate driver of the push to legalise the trade in rhino horn.

I was determined to source some rhinos from him.

Dave and his team did an excellent demonstration of their anti-poaching system and although John described himself as a technology Luddite, he was sufficiently smart to see the benefits of the system. Since Dave and his team landed at Johannesburg airport, they had been lugging around an extra-large steel suitcase. I was dying to know what was inside and finally, at John's farm, all was revealed. The suitcase contained a drone. Neither the authorities in Denver nor at OR Tambo Airport had even enquired as to the suitcase's contents. Eric offered to demonstrate its capabilities and by this time John's sister and a friend, both well into their seventies had come along for a look – not too many drones in Klerksdorp at that time.

The demo was an epic fail. After a slow, controlled vertical takeoff, the drone suddenly developed a mind of its own and, like an Exocet missile, headed straight for Beryl and Meryl who took off like scalded cats. Highly amusing for John and highly embarrassing for Dave and his team. The drone did not see the light of day for the rest of the trip.

Over a cup of tea (without Beryl and Meryl), we discussed the seemingly impossible task of changing beliefs in the supposed mystical powers of rhino horn in countries like China and Vietnam. John murmured that he had personally experimented with rhino horn's ability to improve one's sexual performance and he could categorically confirm that it didn't work. There was stunned silence in the room. There are literally millions of people who believe that rhino horn is an aphrodisiac and here was John, a man in his seventies, who had actually tried it.

The author with John Hume. (Photo credit: Margaret Dearlove)

"*Ja,*" he said, "*one night I was feeling a bit horny – ha, ha, ha – and I shaved off a bit of rhino horn, popped it a glass, topped it up with vodka, added a bit of Tabasco and down the hatch it went . . . I waited for about twenty minutes with no movement – in any direction – so I fell asleep!*". A true conversation stopper.

I'm very pleased and proud to say that the WPS system is now installed at John's farm with excellent security results.

Our next visit was with the Botswana Minister for the Environment, the Honourable Tshekedi Khama, in his office in Gaborone. This was the only time that I had visited a country for a two-hour meeting. We left Johannesburg at 11am and we were back by 5pm the same day. Exhausted but exhilarated.

Tshekedi, who insists on being called TK, is one of three sons of Sir Seretse and Lady Ruth Khama. Sir Seretse was the first President of Botswana and is revered by all Botswanans. TK's brother, Ian, is President of Botswana.

The minister was accompanied by his two senior executives responsible for rhino protection – Dr Cyril Taolo and Tim Blackbeard. Tim is a soldier who clearly knows what is required to keep his animals safe. I tabled an offer for a potential partnership between the Botswana government and WPS stressing that we were not there to "peddle" anything. I had been warned that the government was sick of so-called experts turning up and offering them the world and then not delivering. We certainly did not want to be included in that group.

The government had recently taken a brave decision to reintroduce rhino and they were about to receive their first eight from the Kruger Park. Controlling Botswana's 4,500-kilometre border with four countries was a serious challenge. It was chilling to think that at that time, as pointed out by TK, Australia had more rhinos than Botswana.

I really liked TK. Here was a man at the top of his game who knew exactly what the issues were, who obviously consulted extensively with his people and was open to new ideas. I felt extremely privileged to be given an opportunity to present a solution that could help him, his country and the rhinos.

Dave Weidner, The Honourable Tshekedi Khama
and the author. (Photo credit: Eric Schmidt)

TK also showed a lighter side during the discussion as he said, *"Ray, my job is not to judge the poachers – that is God's job. My job is to arrange the meeting."* Touché.

It is worth noting that the Botswana Defence Force, which has the responsibility for protecting the rhinos, has a "shoot to kill" policy. To further ensure the safety of the animals, they have a one-to-one ratio of soldier per rhino.

The Khama family has made a serious contribution to conservation in Botswana. The Khama Rhino Sanctuary is a community-based wildlife project, established in 1992 to protect endangered rhinos, restoring an area formerly teeming with wildlife to its previous natural state and providing economic benefits to the local community through tourism and the sustainable use of natural resources. Covering approximately 9,000 hectares, the sanctuary provides prime habitat for white and black rhino as well as more than thirty other animal species and more than 230 species of birds.

During this visit, I became aware of another project with goals very similar to mine. The South Africa-based travel company &Beyond and Dereck Joubert's Great Plains Conservation had joined forces to create an organisation named Rhinos Without Borders, whose sole goal was to move rhinos from poaching hotspots to a safer environment. The project aimed to translocate 100 rhinos from high-risk poaching areas in South Africa to the comparative safety of Botswana. The whole project, including ongoing and monitoring and security, required a total budget of US$4.5 million.

Botswana was selected for its low poaching rates and its "no tolerance/shoot-to-kill" policy when encountering potential threats. The people making this happen, Les Carlisle of &Beyond, and Dereck and Beverley Joubert of Rhinos Without Borders, have done a remarkable job in terms of fundraising – Dereck is a marketing machine.

In early 2014, I met Les and Dereck in Johannesburg. It was an exhilarating meeting for me – to converse with two individuals who were also totally committed to translocating rhinos to make them safe. In a far-reaching discussion, their view was that the tipping point had already been reached, that the poachers were highly efficient and were focused on taking out the big bulls, which raised the question of the impact on the genetics of the remaining population. Les and Dereck had undertaken extensive research and concluded that the Okavango Delta was an ideal destination for the rhinos.

When I mentioned the Botswana initiative to Ian Player shortly before he died, he said, *"Ray, Botswana has allowed their rhinos to become extinct in the wild twice in the past, what makes this one different?"* Dereck had a completely different view, saying that the commitment of the Botswana government, led by President Ian Khama, was absolute. The rhinos would have 24/7 one-on-one protection and the shoot-to-kill policy was a powerful deterrent.

I have a deeper concern. Africa's politics are volatile at the best of times. There are any number of examples of this throughout the continent ever since Harold McMillan's "winds of change" blew through Africa almost sixty years ago. Botswana has maintained a strong tradition of stable representative democracy, with a consistent record of uninterrupted democratic elections and the best perceived corruption ranking in Africa. Since independence, the party system has been dominated by the Khama-led Botswana Democratic Party. What will happen if there is a change of government or even a change of president? President Khama is a passionate conservationist as is his brother TK, but there is no guarantee their successors will feel as strongly about endangered species such as rhino. One can see a successful political campaign arguing for more expenditure on education and health and less on protecting rhinos. We pray that this does not happen.

In his role with &Beyond, Les Carlisle has been a steadfast supporter of mine. Unlike some others who seem to resent "competition", Les welcomes any initiative that will contribute to saving rhinos in the wild. After a few beers one night, I must have been sufficiently persuasive for Les to say that, once the Botswana relocation was complete, he would focus on helping TARP.

One of &Beyond's flagship lodges is Phinda Game Reserve, which went through a shocking period of rampant poaching in 2015. I had extensive discussions with Anton Louw, the Managing Director of Phinda and the adjoining Zuka Reserve about sourcing rhinos and Anton was strongly supportive of the plan. Zuka is owned by the grandson of John Paul Getty, who carries the somewhat exotic name of Tara Galaxy Gabriel Gramophone Getty.

Our next stop on the Wildlife Protection Solutions roadshow was at Sabi Sands in the eastern part of South Africa. Sabi Sands comprises some of the best known and exclusive game lodges in the world, including Mala Mala, Ulusaba (owned by Sir Richard Branson) and Londolozi, totalling 62,000 hectares with 72 kilometres of fence line. The reserve is unfenced to the Kruger Park and has a strong population of more than 200 rhinos. When we met, they had lost 51 to poaching. There are 2,800 staff on the reserve which is surrounded by more than 650,000 people in various communities, many of whom live on or below the bread line. Almost 90 per cent of poaching incidents are considered "insider jobs".

Sabi Sands had invested heavily on increasing the protection of the reserve, specifically on fencing; the training of all staff and full delegation of security authority to General Manager Dave Powrie's team – each ranger carried a hand-held radio and GPS.

The rule of engagement became "shoot to kill" but only if the poacher first engaged the ranger. The impact of this focus and investment was immediate and poaching reduced dramatically.

Dave Powrie runs an impressive operation and is a most likeable man. He was immediately taken by the WPS system's power and the benefits of the technology. He showed us his anti-poaching war room, which had a curtain down one wall. He pulled the curtain aside and there was a hierarchical organisation chart which included the names and photos of the known poachers in the area: a true rogues' gallery. Sadly, quite a number of these men had previously worked at Sabi Sands and, as a result, Dave had introduced polygraph – lie-detector – tests every six months for all staff including managerial, administration, labourers and rangers. Nobody was exempt. This was a mammoth task but it had immediate results – a number of employees were fired after they failed two consecutive tests and, lo and behold, the number of poaching incidents reduced sharply.

A few months after our visit, Dave and his wife Loma were asleep at home with their one-year-old son in an adjoining room. At 2am, the bedroom light suddenly went on and there at the foot of the bed were five men, three of whom were armed with machetes and one with a gun. Dave and Loma were completely helpless. Their dog, which slept in their room every night for protection, they subsequently discovered, had been drugged. The poachers demanded that Dave hand over the rhino horn. There was no rhino horn in his house but they would not believe him and after a few minutes, things got really ugly when one of the poachers jumped on Loma. Dave exploded and despite the overwhelming odds he fought them out of his house and then collapsed with sixteen knife wounds to his body including a punctured lung. Loma was also stabbed but fortunately their baby slept through the whole nightmare. I'm pleased to say that Dave survived and he is back on the job. This demonstrates the lengths to which some people will go to get their hands on rhino horn. It also demonstrates the dedication of the men and women on the front line, protecting animals.

Dave and the WPS team agreed that Sabi Sands would become a beta test site for the WPS system, which is now up and running. Saving rhinos. And saving people.

The final meeting in what had been a frenetic week was with Major General Johan Jooste in his office in Skukuza in the Kruger Park. I had previously met Johan, head of anti-poaching operations for all of South Africa's national parks. Many people, and not just his critics, believed that he had an unwinnable task. I really wanted to contribute and I believed that WPS had the technology to do so.

I made exactly these points to the General in my opening remarks – the potential for a partnership between SANParks and WPS and our goal to add value to the General's infrastructure, investment and plans.

The General is a fairly formal man but always polite and gracious (even if he has heard the story many times before!). He confided that his forces were losing the war. The poachers were highly skilled, armed to the teeth, very professional and would strike any day of the week. His primary objective was to identify and catch the poachers *before* they enter the park, making the point that while it was satisfying catching the poachers after they had killed, it did not fulfil the objective, so early detection was vital.

He went further, saying that SANParks are focused on

gathering "intelligence"; following the poaching money trail (agencies such as the FBI and Interpol are engaged); social network analysis and the need for community interaction. *"Without the latter, we will fail."*

The Mozambique government is a key player but seems to neither care nor help. Bearing in mind that this conversation took place in April 2014, not much appears to have changed.

The General stressed that whatever systems were introduced could not be over-intrusive because of the potential negative impact on tourists. More than two million people visit Kruger each year and the General's worst nightmare was a tourist encountering a poacher.

Kruger Park rangers from the K9 unit. Photo Credit (Photo Credit: Kruger Park News)

The subject of drones came up. It was pretty obvious that the General did not have much faith in drone technology. A month did not go by without him being contacted by some organisation that had the latest and greatest drone technology and he just *had* to see it. *"We had another one a few months ago,"* he said, *"a young, confident American lad who was obviously very proud of his invention. I take the view that I have to see them all, in case, just in case, this one is the game changer. Anyway, we took him out to the Skukuza airfield for the demo. It was very hot; it can get to 50 degrees Celsius here in summer. He carefully unpacked his drone and then laid it out on the runway and, you know what, it began to melt in front of our eyes! We haven't seen that chap again."* I gave Dave Weidner a look which said keep that drone in the steel suitcase!

There is a lot of granite in Kruger, mainly in the south where most of the poaching action is concentrated. The high summer temperatures heat the granite during the day, only cooling down again in the early hours of the morning. This rendered some heat-seeking technologies ineffective, where what might seem like a foreign object, for example a gun, is actually just the granite.

The General was very open with us and outlined his battle plan and strategy. Kruger Park is the largest game reserve in Africa. It covers an area of 19,485 square kilometres and extends 360 kilometres from north to south and 65 kilometres from east to west. It is a huge area to protect with limited resources and, given these vast areas, the General had decided to split the area into three protection zones.

He named the southern area the Intensive Protection Zone (IPZ), bordered by the Crocodile and Sabie rivers where most of the rhinos in the Park and hence, in the world, are located. Logically, this is also where most of the poaching takes place – from Mozambique on the eastern boundary and, more recently, from the communities on the western border. The General's intention was to secure this area "like Fort Knox" using the best technology available including seismic cables, portable cameras, fixed cameras and helicopters as well as rapid response rangers and dogs.

The central section was named the Joint Protection Zone (JPZ), bordered by the Sabie and Olifants rivers and there was a heavy reliance on cooperation with the private game reserves on the western side of the Park which could act as a buffer. By definition, there would be less resources assigned to this area.

The northern section is the Joint Management Zone (JMZ), bordered by the Olifants and Limpopo rivers. As the General said, the JMZ would require unprecedented cross-border cooperation (with Mozambique) and deep local community involvement. The General was keenly aware that while there were not many rhinos in this area, it was home to hundreds of elephants and they were unquestionably next on the poachers' menu.

We felt privileged that the General was willing to confide his strategy, which was not yet in the public domain. He was impressed with the WPS integrated approach and asked us to brief the South African Council for Scientific and Industrial Research (CSIR) who do all the evaluations and comparisons of proposals on his behalf.

The meeting with the General brought an end to an exciting and exhausting week. We had certainly added value to everyone that we met and Dave Weidner and the WPS team were delighted with the meetings which set the platform for the establishment of pilot sites for their technology. I had also cemented my relationships, which boded well for gaining additional resources for my rhinos.

As requested by the General, I subsequently met with the CSIR team in Pretoria and demonstrated the WPS system to them. I couldn't understand why they were cautious, almost cagey, until they mentioned that they were working on a similar system. That surprised me, and it also surprised me that they showed no interest in cooperating with WPS in a co-development. I had strong views on this. If the WPS system fit their requirements, why not build on it? I urged them to consider a Public Private Partnership (PPP) which enabled governments and the private sector to work together and share resources on key projects. I knew that Dave Weidner would throw additional resources at such a project – he was so committed to conservation. CSIR were not at all interested and they would not bend. All that they would say was that they were building a similar system. In my view, all the more reason to share resources.

Not long afterwards the CSIR announced the Cmore Surveillance system described as a platform for shared awareness. A system similar to WPS, Cmore covers large geographic expanses, enabling real-time surveillance and analytics of "entities" of interest and "incidents" such as poaching. It is being deployed across the Kruger Park and, to date, with considerable, tangible results.

I am delighted to say that shortly after I returned to Australia, Dave Weidner sent a donation of US$10,000 for my project, which was most welcome.

PREVIOUS IMPORTATIONS

One of my biggest fears was that one or more of the parties involved would see the project as becoming all too hard. As negotiations with the Australian government stumbled along, I researched possible precedents of previous rhino imports that I could reference, with the hope of simplifying what was becoming ever more complex.

Lord Alistair McAlpine, best known as chief fundraiser for Margaret Thatcher's Conservative Party, is widely credited as the developer of the world-renowned Western Australia resort town of Broome and the builder of the Cable Beach complex. He also founded the Broome Pearl Coast Zoo.

McAlpine first came to Australia in 1959, returning in 1964 to Perth – "a big farming town" – as a developer, building office blocks and the city's first five-star hotel, the Parmelia. It was the start of a lifelong love affair with Australia. He headed to "ramshackle" Broome in 1979 with plans to collect seashells, but instead bought a house after he came back from the pub, and went on to sign the deal for the Cable Beach site on the back of a beer coaster. His passion for gardening, especially frangipanis, saw him plant out the city, giving Broome the tropical feel it still enjoys today. He also laid the groundwork for the international reputation Broome pearls now have.

McAlpine managed to import a wide variety of animals into his Pearl Coast Zoo including nyala, sitatunga, sable, gemsbok, kudu, eland, nilgai, lechwe, waterbuck, Angolan springbok, Congo and water buffalo, Grevy's zebra, pygmy hippo, and scimitar horned oryx. Significantly for my project, there was not one incident of any of Australia's fauna or flora being contaminated in any way. Good news.

The 1989 Australian pilot's strike and Prime Minister Paul Keating's "recession we had to have" hammered Broome's fledgling tourism industry and spelt the end of Lord McAlpine's grand plans for the town. Real estate prices faltered and confidence in the town's economy was shot.

Enter one Warren Anderson, a man of grand schemes and sweeping vision, who fell in love with the Northern Territory and bought one of the jewels of the Top End's pastoral belt – the expansive Tipperary cattle station of more than 500,000 acres, which lies in lush landscape along the Daly River. It was swiftly redesigned to Warren's blueprint. He transformed Tipperary into a majestic, modern business, equipped to perfection. But it became more than a mere bush outpost; it was also Anderson's private pleasure dome, a parkland conceived on a grand scale and reflecting his own fascinations and tastes.

At the time, Kerry Packer and Anderson were Australia's wealthiest men. To many who were familiar with the station empires of the far north, Anderson's Tipperary could be read as a response to Newcastle Waters, the hub of the outback empire of the Packer-owned Consolidated Pastoral; a kind of remote version of Sans Souci Palace, deliberately constructed to outdo Packer's Versailles. At the time, Anderson's wealth was estimated at $200 million by the *Australian Business Review* and only Kerry Packer was ahead of him.

Tipperary was on a different scale from anything, anywhere; it was the wildest venture northern Australia had ever seen. It had its own neat town and post office, an equestrian centre, an indoor tennis court, a sealed runway long and wide enough to take a Boeing 727, and single men's quarters decked out in brass and jarrah with a swimming pool and a school.

But the standout feature of Tipperary was the wildlife, roaming pretty much "free" in 400-hectare paddocks. Anderson loved and prized rare animals and bought all of Lord McAlpine's animals from the bankrupt Broome Pearl Coast Zoo.

He collected them and he bred them, and had more than 2200 animals and birds, including zebras, giraffes, several varieties of deer, tropical birds, scimitar-horned oryxes, two white rhino bulls and, in pride of place, luxuriating in their dedicated muddy lake, four precious pygmy hippos.

I tracked down Kevin Langham in Cairns. Langham had arrived from the Mugabe-led Zimbabwe with just $200 in his pocket. A qualified scientist, he did labouring jobs, worked at Western Plains Zoo for a while and then, in 1986, he received a phone call from Warren Anderson which changed his life. Warren wanted Kevin to manage his free-range game park, on which he had already spent $100 million. This was Tipperary Station. The stipulation was that this was not a tourist venture, this was purely for threatened and endangered species.

In Kevin's words: *"Warren was way ahead of his time, not only in a business sense with live cattle export, but also in his views, passion and commitment to conservation. In establishing the Tipperary Sanctuary, Warren had to overcome a raft of 'administrative challenges', not unlike those which you have been through, Ray.*

Tipperary Sanctuary was a project that was on the cusp of making a significant contribution to the conservation of endangered mammals on a regional and international scale. Warren had possibly the largest herd of endangered scimitar horned oryx in the world while the endangered addax, Grevy's zebra, Kafue lechwe and Congo buffalo were all breeding well. CSIRO were working on a research project that had the potential to significantly improve digestion of plant material in cattle, by using rumen microflora from exotic species. A large herd of nilgai antelope was breeding well and showing great potential as a selective browser, controlling broad leaf plants, and the rhino were doing well with plans underway to rapidly increase the number. With just a little more luck, who knows where this would have landed.

One thing is for certain Ray, Warren fights hard, he does not entertain failure, or idiots, and from my experience is more interested in 'how it can be done' rather than 'why it cannot be done' . . . and you need that approach to take on the type of project that you have. Warren demonstrated that it can be done."

Warren Anderson's magnificent Tipperary
Station in the Northern Territory

In 2003, Warren got into financial difficulties and was forced to
sell Tipperary. The property was acquired by Allan Myers QC, in
a move that Warren said broke his heart.

With quite some difficulty, I eventually tracked Warren down
and had a number of meetings with him. Now a very private man,
Warren's story was the ultimate rags to riches and back to rags. He
left school when he was fourteen, after taking exception to being
"strapped" and giving the teacher "a clip".

Warren has been associated with some of Australia's largest
developments including the $1 billion-plus Westralia Square sky-
scraper in Perth; more than 70 Coles supermarkets around Australia;
the Parliament House complex in Darwin, and the redevelopment of
the historic Melbourne Windsor Hotel. At various points in his life
he owned Boomerang, the iconic Sydney waterfront property, and
also the heritage listed Fernhill property at Mulgoa.

When he sold Tipperary, Warren sold many of his exotic animals, including the rhino, to Mareeba Wild Animal Park in Queensland, which was opened in 2003. Others went to Mary River Station, which has now become one of Australia's largest game-hunting reserves.

Warren is extremely supportive of what I tried to achieve but is equally cynical about the future of any such project, believing that the Australian government has little or no interest in conserving endangered species. I must admit that after our conversations, I thought that if Warren Anderson, with all of his financial and political clout could not make a success of protecting the planet's animals in Australia, what hope did I have.

Love him or hate him, and there are plenty of people on both sides, Warren Anderson is certainly one of Australia's most interesting identities. Sadly, his contribution to conservation is unknown and untold.

Warren Anderson and the author

MERCENARIES AND OTHER

VENTURES AND ADVENTURES

During my journey trying to make the "four pillars" become reality, specifically in sourcing rhinos for Australia, I came across a number of interesting people, most of whom had the rhinos' interests at heart.

I had become the go-to man when it came to rhinos in Australia and in early 2014, I was contacted by Dr Andrew Muir, CEO of the South African Wilderness Foundation who said that he and Ian Player had been approached by another group wanting to export rhinos to Australia. Andrew had been contacted by a Simon Witherspoon, Director of the Australian Safari Club (ASC), with a proposal to move rhinos to the Northern Territory (NT). The key elements of the proposal claimed that ASC had met with the NT government and their response was "extremely positive"; that they had the support of traditional landowners who would make available suitable land, and the involvement of the local communities in the project who said that any concept that enhanced land utilisation, created employment and boosted tourism would receive maximum support from all levels of government. Witherspoon also mentioned that *"the Attorney General, (John) Johan Wessel, is an ex-South African and had expressed support.'* ASC also referred obliquely to our project by saying that it was a positive development: *'This can only benefit rhino as a whole, and we support any effort to preserve the species for future generations."*

I read the proposal very carefully. If ASC had achieved all of this, they had done well – very well. Andrew discussed the proposal with Ian and they agreed that they should support only one Australian initiative and that was mine. Andrew passed this message on to me and Ian made it quite clear to Witherspoon that he held the same view.

At Andrew's and Ian's request, I called Simon and we had a long discussion. I then wrote to Ian saying that there was no question that Simon was well meaning in his quest to bring rhinos to Australia and he seemed to have done his homework with the people from the Northern Territory. What he did not grasp was the huge amount of work required to get such a project to the starting line. Specifically, he didn't have the basic governance procedures for doing business in Australia. He would need to register a company and he would need to apply for the DGR status, which allows for a full tax deduction of all donations. This approval is not easily granted – we had been trying to get it for eight months.

Without the DGR status, Simon would find that fundraising in Australia was nigh impossible.

The second major obstacle he would face was gaining the approval of the Australian government. The Australian government would not approve another application for rhinos to be imported into Australia from South Africa, since our approval was seen as a one-off. Also, despite all the work Simon had done with the Northern Territory government, it was irrelevant since biosecurity is a federal government responsibility. I kept the door open by saying there was opportunity to work together with ASC but I did not pull any punches by saying that they were wasting their time (and probably everybody else's) in pursuing a separate initiative and that the best (only?) chance of success was merging with us. Other well-meaning efforts would fail or take a decade to come to fruition.

I also pointed out that Simon's reference to Johan Wessel being an ex-South African was completely wrong. His name is actually Johan Wessel Elferink and he was born in the Netherlands, not South Africa. I know because I spoke to him.

I was troubled by a number of inconsistencies in this proposed venture. I knew how difficult and complex our project was proving to be and I really didn't need the distraction that Witherspoon's plans offered.

As part of my research, I googled Simon and found some worrying information. He had been involved with Mark Thatcher (later Sir Mark), the son of former British Prime Minister Margaret Thatcher, in the abortive coup attempt in Equatorial Guinea. Witherspoon was arrested along with 63 others who claimed to be mercenaries after their aircraft was seized in Harare.

This was pretty unnerving stuff and a subsequent article in the media provided further background. Apparently all 63 mercenaries were uniformed, heavily armed with assault rifles, sophisticated communications and other military equipment. Witherspoon was named as the leader of the group and it was claimed that, if the coup was successful, the group was promised the handsome reward of one million pounds and mining rights in a part of Equatorial Guinea.

With all of this in mind and because of Witherspoon's discussions with the NT government, I thought that I should do some investigating myself. I called John Elferink, Attorney-General of the NT government and briefed him about my project and asked if he had spoken to Simon Witherspoon. He recalled having a brief conversation with him over coffee – that was all – and asked me to send the proposal Simon had prepared. He invited me to call him back in a week or so, which I duly did. It was a difficult conversation. John was angry and also very wary of me. He asked me how well I knew Witherspoon – I said I had only spoken to him that one time on the phone.

In the meantime, Elferink had obviously been doing his own research and discovered that Simon had been involved in yet another coup attempt, again with mercenaries. This time in Papua New Guinea as part of a group calling themselves, "Executive Outcomes". Australians feel almost paternal about PNG and are extremely protective of its people. This was turning out to be like an episode from "Inspector Morse". Apparently the plan was to oust the rebels holding the Panguna mine on Bougainville Island. The plan failed.

John Elferink made it abundantly clear that if I, or TARP,

were in any way involved with Witherspoon, we had an insurmountable problem with any NT projects. I confirmed that we had no intention of working with them. In closing, John invited me to Darwin and said *"If you bring me a proposal to locate rhinos in the Northern Territory, we will support you in whichever way that we can."*

Subsequently, I heard nothing more about or from Simon Witherspoon.

Another person who I thought could be of assistance in sourcing rhinos was Jacques Brits, General Manager of Timbavati Nature Reserve, which borders the Kruger Park and covers around 54,000 hectares. Jacques had invited me to have a chat about moving some of Timbavati's rhinos to Australia and I was looking forward to this meeting since I had always associated Timbavati with hunting and, of course, the internationally famous white lions.

Timbavati has 50 members, each with their own discreet landholding. The pro-hunting faction claims to be the voice of reason; the high ground of "economic sustainability"; the "scientific proof" that the selective hunting of a few carefully targeted animals presents no threat to the species; the return on investment of hunting safaris versus photographic safaris; and the "inescapable fact" that it is only through trade and the commoditisation of wildlife that conservation can be suitably funded and vulnerable species properly protected.

Aside from the "moral reprehensibility" of trophy hunting, many in the "anti" hunting camp would argue, with justification, that the hunting fraternity and conservation officialdom in South Africa is rife with corruption and alive with opportunities for laundering trophies into the global illegal trade for products such as horn and ivory. So, there we have both sides of a very complex situation.

Jacques and Laetitia Brits are lovely people – welcoming, gracious and warm. We had a good discussion which inevitably moved to the subject of Australia. Everywhere I went, people wanted to know what it was like living in Australia as most saw the country as nirvana.

Once these discussions were out of the way, Jacques casually mentioned that he had recently been to Australia to speak at a function in Brisbane. Maybe I was a bit sensitive, but it seemed to me that Jacques was a little reluctant to provide any details of his visit. However, once we had both had generous helpings of Laetitia's delicious quiche with biltong sprinkled over it (for breakfast!), he opened up.

There was a group of South Africans in Queensland who were also looking to import rhinos into Australia. Piet Warren, a wealthy farmer in South Africa, was prepared to fund the entire project by buying land in Queensland, providing a seed population of rhinos and paying all transportation costs to Australia. It sounded like a wonderful plan – very similar to mine. If we could work together, we could make this happen much quicker than I had thought possible. Jacques Brits is a serious and conservative man and I soon realised that he had committed himself to making this project a success. He said that it had significant support and that the head of the Brisbane group, Andre van Zyl, would be in contact with me.

I duly met Andre at the Coogee Bay Hotel and we discussed our respective plans. Within minutes I knew there was going to be one overarching obstacle to us working together. Andre did not try to disguise it – their project was a "commercial" one. To me commercial could mean only one of, or a combination of, three things: rhinos were to be hunted; rhino horns were to be harvested; or the rhinos were to be a tourist attraction. These fundamental differences meant we had a short conversation but we did agree to remain in contact if we could find some common ground.

Soon after, I received an invitation to meet with Andre's consortium in Brisbane. He had spoken to his team and concluded that there were many foundational synergies that should be considered with a joint approach. His expected outcomes of the meeting included understanding the progress and objectives of the two "Australian initiatives", identifying any synergies and exploring the strategies available as a potential unified corporatised entity.

I decided that it was in TARP's interest to attend this meeting, at which there were six attendees, all from South Africa and all from different backgrounds. There was a medical engineer, a former rhino breeder and a corporate lawyer. The laudable common goal was to help rhinos. One attendee who particularly interested me was John Warren, the son of Piet, who was offering to finance the entire initiative. Piet owned 90 rhinos on his farm of which thirteen had recently been poached and he felt that he had to do something. Son John had recently emigrated to Australia.

As the meeting progressed, I became more and more uncomfortable. It was obvious that our objectives were intrinsically different. Some of the more contentious points raised by van Zyl were that the only successful outcome was to link my project and his AARP (Africa Australia Rhino Project) initiatives and that a strong commercial focus needed to be taken in order to ensure that the outcomes were achieved in a "timely and effective manner with genuine stakeholders."

When I was eventually asked to comment I told them that we had conducted a feasibility study which had assessed the logistics, legislation and other issues regarding the importation of rhinos and that the study had concluded that the importation of rhinos would be feasible. Contrary to their view, I did not believe the CITES approval for the legalisation of the trade in rhino horn would occur because the South Africans were unwilling to stand alone on the issue and that the majority of countries did not support the principle anyway. This was one of their fundamental assumptions. I turned out to be correct.

I told them that we had received in-principle Australian government approval to import rhinos under the "conservation" classification of importation. The temperature of the meeting began to rise but I felt strongly that I had to put our cards on the table; the stakes were too high not to. The approval was based on conservation and any commercial trading proposal would need to be approved by the federal Department of Environmental Affairs. And it would fail. I nearly fell off my chair when one of the attendees said, "the importation of rhinos will be easy." Unusually for me, I was speechless. He was either obstinate or he wasn't listening.

I then tabled a letter from the South African Department of Environmental Affairs. This was an important and relevant policy statement and included the criteria that live rhino exports to captive facilities was only allowed if the importing facility was a member of the World Association of Zoos and Aquariums (WAZA) and that live rhino exports would only be allowed if CITES in the importing country confirmed the horn would "*not be used for commercial purposes.*"

In plain terms, they would need to partner with a zoo. As we had done. As far as I was concerned this blew their proposal out of the water but, in fairly typical South African style, Andre ploughed on and asked me to consider a formal partnership. As a courtesy, I undertook to raise this at our next board meeting which I did but it was never going to happen. The key issue was the commercial intent of Andre's group. This was completely against everything we stood for and I was convinced the Australian government would not approve their project. I wasn't being a smartarse; I simply knew what was involved.

I subsequently wrote to Andre advising him that we would not be teaming up with the AARP and wishing him and his supporters well for the future. My understanding is that Piet Warren withdrew his support and the project quietly died.

In 2015, friend Niels Troost put me in contact with Dr Pat Condy, Executive Director of the Fossil Rim Wildlife Center, a not-for-profit based in Texas, which specialised in captive breeding programs for indigenous and exotic endangered and threatened species. Pat, yet another South African, had been approached by a Johannesburg software company with a proposal to move 1,000 rhinos to Texas. He was working with the Exotic Wildlife Association, a US organisation comprising game ranch owners that has more than 125 species of non-indigenous wildlife species, mostly African hoof-stock (ungulates), on their ranches. Most of the ranches were in Texas and varied in size from a few thousand acres to tens of thousands of acres. Pat wanted to know if there was anything they could learn from our experiences.

Well, we all know that everything is bigger and better in Texas but this was something else. One thousand rhino! Although somewhat sceptical, I let Pat know that we would help in whichever way we could. Pat then scaled down the numbers to more like 100 to 200 rhinos, which sounded much more realistic. He ventured that the US had less of a *"veterinary problem than do you in Australia,"* noting that in the past six months there had been three imports of white rhinos into the US from South Africa. How correct he was about the Australian veterinary and biosecurity requirements.

He said that they had already sourced ten white rhinos and they were pushing to get them to the US within the next six months. After some investigation, I established that the Johannesburg company was GroupElephant.com which had a number of divisions including Elephants, Rhinos & People (ERP) which was founded to preserve and protect Southern Africa's wild elephants and rhinos through a strategy based on rural poverty alleviation. In order to accomplish its mission, ERP carefully selected projects based on their potential to create economic engines for impoverished rural communities in areas adjacent to threatened elephant and rhino populations. By having a multifaceted team positioned to tackle poverty, ERP was able to address the welfare of these animals in an unorthodox but effective manner. ERP brought more than twenty years of experience in community relations, poverty alleviation, and impact investment in infrastructure, so as to achieve sustainable, non-lethal wildlife conservation.

In their proposal to the Exotic Wildlife Association, ERP said they had been blessed with many years of aggressive revenue and profit growth. Recent internal strategic conversations about "What's next?" gave birth to the initiative of going beyond corporate purpose with a specific focus on the preservation of at-risk elephants and rhinos, and alleviating poverty amongst rural populations in areas bordering the threatened animals. Like me, they had concluded that if we couldn't take the danger away from the rhinos, then we needed to take the rhinos away from the danger. They viewed Texas as a potential safe haven.

This project had so many touch-points for me in terms of what we were trying to achieve that I reached out to CEO Jon Tager with a request to open discussions since, as far as I was concerned, there were a number of potential synergies. Jon responded by return and I thought that this was an organisation that I could very easily work with (or for).

I subsequently met with several senior executives of EPI-use, the software delivery arm of the organisation, and we seemed to be edging towards a possible partnership. I sensed that Jon Tager and I were on the same wavelength. In principle, we could present one application for export to the South African government; we could share the rhino capture and quarantine costs; if AUSDAFF continued to stymie our efforts to import rhinos directly from South Africa, we could source them through the US (which was acceptable to AUSDAFF). Finally, I sincerely believed that, based on my work, I could save the ERP team a great deal of time and money. I was also prepared to have our project merge with ERP provided that rhinos came to Australia. Over and over again, Ian

Player said that the world needed to spread the risk and to take the rhinos out of the danger zone.

As our talks progressed it became evident that "our" model was being replicated at ERP and I took a potential merger with ERP to our board and was given the go-ahead to continue discussions. Unfortunately, our ongoing issues with AUSDAFF and the subsequent delays made any form of planning or strategising impossible and we eventually agreed to work in parallel with ERP. Although disappointed, anything that could be done to reduce the threat to rhinos had my full support.

The blatant shooting of a rhino and the removal of its horn at a Paris zoo in 2017 startled the executives at ERP. They now realised there was nowhere safe for rhinos. If this could happen at a Paris zoo, it could equally happen at a property in Texas, so they decided to pause the rhino relocation plans and concentrate their efforts on the communities within South Africa.

The folk at ERP are a determined and focused bunch and Jon Tager is an outstanding leader. I have no doubt that their efforts will bear fruit. I would love to be a part of that.

THE TED TALK

TED is a non-profit organisation devoted to spreading ideas, usually in the form of short, powerful talks. It began in 1984 as a conference where Technology, Entertainment and Design converged, and today covers almost all topics – from science to business to global issues – in more than 100 languages, and has a massive global following.

In late 2015, I was approached by Siobhan Moylan, who asked if I would be interested in doing a TED talk about The Australian Rhino Project at the Sydney Opera House. Would I ever! Siobhan sat on the panel that decided who should be on the following year's TED Sydney program.

I am a huge fan of TED talks and never, ever did I think that I would have such an opportunity. It would be a real coup for the project with a reach that we would never have expected to achieve. Siobhan was measured in our discussions. To reduce my expectations, she regularly pointed out that the final decision had not been made about the speakers but that I had a chance. Well, I threw in everything I had to ensure that I was selected. Outside of my family, I did not mention this to anyone, just in case it all fell in a heap. Siobhan was my official coach and mentor and she did an amazing job. She asked me to send through a draft talk, which I did, not realising that this was going to be the first of many drafts.

Finally, Siobhan called and said, *"You're in."* I was at once elated and terrified. Siobhan was my rock in terms of guiding me as the intensity of the "editing" of my talk increased. *"Rehearse, rehearse, rehearse,"* she said – over and over again.

I did a practice run with senior executives at JB Were. Donna Gulbin and her colleagues were honest in their critique of the talk; it was uncomfortable, but invaluable. This was but one example where the JB Were team of Donna, Shamal Dass and Alex Kalcheff were unwavering in their support for me.

When the day of the final dress rehearsal arrived, I gave my talk in front of a small group of TED staff – all experts in their fields. It was tough. One person was responsible for commenting and advising on content and another on presentation style, mannerisms, etc. I was told to speak more slowly, breathe in and use pauses for effect – all extremely useful advice. It was very positive, motivating and encouraging. And direct. No room for egos at this session.

I was mortified to hear that there would be no teleprompter. All I would see in front of me on the stage were two screens – one showing what was being projected behind me and the other a clock timing the talk – now that was really distracting. When I asked how long I had, I was told that twelve minutes was the standard, but that I could go to fifteen. I was also told that I was last on the agenda. Another shock – I had really hoped that I would be speaking early in the day, rather than having to wait all day to speak with my nervousness increasing and blood pressure rising. Siobhan said that the last two presentations were really important and that the organisers wanted to end on a high note. Gulp.

I was offered a "good seat" in the Opera House to watch the other speakers but I declined. I really did not want to see or hear other presentations and then be thinking "Oh God, why didn't I think of that?" or "What a great line – I should have used that" or that my talk would be dry. Or boring. Or not at all enjoyable. As a result, my wife and I drove into the city in time for Margie to watch the afternoon session while I tried to read a book and, for the umpteenth time, rehearse my speech.

What terrified me most was that I would forget the opening line "*I want you to imagine that you are a rhino – a grandma rhino.*" I was confident that once I got past that opening line, I would be OK. And so, I sat waiting, nervous, taking deep breaths in the green room.

This event is superbly organised, the TED team thought of everything – drinks, food, the lot. What was especially noticeable is how well each member of the TED team – most of whom were volunteers – cared for the speakers. Very comforting indeed. I don't care how many speeches or presentations you've made, this one is very special.

Finally, I was called to the make-up room. Again there was this calm with light-hearted banter, all of which settled the nerves.

In a flash, I was standing on the edge of the stage watching the speech before me finish. In some ways I wanted them to hurry up, in others, please take as long as you like. Then it was *"Ray, you're on, good luck, wow them."* Out I walked to the designated spot. I looked up and all I could see was the first few rows and then just people – a lot of people – 5,000 people. In addition, the whole day's event was streamed live on the internet and was being piped into a number of the offices of major firms.

"I want you to imagine that you are a rhino – a grandma rhino." I had barely started my talk when I noticed a woman in the front row crying with emotion. That was all I needed. I'm a pretty emotional person at the best of times and I knew that when I came to the line," and *"I want to say to all of the people in Africa who are fighting this undeclared war – you do not walk alone,"* I would probably choke up. For the rest of the talk, I avoided looking at the lady – I really hope that she actually enjoyed it.

The line about Johnny Depp was very well received. Depp, the famous film star, had recently been in Australia to make a film. The trouble began when his wife, Amber Heard, arrived to visit him with their two Yorkshire terriers, Pistol and Boo. Amber had disembarked from their private jet without declaring the presence of the dogs, which were supposed to be placed in quarantine upon arrival – standard practice in Australia. The Australian authorities were not happy, and set down the conditions for the couple to rectify matters.

Australia's Minister of Agriculture, Barnaby Joyce, a fairly fiery individual, had strong words for Depp: *"It looks like he sneaked them in. He either has to take his dogs back to California or we're going to have to euthanise them."*

That struck Johnny and Amber as a tad extreme. Sympathetic observers started a hashtag, #WarOnTerrier, and created a petition asking for canine leniency. But celebrities aren't above the law, Mr. Joyce maintained. *"If you start letting movie stars, even though they've been the 'sexiest man alive' twice, to sneak dogs into our country, then why don't we just break the laws for everybody?"* In the end, Heard and Depp agreed to send the pups back home but they were still charged and in court they acknowledged their transgressions after pleading guilty to illegally bringing the dogs into Australia.

Mr. Joyce was unimpressed, mocking the couple's apology by saying that it looked as if Mr. Depp was *"auditioning for* The Godfather." Never one to mince his words, Barnaby added, *"It's time that Pistol and Boo buggered off back to the United States."*

Later, appearing on the US talk show *Jimmy Kimmel Live*, Johnny got his own back by saying of Mr. Joyce, *"He looks somehow inbred with a tomato. It's not a criticism, I was a little worried that he might explode."*

And then everybody lived happily ever after. Sort of.

I am delighted to say that I was given a standing ovation at the end of the presentation. A proud moment for me and my family all of whom were present.

Judging by the emails and texts received from all over the world, I am very confident that we significantly increased awareness of the rhino crisis that day.

The TED talk was one of the highlights of my life and resulted in significant publicity and a spike in donations to the project.

DR IAN PLAYER

Ian Player was many things to me. He was the father of rhino conservation, he was a mentor and he was an active supporter. In short, he was my hero.

Ian was internationally recognised as an environmentalist and a conservationist, but he was also a man of many facets and contradictions. Not just a ranger, a man of culture and the arts, a deep thinker and Jungian, an irascible campaigner and a maverick, he was a writer, a lecturer and an international diplomat. A man deeply committed to all he believed in.

Born in Johannesburg in 1927 and educated at St John's College, the same school I attended, he served with the South African forces in Italy in World War II and returned to South Africa aged 19 with no idea of what he wanted to do with his life. When he pioneered the Dusi River Canoe Marathon in Natal

Dr Ian Player, the father of rhino conservation. (Photo credit: Alchetron)

in 1950, he expected to see an abundance of wildlife along the riverbank but, to his dismay, he saw almost none. Then began an epic personal journey to fight for nature conservation.

He joined the Natal Parks Board in 1952 and established Operation Rhino, which succeeded in saving the white rhino from extinction. He also founded the Wilderness Leadership School during the troubled days of apartheid, a multi-racial and experiential program that was to spawn a global network of conservationists committed to saving wilderness and wildlife throughout the world.

I first met Ian Player in 1977 when he and Sir Laurens van der Post (godfather to Prince William) conceived the first World Wilderness Congress in Johannesburg at the suggestion of Player's friend and mentor, game ranger Magqubu Ntombela. My wife Margie and her business partner, Bill Mounsey, had the privilege of being selected as the event managers for the conference, which was attended by 2,700 delegates from 30 countries.

What was quite extraordinary was that when Margie and I met with Ian shortly before his death, he remembered not only her name and that of Mounsey, but also the name of their company – Festivals and Conventions Trust. That was almost forty years later.

I wrote to Ian soon after the launch breakfast, briefing him on what I was trying to achieve and inviting him to be a patron of the project, which he kindly accepted. He wrote, "*I was delighted to see the progress that has been made and you can rely on me to do everything I can to help you make the project a great success. In the 1960s I was trying desperately to get a decent herd of rhino into Australia, but only succeeded in getting a pair to Taronga. With the situation in this country and the consistent killing of rhino there has been worldwide revulsion so your Project could not come at a better time and I am certain that with the right publicity (which you have already started) that you will be inundated with offers of help, including financial help. In South Africa, a great deal of money has been raised, estimated to be over R200 million ($20 million), regrettably most has not gone to the rhino.*"

If ever there was an endorsement that mattered for what I was trying to achieve, this was it.

Ian was particularly proud that someone from his alma mater was working to save the rhino. He mentioned that he had recently arranged with the Wilderness Leadership School to take a group of young St Johns boys on a two-week Rites of Passage course. He said that it had done wonders for them, camping in the bush for a fortnight "*but not without a great deal of squealing; most of them never having had to struggle for anything in their lives, let alone going without food for a day*". He was a hard man but he loved St Johns College.

Recalling the first World Wilderness Congress in 1977, Ian mentioned that the 10th Congress had just been held in Spain, saying that it was an idea whose time had come and that it had now become the longest running environmental congress in the world.

Ian and I had another connection which he alluded to in a subsequent exchange: "*I was very pleased to read that you are a relative of Trevor Dearlove, who also used to work with me as a ranger in iMfolozi and then went on to do an outstanding job in Kruger. He must be delighted that you are involved in this whole exercise which, pray God, will get a decent population established in Australia."*

My cousin Trevor conceived the idea of wilderness trails in the Kruger Park in 1978. It was a novelty that appealed to every wildlife enthusiast and which satisfied an intense longing in visitors to the Kruger Park; to be able to walk in the bush instead of seeing it all from inside a hot and cramped motor vehicle.

As Ian's health deteriorated, the tone of his notes to me took on more and more urgency. *"I am glad that you have met the Canberra officials – all bureaucracies are a nightmare and the only way to get anywhere is to keep hammering on the door. Let us hope that we can keep this urgent task of moving the rhino to Australia on the road. The poaching has not stopped at all and in fact has got worse and the animal is now under greater threat than ever and it would be a crime if we did not succeed in getting them relocated to a safe haven, like Australia. Hopefully, we can also make this relocation the beginning of sending other African endangered species to Australia as well."*

He went on, *"You have a great missionary task ahead of you in Canberra, Ray, but you must take heart and keep up the fight."*

He finished his letter on a sobering note: *"I regret to say that my decrepitude is getting progressively worse and the old rhino capture injuries, as well as the onset of muscular dystrophy, places more and more restrictions on any movement. It is unbelievably frustrating, but if the situation ever demands it, I will get into a wheelchair and travel with you to beard the bureaucrats. I know only too well how their minds work and there are ways of dealing with them."*

Here was a man who had travelled this road and just could

not believe that it was happening all over again. He read the situation perfectly with regard to the Australian government bureaucracy. God, how I wished that some of the bureaucrats from the Department of Agriculture in Canberra, with all of their delaying tactics, could have had just 30 minutes with Ian Player. Perhaps we would now have had a crash of rhinos safe and successfully breeding in the outback of Australia.

What is not widely known is that Ian and Gary Player are brothers. The Black Knight, as Gary came to be known, accumulated nine major golf championships, including a golf Grand Slam. Gary won 165 tournaments on six continents over six decades – an extraordinary achievement. A talented family by any measure.

Famous brothers Gary and Ian Player. (Photo Credit: Ulf Doerner)

Margie and I visited Ian and Ann Player at their farm near Howick in Kwa Zulu Natal in October 2014. Ian's eyes were misty but alert and his handshake strong although he was not at all mobile. I had written a poem for him and presented it to him. He asked me to read it to him, which I did, finding it tough and emotional. I called the poem "For Dr Ian Player – the Father of Rhino Conservation". Ian had tears in his eyes as he gave both me and Margie a big hug.

On the day we met Ian, there was a delegation of game rangers from North West Parks who had travelled 1,600 kilometres to pay their respects. In an incredibly moving show of love and respect, each one of these men, young and old, knelt in front of Ian, took his hand and held it.

A month later, Ian had a severe stroke which signalled the beginning of the end. Good friend, Sheila Berry, penned this beautiful note on behalf of the Player family, *"A week ago, today, Ian cast his canoe on to the river that would take him across to the other side. He is a strong man but there are signs he is approaching his destination. His pulse is regular and his grip is firm but not as sustained as it has been. It is more like a comforting squeeze, as if to assure those he loves he is still here. And so, he is being caring, considerate, generous and thoughtful of the needs of others to the end."*

A week later, Ian died resulting in tributes from all over the world. I wrote to Ian's family, *"Although expected, this news is crushing. Ian's contribution to conservation has been immense. When I first started out on The Australian Rhino Project, Ian was intensely supportive, insisting that spreading the risk – as he had done before – was vital in the attempt to preserve the species. Ian has been our greatest supporter and my wife and I were blessed to meet with him and Ann a few short weeks ago. He was resolute in supporting our project and we will do everything that we can to play our small part in keeping Ian's dream and passion alive."*

Sandile Masondo is a young Zulu man who went on an Ian Player wilderness trail a few years ago. He is from a humble township in Howick, about 25 kilometres from Ian's farm. He arrived at the farm the morning after Ian's death. Sandile leads a deceptively simple life, while actually being extraordinary. After the wilderness trail, Sandile climbed Kilimanjaro with the South African Rhino team to draw attention to the plight of rhinos and to encourage South African youth to become involved in trying to stop the slaughter of these magnificent animals, traditionally royal to the Zulu people. In 2015, Sandile walked 3,500 kilometres to promote the Zulu language and culture, strongly believing that African people who have lost contact with their traditional roots have no moral or spiritual compass to guide their lives.

Sandile explained the purpose of his visit to the Player homestead. According to Zulu tradition, one's burial place is one's final house. Sandile had come to ask if he could be given the honour of digging Ian's grave. He wanted to prepare a comfortable last room for Ian's body. Sandile's wish was granted. He was grateful to be able to assuage his pain and shed his tears through the sweat of his body as he dug the grave for this giant of a man, who he deeply revered, respected and loved. And so, very early, before any rays of sunlight touched the eastern horizon, Sandile arrived at the little church where Ian's family and closest friends gathered to bury Ian's mortal remains.

In many ways, I am pleased that Ian was not here when I left the project. I would have hated to explain to him that the Australian government and internal politics within TARP had destroyed his and my dreams.

I am truly blessed to have had Ian Player in my life.

"MY PEOPLE HAVE

NO CONNECTION"

Engaging with people who could influence the progress of The Australian Rhino Project and curtail the massive surge in poaching that was threatening the very existence of rhinos was a high priority and, not surprisingly politicians and bureaucrats were high on my list.

A few years ago, I met with the South African High Commissioner to Australia, Her Excellency, Koleka Anita Mqulwana, who, in conversation, said, *"Ray, it is vital that you understand that the communities in South Africa have no connection to wildlife – they see no value. It is the same with trees. My people have no connection with trees – they see them solely as sources of light, of warmth and for cooking. So, they cut down the forests."*

In our conversation, she used the word "connection" several times. It was a difficult discussion. Her Excellency seemed to hold the apartheid regime responsible for this situation and, by definition, as a white 60-something year old who spent the first forty years of his life in South Africa, I was part of that group. Without going into the whys and wherefores, she is absolutely right. For decades black communities were barred from national parks and the benefits of the wilderness. I can clearly remember when Balule Camp in the Kruger Park was reserved for "non-whites" only. It was the only accommodation in Kruger that was available for people of colour.

Her Excellency's statement is spot on; the only way to reduce the poaching rate is to engage and educate communities to understand that animals such as rhinos and elephants are worth more to them alive than dead. This is a huge task and, unfortunately, it will take a generation or more to achieve. In my opinion, that will be too late.

Lennox Mathebula, of the Shangaan tribe, is employed at the Sabi Sands Game Reserve, bordering Kruger, as its community liaison officer. He has responsibility for educating locals about how important it is to protect the rhino. There are 650,000 people who live in very basic conditions on the borders of Sabi Sands. When we met, Lennox proudly said, "*For the first time, we recently had a call from villagers giving up a poacher.*"

He then related a less encouraging story. He spends much of his time with the local Indunas – the tribal chiefs, who still wield significant influence and authority over the communities. He described how he was making definite progress with the indunas until the day a 23-year-old young man drove into the village in his sparkling late-model BMW. The source of his windfall? Poaching. *"We had to start all over again,"* said Lennox. The other youngsters see the fruits of poaching, ignore the risks and sign up for the next foray into the Kruger Park.

Reams and reams have been written about poaching and the international market for rhino horn that it has spawned. It is a highly complex issue. The ranks of rhino poachers are best illustrated as a five-level pyramid. Number one is the hunter, usually a highly trained tracker and excellent marksman, probably with a military background. Number two is the handler who provides the hunter with resources such as the weapon and ammunition. Number one hunts the rhino, saws off its horn and hands the horn to number two in exchange for payment.

From there the horns make their way to number three, who would typically live in the town or the city. He delivers the horn to number four, who ensures that it reaches number five, the end-buyer in countries such as Vietnam, Laos or China.

Anyone involved from level two upwards is typically called a syndicate member. At level one, there will also be the runners, usually two, who carry the food, mobile phones or have some knowledge of the area to be targeted. One of these runners is the fellow who needs to feed his family, who is literally picked up on a street corner on the day and made an offer to join the hunt. The reality is that poachers are still running amok throughout the country, seeking and killing rhinos.

Authorities also define five levels in the illegal supply chain. Members of level 1 are poachers paid per hunt; members of level 2 are paid per transporting event; level 3 are local middlemen who often oversee a number of poaching teams and transporters and are paid per kilogram of horn; level 4 are exporters who transport rhino horns via airports or harbors to destinations in Asia and receive payment per item. Finally, members of level 5 are traders who sell trafficked rhino horn directly to consumers in end-user states.

Ultimately, the ability of the traders to make a profit depends on the price demanded by poachers and the black-market price that consumers are willing to pay. As long as the unit cost to this cooperative is lower than consumers' reserve price, the illegal trader will stay in the business of rhino horn trafficking. To continue to make a profit, these illegal traders will lower or raise their black-market price in response solely to the purchase decision-making of consumers.

We must not forget that we are dealing with international organised crime, backed by foreign criminals. These syndicates are so wealthy that they could be a Fortune 500 company in their own right. They don't have any conscience, laws or rules of engagement, and they have good intelligence and unlimited resources. They will always assist poachers who have been arrested by providing bail and legal defence.

The other frightening element is the link to global terrorism. The Kenyan Wildlife Service (KWS) recently reported that Kenya was losing two elephants every week to poaching with some of the proceeds said to be used to finance Al-Shabaab and other criminal groups. KWS director Julius Kipng'etich revealed the link between the surging illegal trade in high-value wildlife products and transnational criminal networks that are funding militant insurgencies: *"Poached ivory travels through the same channels as drugs and people who are being trafficked. Terrorist organisations like Al-Shabaab have been linked to poaching in Kenya.*" The problem is in the relatively new poaching grounds in northern Kenya, where unlike the traditional poaching areas of Tsavo and Amboseli where poachers mainly used spears and arrows, rangers now have to contend with poachers using deadly weapons. Al-Shabaab is said to be crossing the Kenyan border and killing elephants using powerfully lethal guns like the M16.

At a recent US Senate hearing, committee chairman John Kerry cited evidence presented by the *Independent* indicating that Al-Shabaab has connections to the illicit poaching and trafficking of both ivory and rhino horn. Together with drug trafficking, illegal wildlife trading is among the main sources of revenue for terror groups such as the Lord's Resistance Army in the Central African Republic and the Sudanese Janjaweed.

The whole poaching situation is extremely complicated. In some communities, poachers are seen as heroes because they share their wealth within those communities. So it was with ranger Sean van Niekerk who was badly assaulted by one such community in Corruman in Mozambique, one of the poaching hubs. He was the target of such a poacher-supporting community when he and two colleagues escorted a group of apprehended poachers to the local police station. An angry mob turned on them and during the fight he was hit over the head with a panga and severely beaten. He was very fortunate an off-duty policeman saved him from certain death at the hands of the mob. The poachers walked away.

Anti-poaching teams are having increased success and part of that is due to the increasing use of technology, intelligence and weaponry. Across Africa, drones, night-vision equipment, helicopter-borne intervention teams, automatic weapons and special forces trainers are all being brought in to try to stop the poachers.

Poaching is also evolving tactically. A recent investigation determined that criminal networks smuggling rhino horns out of Africa are now turning them into jewellery to evade detection in airports. While previous seizures have typically comprised whole horns or horns cut into pieces, Chinese ecommerce sites are now selling rhino horn beads, bracelets and other similar jewelry – all status-symbol products.

Be assured that there is also personal risk across many levels in this dreadful situation. We have talked elsewhere about the risk to the poachers who kill the rhinos; there is also a risk to well-meaning conservationists who pay thousands of dollars to defend their rhinos and there is risk to the rangers who seek to protect them.

I agreed to meet a vociferous opponent of wildlife corruption in Pretoria. I was a little nervous about the meeting and asked a friend to join me. When we met him, he was obviously very well connected in government circles but was neurotic about secrecy and adamant that his phone was bugged by one of the syndicates. As we sat, me somewhat nervously, in his living room, in walked another man, let's call him Dieter. Dieter was one of those people who your instinct tells you to be very wary of. We chatted for a while and I explained to them what I was trying to achieve. When I was finished, he looked at me and said in Afrikaans, *"Ray, jy moet pasop."* Translated, *"You must be very, very careful."* I asked why and he responded, *"These are ruthless people and some will see what you are trying to achieve as a threat to their livelihood by taking rhinos out of the country."* We had a very quiet trip back to Johannesburg.

In January 2018, when gunshots rang out in the Maswa Game

Reserve, a protected area bordering Tanzania's Serengeti National Park, an anti-poaching ground patrol unit was called in to investigate. The team trekked through thick bush until morning, when they radioed for air support to help locate the suspected poachers. Helicopter pilot Roger Gower and safari guide Nick Bester took off, and soon saw a fresh elephant carcass with its tusks still intact—a sure sign that the poachers were still around. Flying low, Gower looped the chopper around the area to get a better look and spotted what looked like a pile of ivory balanced atop a small, rocky hill. Knowing they'd been discovered, poachers emerged from the bush and fired high-powered rifles at the helicopter. One of the bullets scythed through the floor of the helicopter up through Gower's seat, hitting his leg and piercing his shoulder, before tearing through the roof. Gower somehow managed to land the aircraft but he subsequently succumbed to his injuries.

I have previously referred to Ingwelala, where I have a home. One night in February 2018, three poachers were hunting rhino in the area when they walked into a pride of lions. Two poachers escaped while the other was eaten by the lions. The newspaper article was headlined, "Poetic justice?"

In April 2019, a group of five poachers entered the southern section of the Kruger Park and, in their search for rhinos, they ran into a herd of elephants, which attacked them, leaving one poacher dead. The remaining poachers advised the man's family who alerted the park's rangers. They undertook a search but by the time they found him, lions had devoured the body leaving only the skull and his pants.

SOURCING THE RHINOS

Our monthly board meetings were both formal and lively. One of the contentious issues was what we should focus on – sourcing the rhinos or securing the Australian government's approval. I insisted that they must be parallel activities. A perennial question asked was if I had a Plan A and a Plan B for sourcing the rhinos. The question annoyed me because there was little appreciation of how complex and difficult sourcing rhinos was and how much time I was spending on this issue. In truth, I had Plans A to Z!

While the overall goal of 80 rhinos over a four-year period remained, we decided to go for a lesser number for the first shipment: between six and ten. I was certain that once the first animals were in Australia, the process and the funding would be a lot more straightforward. I therefore viewed the first shipment as a "proof of concept" or "pilot".

We were all keenly aware of the two most recent shipments of rhinos from Africa to Australia, in 1994 from Zimbabwe and in 2005 from the Kruger Park. These shipments suggested that there was a precedent and, working from that assumption, I approached a number of people within SANParks, relatively confident this would be something of a formality. I had first spoken to Dr Markus Hofmeyr, head of SANParks Veterinarian Services and Dr Michael Knight, Chairman of The IUCN African Rhino Specialist Group and both were cautiously optimistic about such a plan.

I then met Mike Knight's superior, Dr Hector Magome who was the second in command at SANParks. I explained my plan to him which assumed that SANParks would catch the rhinos and also quarantine them. We would do the rest.

"*So, Hector,*" I said, "*the transaction will be cost neutral for SANParks.*"

He paused and said, "*No, it's not.*"

"*How's that?*" I asked, wondering what I had missed.

His response "*Because rhinos have a value.*"

I could not help myself and retorted "*Not if they're dead, they don't.*"

At this point, Mike had a fixed gaze out of the window, I'm sure he was thinking, "*You're on your own, Ray.*"

Dr Magome didn't react but I sensed the meeting wasn't going particularly well and thought I'd try and introduce a bit of levity. The Australian Cricket Team were touring South Africa at the time and the previous week, contrary to expectations, they had walloped the national side, the Proteas. South Africans love their sport and the loss had not been well received. I asked Hector if his reaction had anything to do with cricket? Laughing, he said, "*Yes, actually it does. We hate losing and we hate losing to you Aussies even more.*" (It always amused me that South Africans saw me as an Australian, whilst Australians considered me a South African.)

This cracked the ice and he proceeded to make suggestions to progress the plan. He also asked me about the "Queensland Plan" which I have addressed in Chapter 11. He was not very complimentary about their intentions saying that it seemed to be "*back of the cigarette packet planning.*"

Hector is an impressive executive who knows his stuff. He earned his stripes in the previous Bophuthatswana "homeland" government. He insisted that any rhinos exported to Australia had to be free range, not go to zoos – a point I agreed with completely – and he emphasised that we are all custodians of animals such as rhinos. Again, total agreement from me. We touched on disease management and I assured him that AUSDAFF saw this as a critical component of our plan.

Then there was the inevitable question: "Why Australia?" I explained my reasoning, which included the remoteness of the planned location of the rhinos at Western Plains Zoo in Dubbo, five hours west of Sydney, and there was no comparable poverty or corruption in Australia. Clearly, I had to tread very carefully on this since nobody wants their country criticised. Hector nodded without offering comment.

Dr Ian Player was an idol for anyone who was in conservation and his endorsement of TARP influenced Hector. We concluded the meeting with a soft endorsement from Hector.

Pod introduced me to Norman Adami, former Chairman and Managing Director of South African Breweries. Norman is a strong conservationist who has his own private lodge with multiple rhino. I met Norman in his Sandton office and immediately liked him – a straight-shooting, no nonsense executive. I told him my story and he became quite animated – in between smoking cigarettes with one foot in the garden and the other in his non-smoking office. He reached for his phone saying that this was one of the best ideas he had ever heard to help save the rhino and asked *"Have you spoken to Zuma?"* Jacob Zuma was then President of South Africa.

"Wait, wait," I said, *"it's probably a bit premature, I need to work my way through the bureaucracy."*

"Bugger that, this is far too important for that", he said and started dialling another number, this time to a member of the SANParks board. The call went to voicemail and Norman was quite succinct and direct in his message *"Gert, call me back. I have a bloke here in my office from Australia who has a fantastic idea for helping the rhinos."*

Out of interest, I asked Norman what Zuma was like. He said, *"Ray, do you know that he only has a primary school education, but I can tell you that he is the most street-smart and cunning person I have ever met."* As South Africa was yet to find out.

Norman questioned me closely about my plan and when I said that there were already about 55 rhinos in Australia, he murmured, *"Australia has more rhinos than the rest of Africa north of the Limpopo"*. No doubt an exaggeration, but not far off and a sobering point. He really was captivated by the plan and that was also, I'm sure, because of Pod's involvement and support. Like many successful senior executives, Norman was able to cut through and see things so clearly. *"What you now need to do, Ray, is get five to ten rhino owners to each donate two rhinos to your program. Simple, count me in."*

Norman Adami was the type of person I would have liked to join our board. He would make an outstanding contribution. He later linked up with the team from ERP.

In my ongoing quest to source rhinos, Godfrey Abrahams introduced me to Allan and Myra Salkinder, who owned a private game reserve in the north-west of South Africa. Allan ran a creative agency with the somewhat oddly named "Ballz'n'Brainz Partnership", while Myra is a senior executive in the Kirsch Group. Their story still haunts me.

Originally, they owned sixteen rare black rhinos but after a series of poaching incidents, they were left with just four, one of which had been relocated to Johannesburg Zoo. This particular rhino is named Phila and she had become something of a celebrity in the hearts of South Africans. An article by CJ Carrington about Phila takes up the story.

"Although I've always loved and respected all animals, the first time I was emotionally affected by a rhino was when I met Phila, the poster-child for rhino survivors everywhere. Phila is a black rhino who had been shot nine times in two different poaching attempts. I met her while she was still at her temporary home at the Johannesburg Zoo, when I brought some special food for her. Despite the brave girl's horrendous injuries and poor health, she still trusted us vile humans, and

came running up to me when I called her name. I hand-fed her, and through my own tears, I could see the ancient pain and loss in her sad, dark eyes. A child's balloon popped, and Phila bolted to go and cower in her sleeping enclosure. I cannot call Phila a survivor in the true sense of the word, because to me survival needs an element of a fighting spirit. And that flame was gone from her wise old eyes.

Phila is as happy as possible now, at a very special, highly guarded, secret sanctuary where other severely traumatised rhinos quietly share their tragic tales of horror with her in the calm, defeated way of silent despair."

I met Phila about a year later at that sanctuary and I can vouch for every single one of Carrington's words. I weep every time I read this story and am reminded of Martin Buber's words, *"An animal's eyes have the power to speak a great language."*

Phila the black rhino. (Photo Credit: Allan Salkinder)

Allan told me that in 2010, in a poaching incident, he lost two black rhino cows and Phila was shot. Fast forward and now only four remained – one bull, one calf and two cows, one of which was Phila. The rest had been brutally slaughtered by poachers. With tears welling, Allan pleaded with me, *"Ray, there is no alternative, these remaining rhinos must be moved and placed in a protected environment."*

I tried everything to help Myra and Allan get these four rhinos into Australia. I was advised by Taronga that I should refer this dreadful situation to the International Rhino Foundation (IRF) for assistance. The IRF's mission statement claims: *"IRF champions the survival of the world's rhinos through conservation and research. We do what it takes to ensure that rhinos survive for future generations. We operate on-the-ground programs in all areas of the world where rhinos live in the wild. In five countries across two continents, we support viable populations of the five remaining rhino species and the communities that coexist with them."* Very noble goals.

It seemed to me that Allan and Myra's situation was a perfect fit for the IRF's strategy and I immediately took the matter up with the local IRF board member. I followed up a month later. No progress. I followed up again another month later. Not a word.

Two months after asking for assistance, I received a response, *"There have been discussions with IRF Executive Director, Susie Ellis about this . . . Although expressing some initial interest, they have landed on establishing a need to carry out some considered background work on the existing program within the US. They are hoping to complete this in the next couple of months, following which, they will have a better handle on the overall opportunities and requirements of new founder animals to ensure success in the long term. So, at this point, timing is not aligning to enable them to consider the request from Allan Salkinder."*

Seldom in my life had I heard such bloody mumbo jumbo and bureaucratic rubbish, my blood pressure rose, but I bit my tongue. So many people who purport to want to save rhinos have blood on their hands. A month later, the Salkinders lost yet another rhino. I advised the IRF whose reply was, *"A great shame, and unfortunately even with all the intent in the world we won't prevent these examples."* How I hate being patted on the head. In the four years of my work on this project, I found the IRF completely and totally ineffectual. The rhinos need action, not championing – this is yet another example of the industry surrounding rhinos suffocating the people who are really trying to make things happen for rhinos. Like us.

In 2015, the last of Allan's and Myra's rhinos was slaughtered. Not wanting to share the spoils, the greedy poacher went hunting for the black rhino on his own. Black rhinos have the reputation of being very aggressive animals, in fact hunters are on record as saying that the most dangerous animals to hunt are black rhinos and buffaloes. In an ironic twist, Allan's rhino died from the gunshots, but not before the rhino killed the poacher. In his note to me, Allan said, *"I am sick to the bottom of my soul. To say I am devastated is an understatement."*

I referred to Allan's and Myra's terrible experience in my 2015 speech at the Sydney fundraising dinner. I said: *"In the audience tonight there is a family who contacted me two years ago. They told me they had owned sixteen black rhinos, but twelve had been poached and all that remained from the herd was a bull, a cow with a calf and another female. They were very emotional when they told me the story and begged for their remaining four rhinos to be amongst the first batch to come to Australia. People, I promise you, I tried everything I possibly could to get those rhinos into Australia including going to the IRF and I failed. I had an email from Allan last week which had some harrowing photos in it outlining how the last of these sixteen rhinos had been slaughtered. Myra and Allan, I'm sorry, I really did my best."*

You could have heard a pin drop in that room.

In my ongoing quest for identifying sources of rhinos, I was given the names of many people and organisations. I pursued every single one of them.

One such person was Dr Bandile Mkhize, CEO of KZN/Ezemvelo Parks Board – previously the world-famous Natal Parks Board – famed for its rhino populations. Ian Player strongly suggested that I meet with Bandile. During a 2015 visit to South Africa, I made a special trip to Durban to meet him. Initially guarded, he soon warmed to what we were offering. In essence, I wanted them to provide us with ten rhinos (two males and eight females), all under seven years old, on a custodial basis. He really liked our objective to *"reinforce survival of the southern white rhino sub-species in the wild by augmenting the gene pool outside South Africa."*

We also discussed my offer to include the communities surrounding the game reserves in combating the onslaught and I briefed him on another component of our offer, that we would like to establish a series of agreements with communities surrounding KZN/Ezemvelo conservation areas whereby we would purchase crafts, such as beads, artefacts and carvings, made by the communities, at a good profit to them, and establish retail opportunities for such products throughout Australia.

In time this could provide a significant cash injection into the communities. Apart from the obvious financial benefit, I hoped that this would encourage them to further understand the negative impact of poaching on conservation. A further offer was to work with the makers of such crafts to improve their general financial and management skills using graduates from the University of Sydney Business School. Finally, I proposed funding a joint research food security project in one of the communities neighbouring a conservation area or park, using the considerable resources of the University of Sydney Veterinarian Faculty, Charles Perkins Centre and Business School. I pointed out that there were similar existing projects with countries such as Nepal where the pressure on conservation areas is also intense. Fellow director Professor Leanne Piggott, from the Business School, had agreed to lead this piece of work. To strengthen my offer, I mentioned that I also had preliminary discussions with the Australian High Commission to South Africa and they were very keen to be involved in such a project under the Foreign Aid program.

At this, Dr Mkhize stood up and banged his fist on the table. Oh Lord, I thought, what have I said to upset him? *"Ray,"* he said, *"if you can do that you can have as many rhinos as you want."*

Job creation is paramount in South Africa and it reminded me of the Nelson Mandela quote, *"Poverty is not an accident. Like slavery and apartheid, it is man-made and can be removed by the actions of humans."* We parted on a really positive note and agreed to catch up in Sydney at the upcoming National Parks Congress. We duly met in Sydney and Dr Mkhize was one of the stars of the show at the

Michael Knight cocktail party, hosted by the Business School, to coincide with the Congress.

Alas, within weeks of returning to South Africa Dr Mkhize was suspended from his role as CEO to face disciplinary proceedings over the restructuring of management salaries at a cost to Ezemvelo Parks of about R20 million ($2 million). Mkhize claimed that the entire process was overseen by the board and, sure enough, a year later, he was paid out a year's salary in compensation. Not for the last time, I felt that I had this gold in my hand that I wanted to share, but inevitably, politics got in the way.

I first met Dr David Mabunda at the same Parks Congress in Sydney. Certainly, his name was familiar to me. He had been CEO of SANParks and had performed that role with distinction. David had received a lot of negative publicity about his role as a shareholder in the world-renowned private game reserve Mala Mala, which the government had bought for R1 billion ($100M) in its most costly land settlement deal. David was a director and shareholder of Mala Mala and resigned from the board a month after the property was transferred to the local community. His role in the deal made headlines after he allegedly received R81 million ($8.1 million) from the settlement. The subsequent investigation unearthed *a serious conflict of interest* as he was head of SANParks, as well as being a director and shareholder of Mala Mala. No charges were laid.

We got on really well and that friendship is still strong today. Our discussions centered around the Mpumulanga Parks Board of which David was chairman. I sent him a comprehensive proposal to source rhinos. David's response was most encouraging. He had introduced the proposal to the board and it had been "very favourably received," and once board approval had been obtained the proposal would be referred to the Provincial Cabinet for final approval. He concluded by saying, *"My observation is that the appetite to do the project in the Mpumalanga Province is better than at any other tier level of government."* I couldn't have hoped for more. In a later note, David wrote, *"Be assured of my support until the rhinos are delivered on Australian soil as a future endowment just in case the inevitable happens."*

Soon after the news broke about Bandile Mkhize's suspension, I had a note from David saying that he had been appointed interim CEO at KZN/Ezemvelo Parks board replacing Bandile and that he would very much like to continue our discussions. We now had two irons in the fire. Better still, Maurice Mackenzie, a good friend, sat on the KZN board. Soon after, David and I exchanged correspondence and he wrote, *"I have approached both provinces to come to the party with the rhinos, Mpumalanga and KZN."* He said that the management of the Mpumalanga board was in crisis and that I should not expect anything from them in the foreseeable future but that he had placed the matter on the agenda of the board at KZN and that he had the support of most board members. He concluded by saying, *"We should have the deal approved in early February to enable us to move during the cold winter months."*

At our board meetings, it was occasionally suggested that I was going down blind alleys in terms of sourcing rhinos and I was told that this was one.

I later met David in Pretoria and he brought along two

colleagues which I took as a really positive sign. Bheki Khoza, now CEO and Sifiso Keswa, the GM of KZN/Ezemvelo Parks. After this meeting, David wrote: *"My first target is to get approval for the 12 pilot rhinos and then we can look at the rest of the issues and sub-categories of the project. Please explore the possibility of us visiting the final destination of the proposed sanctuary in Australia and the ecological assessment. The board has added the matter on their 17th March agenda for consideration."* I was over the moon.

In situations like this, time seems to fly, but it also seems to drag and perhaps that is the definition of the word bureaucracy. Six months later, after chasing David, I received a response, *"The project is still on the table. The challenge is getting national endorsement from cabinet to move rhino to Australia. At the moment we have your proposal, that of the Government of the Northern Territories and the Texas bid by ranchers in that region. It's confusing, Ray. Policy dictates that national government gives consent for the animals to be moved."* I sensed the issue was cooling in David's world and I was right. The South African Government had clearly decided to play a more active role in the export of rhinos and this caused even greater delays. I assured David that the Northern Territory project was dead, one less to worry about.

David and I continued to correspond and, separately, I assisted him with a domestic violence case in Australia regarding the daughter of one of his colleagues.

David also suggested that I contact Piet Warren as a source of rhinos. Piet was the driving force in what we referred to as the Queensland rhino project. He is a successful farmer and rare species breeder in the north-eastern part of South Africa.

The increasing demand for rare game species initially attracted his attention and while he breeds rhinos and other exotic species, his personal pride and joy is an intensive and extremely successful sable antelope breeding program. He, like John Hume, started harvesting rhino horn in the hope that it would be legalised in the future. With supplementary feeding, his rhinos now calve every two years, instead of every three years or more in the wild. This was exactly my plan for our project. By keeping them safe and with careful management of diet, we could decrease the period between birth and weaning of the calves and rapidly build up our herd.

I already knew that Piet was willing to donate rhinos for export to Australia and Margie and I visited Piet and his delightful wife Christine at their game farm near Gravelotte to brief him on my plan and hoping that he would join our team. Inviting us in for a cup of tea, we entered his lovely home only to be greeted by a room full of dead animals – the room's walls were covered with animal trophies. It felt as if we were in a mausoleum.

He drove us around his property and we saw plenty of rhinos and also Piet's world record-holding sable horns – which, I'm pleased to say, were still attached to the sable. Piet glumly mentioned that he had recently become a target for rhino poachers and had lost two rhinos in the past three weeks. In one instance, the poachers had placed a mattress over the electrified fences and jumped over and in the other case, they had climbed over the fence via a tree's overhanging branches. That tree was subsequently heavily pruned.

Piet asked if we would like to see the remains of the rhino. Margie declined but I thought that I "should". A heartbreaking sight. This magnificent animal reduced to a skeleton. The poacher was obviously a very good shot. A single bullet killed the rhino.

What really angered Piet is that he (and everyone else) knew exactly who the poacher was but no action was taken by the police. He told us that the poacher had passed on a warning to Piet, saying: "*Tell Oom (Uncle) Piet to stay out of my way, if he gets in the way of my rhinos, I will shoot him.*" Note the use of the words my rhinos. Lovely.

Piet declined my request for rhinos, saying that he was building up his stocks for when the trade in horn was legalised. At that time, he had about twenty rhinos on his farm. The last time that I spoke to him he had more than three hundred. And international trade in horn was still banned.

In the context of rhinos – poaching, conservation, trade in rhino horn and so on – probably more words have been written about John Hume than any other individual. John is admired in some circles and reviled in many, many more. John is unfazed by the latter – he is comfortable in his own skin and convinced of his cause.

I have met John on several occasions and had many a conversation with him. Our first meeting is described in detail in chapter four. He is a charming man with a gruff exterior. He lives for his rhinos. At the time of writing, he owned 1,735 rhinos, thus getting very close to his goal of producing 200 babies a year. Who can argue that this is not a great achievement? Those who can find nothing good to say about John argue that he is breeding rhinos purely for commercial profit. There is some truth in this since John dehorns all of his rhinos and stores the horns in bank vaults.

John was always willing to help me with advice and guidance.

He gave me his confidential rhino database in which he kept detailed records for each rhino, including birth and death data, calves, dehorning details, feed, medical history – the lot. I think he quietly admired what I was trying to achieve. He called it '*ballsy*'. While I would never give up, my view was that sourcing rhinos from John Hume, unless we paid the market price, was not going to happen.

In 2017, domestic rhino horn trade was legalised in South Africa – a decision that was greeted with dismay throughout the conservation world. This decision followed the Constitutional Court's ruling against an appeal by John Hume and others to maintain the 2009 ban on domestic trade. For many years, South African rhino breeders had been pushing for the ban on domestic trade to be lifted, claiming that trade needed to take place and that this would curb rhino poaching. Soon after the court's decision, Hume announced that he planned two global auctions to sell 500 kilograms of rhino horns. The auction turned out to be a damp squib and there hasn't been one since.

Although domestic trade is legal, international trade of rhino horn remains illegal. Despite this, there is concern that domestic trade could serve as a platform for smuggling rhino horn internationally, since there is virtually no market for rhino horn in South Africa but a huge market in Asia.

My view is that the legalisation of trade would have the opposite effect and that poaching would actually accelerate. Illegal trade will still be profitable. The demand is there and poaching will continue. The bureaucratic process that Hume had to go through for the first auction of his rhino horn suggests that the South African government will make it exceptionally difficult to obtain permits to trade horn in South Africa and it is likely that legal trade will only create avenues for illegal horn to be traded. Realistically, who are the likely buyers of the horn in South Africa? Investors and speculators, maybe a few. The only true demand is from the suppliers to the illegal traders.

Those arguing for legalisation suggest a De Beers Central Selling Organisation (CSO) type model. In the late 1800s after a massive diamond discovery in South Africa, a diamond rush was born, and Cecil John Rhodes bought as many diamond mining claims as he could, including farmland owned by the De Beer family. By the turn of the century, Rhodes had accumulated enough properties that his company accounted for the majority of the world's supply of rough diamonds. He called his company De Beers Consolidated Mines Limited. As De Beers maintained a hold on the worlds rough diamond supply through the first quarter of the 20th century, rival financier Ernest Oppenheimer began accumulating shares of De Beers and reached a controlling stake of the company by the mid-1920s. Under Oppenheimer's control, De Beers further expanded into every facet of the diamond industry, intent on monopolising distribution. De Beers successfully convinced most of the world's suppliers to sell through their channel, gaining control of the global supply not produced by De Beers mines. The cartel was born, giving Oppenheimer the power to influence diamond supply and thus diamond prices. The De Beers CSO distribution channel had the power to sell diamonds when and where they wanted to. In order to maintain a stable but rising diamond price, De Beers had the power to stockpile inventory in a weak market or, in an excessively strong price environment, they had the excess supply on hand to release to the market when needed, repressing disorderly price increases.

It was a brilliant business model that served De Beers well, but could it work for rhino horn? The rhino "industry" is so fragmented and, in truth, probably controlled by the international crime syndicates. There would be immense suspicion if any private organisation started such a channel. Could the government control such an organisation? Possibly, but there is no way that the South African government could do so – the corruption within the government flows deep and a "Central Rhino Selling Organisation" would fail.

The South African government needs to first tackle the issue of corruption before any trade can be properly regulated, while the cynics would argue that the syndicates effectively run a CSO today. As the conservation organisation Save the Rhino says, *"There is no single silver bullet that is going to solve the rhino poaching crisis."*

With regard to John Hume, given that rhino horn trade is highly unlikely, it is inevitable that he will run out of money and what does the future then hold for his 1,735 rhinos? Plans are afoot to buy John out and ensure that his rhinos do not fall into the wrong hands.

THE DESILETS RHINOS

In early 2015, David Desilets' name cropped up as a potential
source of rhinos. After quite some email traffic, Pod and I flew
to the Sunshine Coast to meet with David at his lovely home on
the Noosa River. David is a patriotic South African who successfully sold his business, banking a tidy sum which enables him
to split his time between South Africa and Australia. We spent
an enjoyable two days with David and his wife Di. They own
a game farm northwest of Johannesburg and started out with
twelve rhinos until three were poached in a single attack. When
this happened, David sent the remaining nine to be cared for at
another farm in the Bela Bela area, where another three were
subsequently killed by poachers. I had visited this farm a month
before. It was owned by Hans Kooy, who offered a service of

caring for the rhinos whose owners found it too dangerous and expensive to keep them.

We left David and Di with a handshake agreement that, if we could secure all of the necessary approvals, they would be happy for their rhinos to be moved to Australia, at no cost to us. Pod and I were ecstatic and shared this joy with the board. David's rhinos were two adult cows aged thirteen and eighteen years; three heifers aged one, three and four years and a young bull of five months. This looked to be an excellent mix since the key criterion for us was that all imports were capable of breeding.

For the next while, we tried to bed down our plan and come up with a realistic budget. The key assumptions were that we would source the six rhinos and move them to a known quarantine facility outside Pretoria. Since the animals were already in captivity, there was no need for the expensive business of locating, darting and transporting rhinos from the bush. We would also meet AUSDAFF's requirement of twelve months location history knowledge. We estimated that the rhinos would spend two months in quarantine and then be crated and shipped to Australia.

Pod and I were in regular dialogue with David and, in one particular conversation with Pod, David said that his major worry was that if the delays were ongoing, his rhinos *"may not be there anymore"* – it was a sobering thought that there was a realistic possibility that they could all be poached. One option was that we shortened the quarantine period in South Africa and lengthened it in Australia, given that is a safer environment. He also had no problem with Western Plains as a destination – like the Salkinders, he just wanted them to be out of South Africa and safe.

In May 2015, I drafted a Memorandum of Understanding

(MOU) between the project and the Desilets family for the supply of rhinos and passed it to Taronga, ZAA and Ashurst for review and comment. Simon Duffy, as always, responded quickly and suggested a few changes. Nothing from ZAA – this was not unusual as several follow-ups were always required from them – but Simon generally represented ZAA's view anyway since, to the outside world, Taronga and ZAA seemed to be joined at the hip.

I was really troubled by any delays since everyone was acutely aware that Desilets was in a very difficult place. He and his family saw their rhinos as part of their family. He was desperately concerned for his rhinos and wanted them to be safe but he was uncertain if the Australian government shared his urgency and wanted some assurances. In South Africa, "now, now" means soon, while "just now" means sometime in the vaguely foreseeable future, but "now" means right now, and David and I wanted action now.

How we could help was to move quickly, but six months later, after I had followed up for the umpteenth time, I had still not received any input for the MOU. Finally, in early December, we received an updated MOU for Desilets, but it wasn't released until I wrote to the board saying that David wanted to see an MOU before having any further discussions. We were in a stalemate situation.

Pod chipped in, *"I understand and appreciate David's frustration. He asked for this ages ago and it's not an unreasonable request. I think his concern is around ownership once they get here and he wants to make sure that he will still have some access to the animals and their offspring. I don't think he is being unreasonable at all."*

What Pod and I stressed was that we were actually being gifted these rhinos and that their owner was deeply concerned that while they were in South Africa, they were at risk.

It was even more complicated in that we had advised the Australian government that these were the specific rhinos that were to be imported into Australia and they were working to that plan.

Finally, I sent it to David who reiterated that he had two non-negotiable issues. He would not bring the animals to live in an enclosure, like a zoo, and he wanted to retain ownership with an ability to move them to his farm if/when circumstances changed. The legacy of perception that zoos are a series of cages is still widespread although Western Plains Zoo is not like that at all.

I was pretty sure that David didn't believe that we would get the approval and he would therefore be saved a decision, so I recommended to the board that we back off for the moment and focus on getting the AUSDAFF vets over to South Africa to check out our designated quarantine facility and let them list any requirements to meet their protocols. This had been long agreed. To be blunt, until we had AUSDAFF's certification of the South African quarantine facility, we had nothing.

As far as AUSDAFF were concerned, and other stakeholders as well, we would still be focused on only the Desilets rhinos. All of our efforts should be on getting AUSDAFF on the plane to Johannesburg. Once we had secured this approval, my sense was that David would then actually put his mind to the project. I was convinced that this was the way to go.

In June 2016, I had one last go at David: *"The time has come. We now are pretty much ready to move the rhinos into quarantine, and we need to finalise arrangements, please can you let me know if you are willing to permit your rhinos to be moved to Australia as part of our project.*" I couldn't be more direct than that, given that we had now become friends.

Frustratingly, David did not respond for a month, but when he did, he didn't mince his words. He would not confirm that his rhinos would be part of the project and now he had to reconsider the conditions that we had put forward. If we could not agree on terms, the rhinos were not moving. Then the pointed jibe that he regretted the delay but *"as it has taken so long to date, another couple of weeks is no big deal."* That really hurt, but David was exactly right, we had stuffed him around for more than eighteen months.

A huge effort had been put into trying to get Desilets' six rhinos to Australia and since this was, by far, our best option, the question must be asked, what went wrong? The most obvious reason is the length of time it took to review the MOU on our side. The delay of a year made us look like amateurs in the eyes of the Desilets family. With the benefit of hindsight, perhaps I had not given our board a clearer understanding of the urgency of the situation and of David and Di's deep concerns about trans-locating their rhinos, their desire to be able to visit them on a regular basis and, vitally, their abhorrence at the thought of the rhinos living out their days in a zoo. In my view, another factor was AUSDAFF's regular moving of the goalposts when it came to the length of time required about the knowledge of the rhinos' history and movements.

Sadly, we blew this opportunity and yet it could have been so different. Now the search would continue to try and satisfy AUSDAFF's ever more stringent requirements. In the meantime, three rhinos a day were still being slaughtered.

POSSIBLE DESTINATIONS

I did not spend almost four years of my life trying to bring rhinos from Africa to live in zoos in Australia. My intention was always to have our rhinos running in the wild in Australia. By "in the wild", I meant not caged in a zoo – however big the cage.

In setting up the project, I had made a commitment to Cam Kerr that the first group of rhinos would go to Taronga and I always intended to fulfil that commitment. It is important to understand that neither Western Plains nor Monarto are "traditional" zoos – where "zoo equals cage". Both are more like safari parks. Western Plains covers an area of three square kilometres while Monarto covers an area of ten square kilometres. They are truly modern zoos and the quality of animal care is world-class.

There was general agreement from all stakeholders that all subsequent shipments of rhinos would follow the same quarantine process but that the destination after fulfilling our commitments to the zoos would be what we referred to as "open range". There were a number of such potential destinations and I worked really hard on these, some of which are described in the following pages.

The criteria we considered for the placement of the rhinos included safety and security, suitable vegetation and feed, appropriate veterinary care and tourism potential – all focused on ideal conditions for breeding.

The late Tony Greig, former England cricket captain, was born in South Africa, although he spent much of his life in England and Australia. He was a regular visitor to South Africa to keep in touch with his family and during those visits he would take as many opportunities as possible to get out in the bush and see the African wildlife. I recall one conversation with him at Sydney Airport when we were comparing life in Australia and South Africa and I suggested that Australia would be an even better place if we could see African wildlife such as elephants, lions, leopards, multiple antelope species and, of course, rhinos, running in the Australian outback. He laughed and said, let me tell you a story about Kerry. Tony was referring to the late Kerry Packer, a close friend and mentor, and also Australia's wealthiest man at the time.

In the mid-1980s, Packer asked if Tony had ever done any hunting. It turned out that Packer wanted to bag an elephant. Tony had never hunted but found himself supplied with special boots, hunting outfits and oilskins while Packer brought an armoury. Greig recalled that they had enough guns and ammunition to supply a small army as the two boarded Kerry's private plane bound for Johannesburg.

Accompanied by two professional big-game hunters, they set off into the Okavango Delta in Botswana in search of the elephant Packer had paid tens of thousands of dollars to pursue. There are about 140,000 elephants in the Delta, and Botswana issues up to 100 hunting licences a year for trophy elephants. Packer had to find the exact elderly bull nominated on their licence. The elephant remained elusive and on the second-last day of the safari, Packer had had enough and said that he was sick and tired of trying to find this elephant, and was prepared to release the right of shooting the elephant to Tony Greig – if he could find it. The good news was that Tony and the trackers never found that elephant.

In his book *Love, War and Cricket*, Tony's son, Mark, adds a story about the same trip. Packer got the trackers to place a dead crocodile in Tony's tent early one morning. The tracker found a stick and propped open its mouth sufficiently to make it look alive – and threatening. The story goes that Tony saw it just as he got out of bed and then broke the world long-jump record to evade the crocodile. Boys will be boys.

After the trip and emboldened by Packer's obvious joy to be among wild animals, Tony suggested that he should use some of his vast pastoral holdings in northern Australia to set up a "mini-Serengeti" which would be a major tourist attraction. Tony really pressed the point with Kerry who finally relented saying, "*Get it done.*"

A year or so later, I mentioned this story to Ken Warriner. Ken, considered one of the best cattlemen in Australia, had Packer's complete trust. They became good friends in the 1970s spending time bull running and buffalo shooting and Packer especially loved the chance to get away from city business pressures with Ken and mix with the rough-and-tumble bush characters. Over time, Ken managed the entire Packer-owned Consolidated Pastoral Holdings, which ran more than 300,000 cattle on more than five million hectares – an area slightly smaller than Belgium. Picking up on Greig's story, Ken said that once Packer had made a decision, he typically wanted action. He committed $50 million to the project to be kept in trust "so that no bloody politician" could get his hands on it or, in future years, say that it was unaffordable.

Things moved fast as they focused on property in the north of Western Australia and discussions commenced with Premier Richard Court's state government about establishing the sanctuary. According to Ken, plans were well advanced with the government very supportive until, as happens, there was an election and Court's Liberal National Party lost power to the Labor party which saw no merit in the proposal. Sadly, the project simply died. Not for the first time nor for the last time, the politicians had the final say.

Recently, I was talking to Michael Hawker, the former Wallaby, and I mentioned Kerry Packer's ambitious plans for a "Serengeti" in the north of Australia. Michael, who is a regular visitor to African game parks, became quite animated proposing that we should revisit this concept with Kerry's son, James, also one of Australia's richest. James Packer's focus was on gaming and he owned casinos all around the world. *"Picture this, Ray, James builds a casino in the Northern Territory – he owns plenty of land there – and around it, is this huge game park where, within reason, the animals can run free. Darwin is so close to Asia – the Asians love their gambling and they love visiting the game reserves in Africa, everybody wins. I know him quite well and I would be happy to approach him."*

I just love people with vision and "big-picture" ideas. Just imagine.

Talking of people with vision, I first met Jake White in Cape Town in 2002 when he was coach of the shadow South African Super Rugby team. Jake subsequently went on to win the Rugby World Cup as Springbok coach in 2007. Our son Paul had set his mind on being a professional rugby player and Jake kindly assisted in arranging a trial with the Natal Sharks rugby team. We remained in touch and Jake was always willing to be the keynote speaker at a number of fundraising events I organised in Sydney. Jake married Lindy Taberer, whose late husband Tony amassed a fortune in the tobacco industry in Rhodesia. Tony showed considerable foresight by acquiring significant tracts of land near Cape Town and also in Western Australia. I worked with Jake at the Brumbies in 2012 and got to know him and Lindy really well.

Margie and I were travelling through the Kruger Park in late 2013 discussing where we could locate the rhinos when they got to Australia. This was after we had encouraging talks with a number of South African parties who were willing to provide rhinos for the project. Margie said, why not ask Jake and Lindy about their property in Western Australia?

I called their Avontuur stud farm outside Cape Town and was told that the Taberer family were actually in the process of selling the Western Australia property – the Yeeda Cattle Station – and suggested that I called a Mervyn Key, who was buying the property. I called Mervyn as soon as I returned to Australia and told him what I was planning. He was keenly interested and we agreed to meet when he was next in Sydney.

Mervyn is a South African who lives in Perth. A lawyer by profession, Mervyn is a fascinating man. Clearly an entrepreneur, he was almost single-handedly responsible for arranging the 1986 All Blacks "Cavaliers" rebel rugby tour of South Africa. It is a gripping story with Mervyn spending three months in New Zealand securing the signatures of all but two of the All Blacks team. (An oft-asked trivia question is "Who were the only two All Blacks who refused to sign up for the Cavaliers Tour?" Answer is Sir John Kirwan and David Kirk MBE.)

I sent Mervyn the details of the plan to import the rhinos into Australia and when we met, he was fully prepared. He asked a few probing questions, made some very valid points and then offered to host the whole herd at his Yeeda property. The size of the property was a jaw-dropping four million acres on which he ran 95,000 cattle. He had previously owned a game farm in the Karoo area of South Africa, which included rhinos and other Big Five animals, so this would not be a completely new venture for him. Mervyn offered a fully packaged "solution" – fencing, security, veterinary services – the lot. I became pretty emotional with this astonishing offer as it addressed one of my biggest concerns – where would we house the rhinos after fulfilling our obligations to Taronga. Mervyn was very sceptical about the Australian government's willingness to make this happen. This was way back in 2013. Mervyn turned out to be spot on.

In July 2015, out of the blue, I received a phone call from the Pilbara Regional Council (PRC), an amalgamation of four Western Australia councils: the shires of Ashburton and East Pilbara, the City of Karratha and the Town of Port Hedland. Amelia Waters introduced herself as the project manager for a rhino project in the Pilbara. The Pilbara is a large, dry, thinly populated region in the north of WA and covers an area of approximately 508,000 square kilometers.

After the steep fall in the iron ore price in 2014, the PRC moved quickly to explore opportunities to increase employment in the areas most affected and one of the key focus items was tourism. Amelia had read about our project and recommended that the PRC assess the feasibility of introducing rhinos to the region as a catalyst for tourism and to "develop the Pilbara and engage its community to assist in the protection of the African rhinos." Amelia wrote to me that their next steps involved reconnecting with a number of stakeholders including the Buurabalayji Thalanyji Aboriginal Corporation, which had expressed great interest in being involved. Negotiations would refine the geographical range within their native title area that may be suitable. The corporation had also expressed interest in developing training and employment opportunities for Indigenous rangers at a later stage to provide care and protection for the rhinos.

The full PRC had met and passed a resolution to support the council executive in exploring such a project through to feasibility stage. The PRC had a number of avenues of enquiry to secure sufficient funding for hosting the rhinos and wanted to meet with me.

As a board, we were still in conversation about possible

destinations for the rhinos so this was a very exciting proposal. The concept of working with a committed government and the original owners of the land appealed strongly. I had lengthy conversations with Amelia and we agreed that, with the approval of our board, I should visit Perth, meet the executive of the PRC and help assess if such a project was viable. I was surprised how advanced they were in their research and I was impressed by their passion and enthusiasm for this project. After considerable correspondence, the PRC asked if they could have a copy of our feasibility study as it would be very useful as they went through their own requirements. I reviewed the request with Nick Boyle from Taronga – who had led the study – and he sent it to the PRC.

The PRC then advised that they were about to issue a request for a quotation (RFQ) for interested parties to do their own feasibility study and asked if they could use our Executive Summary as a part of the RFQ. I checked with our board secretary, David Humphreys whose view was that, since the document was in the public domain on our website, this was not an issue.

The PRC were proving to be an excellently run organisation and were keen to strengthen our partnership by requesting that we consider signing an MOU which I passed on to Mark Stanbridge. The item was on the agenda for the board meeting which I would unfortunately miss because I was in South Africa. When the matter was raised, Mark suggested that we licence PRC to use the study, which would require them to acknowledge our copyright. The alternative would be to ask PRC to sign a deed of confidentiality. Both good, pragmatic suggestions.

From South Africa, I asked if the proposal had been approved. I was told that it hadn't as it was seen as a possible risk to our project and had minimal plusses. I saw this differently, pointing out that the PRC doing a thorough ecological, habitat, fauna and flora review would save us a lot of time and money. I also firmly believed that we had responsibilities as good corporate citizens to support any such endeavours. I mentioned that the demands on my time were minimal and we had built up excellent relationships in the West and these should be maintained. Unfortunately my view was not supported and the PRC were requested to return all the documents that had been sent to them, on the basis that it was our IP and not to be shared.

This surprised me since the full study was on our website for all to see. Soon after, the study was removed from the website. It was a real pity since, in my view, the PRC could have been the ideal partner particularly since it was increasingly obvious that we were in for a long, hard battle with the federal government. With a state and local government backed organisation in our corner, we would have had considerably more firepower. I stewed over this opportunity and concluded that I should have better briefed the board as to the advantages of the partnership.

I was introduced to Mark Carnegie by actress Rachel Ward, who thought that he could potentially be a funder of the project. Mark has a reputation as a hard-nosed businessman and within five minutes of meeting him, I could see why.

After the introductions, and before I could tell my story, Mark said, "Mate, unless this thing can make a buck, I'm not interested". Well, I knew better than anyone that this was a costly exercise and there were only three ways in which a buck could be made: the rhinos were to be hunted, the rhino horns were to be harvested or the rhinos were to be a tourist attraction. None of these were in the plan.

As I explained he came right back saying that the only way to proceed was to locate the rhinos on Aboriginal land and, on an annual basis, grant limited licences to hunt the rhinos. I said that was not going to happen. Undeterred, Mark was in full flight; *"How much does it cost to get the rhinos to Australia?"* I said that it was $80,000 per rhino. *"Ok"*, he said, *'how much can we sell the licences for?"* Usually I get very excited when people say "we", because there is buy-in. In this instance, I went cold and told him the story of the American who had paid $300,000 to shoot a black rhino in Namibia. Triumphantly he said, *"There you are – the model can work."*

Mark mentioned that the laws for hunting in Aboriginal areas were very specific and very different from anywhere else and that this could work in our favour. (I later checked and the Act in WA is indeed very specific but it relates to "hunting for food"). *"The Wildlife Conservation Act 1950 s 23 (WA) exempts Aborigines from conservation laws when hunting for food on land not being a native reserve or wildlife sanctuary".* Warming to his subject, he said, *"Let's have a chat to Warren and see what he thinks. I had dinner with him last night."* He was referring to Warren Mundine, the highly respected Aboriginal leader. Fortunately, Mundine did not answer the phone. I tried to explain that the Australian government would never give their consent to such a plan. Undeterred Mark said he would also talk to Wayne Bergmann who is one of Australia's leading advocates for Indigenous self-determination through economic empowerment and opportunity. His vision is for long-term economic independence for Aboriginal people.

After our meeting, Mark sent me a note saying that he had spoken to Wayne and that, *"If it works economically, he is up for it and he has the land."* I called Wayne who was very upbeat and willing to help, but we agreed that while the Kimberley was a good option, it was too soon to work out any detailed plans and that the first priority was to get the initial batch of rhinos into Australia.

In May 2015, I received a lengthy note from Amanda French, representing the Bob Irwin Wildlife and Conservation Foundation. Bob is the father of the late Steve Irwin, "The Crocodile Hunter". Amanda had seen my interview on Channel Seven's *Weekend Sunrise Program a*nd she outlined the relationship that the foundation had with a private property in Broken Hill in New South Wales. The property is called White Leeds Station and is owned by Margaret McBride and Steve Radford whose main conservation project had been in developing a man-made wetland that had transformed an arid zone into an oasis in the outback using Broken Hill's sewage water. For some years they had thrown around the idea of utilising the land for an elephant breeding program within Australia to safeguard endangered populations. Amanda wanted to know if I thought this land would be of use for my project. She described White Leeds as a part of the Broken Hill bioregion complex with an area of approximately 10,000 hectares – all of which is gazetted as a wildlife refuge.

I was blown away. It was no secret that the key survival

element for animals such as rhinos was the availability of water, since rhinos drink every day. The basic checklist for suitable rhino habitat included moderate-to-dry savannah, which should meet basic parameters such as an herbaceous layer of sweet, short, grass; surface drinking water; mud-holes for wallowing; patches of dense thicket vegetation for refuge; scattered tree foliage for shade and resting; and relatively flat terrain.

One thing I could never be accused of was missing an opportunity and I immediately contacted Amanda. After our conversation, I was even more convinced of the potential synergy between White Leeds and the project. I received a subsequent note from owner Steve Radford, saying that White Leeds was large enough to handle the rhinos, far enough out of Broken Hill to make it remote from a security point of view, but close enough to receive the community's offerings and services. His core business is earthmoving, so they could make any animal habitats as required. They also operated five of their own aircraft, so getting people in and out of Broken Hill was no issue. He and his wife Marg have pastoral backgrounds and with the abundance of water and opportunity for a number of waterholes, and the open grazing, he was sure that they had something to offer. He also offered to sponsor the project in kind to make it successful. Once again, I marvelled at the generosity of the Australian people: "*We are happy to sponsor the project in kind!*"

All of these conversations took place in the second and third quarter of 2015. I then met Steve and Marg at the fundraising dinner, which reinforced their commitment to the project. We had pointed out to them that White Leeds would need to be registered as a zoo for the plan to succeed. Demonstrating the determination and resilience of this couple, nothing seemed to faze them and they engaged a suitably qualified professional to prepare the documentation to become a zoo.

The name Kevin Humphries had come up a number of times during my discussions with Steve and Marg and in July, I received an email from him: *"I'm a member of the NSW Parliament. Broken Hill is in my electorate as is 45 per cent of NSW. Steve and Marg have done a great job on their wetland project with water recycling and building an ecosystem. Their conservation project and potential link up with the rhino resettlement project is one of the best I have seen. If there is any way I can be of assistance please let me know, this is really exciting."* I realised that these folks were deadly serious. Getting a politician's attention is difficult at the best of times, but here was a highly respected politician actually chasing me to get things done. On the same day, I received a note from Steve Radford saying that after seven tough years, the water project was complete. How refreshing to work with people who were willing to give, give and give.

Soon after, I arranged a meeting with Troy Grant, the Deputy Premier of NSW and also MP for Dubbo, home to Western Plains Zoo. Troy had been well briefed about our project. I reiterated that we would not be successful without Taronga – that they were critical to our success. Troy offered to brief federal ministers Barnaby Joyce and Greg Hunt, when the time was right. We also met with Kevin Humphries. His enthusiasm and support for the project were so obvious. He undertook to brief Deputy Prime Minister, Warren Truss, about the merits of our project. Kevin was true to his word. He contacted Truss whose chief of staff, Damian Callachor, off his own bat, did some discreet background investigation about the status of the project with AUSDAFF – the department fell into Truss's area of responsibility. He confided that things appeared to be moving forward and that there were yet to be any red flags raised with our project. Good news all round.

In mid-2016 I had a note from Professor Lloyd Reeve-Johnson who has the longest title and pedigree I have ever seen. He is a veterinary surgeon and has worked all over the world as well as with the Queensland and Federal governments. Lloyd wrote, *"If you ever need an 'isolation site' in Queensland, we would be happy to volunteer our property outside Esk. We have 185 acres of undulating grassland surrounded by other 1,000-plus acre properties with single private road access, a permanent creek and four dams. Both my wife and I are veterinarians and I grew up in Southern Africa with rhino and also worked for a while with a zoo in the UK where we kept breeding rhino. Aside from that I wish you well and am delighted that this project is now moving forward."*

Lloyd and I exchanged correspondence on a regular basis and I also introduced him to Allan Davies, noting that Lloyd was someone who not only had the intellect and "on the ground" experience but a passion that matched mine.

My heart breaks that there were so many people who really believed in my vision and yet the bureaucracy seemed to be determined to place obstacle after obstacle in our way. All of these potential destinations had their own distinct advantages and very little downside. Innovative and perhaps even radical, but each one had strong merit, and, in most cases, we were being offered land or services for free.

RHINO ORPHANS

AND OTHER STORIES

I had a burning objective to secure one or more reliable sources of rhinos to translocate to Australia and, in truth, this should have been a fifth pillar. I have detailed the discussions and negotiations with SANParks, the Salkinders, Piet Warren, David Desilets, David Mabunda, Bandile Mkize, Norman Adami and John Hume – a total of eight different individuals/organisations. All of these were smart, successful and serious people and organisations who wanted to help. And there were others who offered to help. Pretty much everywhere I went, people understood the urgent need to act and, with very few exceptions, were prepared to get involved.

One such gentleman was Gianni Ravazzotti. Gianni, an

immigrant to Johannesburg from Italy after World War II, saw the need for affordable tiles and ceramic products in an increasingly urban South Africa. He began importing and retailing them through the company he founded, Italtile. Ten years later, with the first hints that there would be trade sanctions against South Africa in the wake of the 1976 Soweto uprising, he began manufacturing ceramic tiles domestically and, in 1992, his company was listed on the Johannesburg Stock Exchange. Gianni is now one of the wealthiest men in Africa.

In July 2015 I received a note from Gianni's daughter Gia, who lives in Sydney, asking for details of my project. She wrote that her family was entirely committed and prepared to conserve the world's rhino population and would like to assist in the most "hands on" way possible, and that they had many resources at their disposal. Gia concluded by saying that they would like to assist. *"As South Africans and conservationists, your project holds great interest."*

How exciting was this! I gave Gia and her sister Luci, who also lives in Sydney, a full briefing and we agreed that I would meet their dad when I next visited Johannesburg. I met Mr Ravazzotti at his office in Bryanston. Not a young man, he has his own private work area/gazebo outside his expansive office. The building is non-smoking, so he sits outside quietly smoking his cigars and drinking strong Italian coffee. Apart from all his other qualities, Mr Ravazzotti is an ardent conservationist: he founded the 36,000 hectare Lapalala Private Game Reserve in the North West Province, which became the first private reserve to acquire black rhino as the threat to these highly endangered animals increased. Lapalala's commitment to preserving these magnificent creatures continues to this day, and it is now one of the leading private black rhino sanctuaries in the world. I was certain that as soon as we had the government approvals, he would be among the first to offer us rhino.

Black rhino. (Photo credit Gianni Ravazzotti)

It is fair to say that if you see a female rhino in the wild, she is likely to be pregnant or have a calf running at her side. With the mass killing of rhinos in the Kruger Park someone asked the question, "*What happens to the calves when the mothers are shot?*" There were several answers to the question, all uncomfortable: the calves could be shot by the poachers or by the rangers – to prevent them being taken by predators, which was the most likely fate of these defenceless young animals. Once this knowledge became public, there was international outrage and, in true South African style, an enterprising young woman decided to do something about it and "maak a plan": the Care for Wild Rhino Sanctuary was established by Petronel Nieuwoudt. With the dramatic increase in the number of rhinos poached, there was a need to care for and rehabilitate the injured and/or orphaned rhinos. Petronel's mission was to provide this service for all orphans, but rhinos far outnumbered any other species.

The more that I learned about her efforts, the more enthusiastic I became. I just had to meet Petronel since I surmised that her program would be an absolute winner for us. If we could secure some orphans, we would be guaranteed success. Emotionally, it would be an even easier sell to potential donors; the orphans would cost much less in terms of transportation and we could then pair them with the existing population of rhinos in Australia to wean them.

My first visit to meet Petronel was an eye-opener. Outside Nelspruit, Margie and I drove down a dreadful gravel road for about fifteen kilometres to be met by this slight but dynamic young woman. She showed us around the facility (which also housed an orphaned white lion cub) and we then moved to her house for a cup of tea. We were sitting in her lounge room when the door flew open and in waddled a baby hippopotamus. Ellie was her name, yet another orphan Petronel had adopted. Ellie didn't give us a glance and headed straight for the kitchen for a snack. I've seen some pretty interesting things in my time, but this encounter with Ellie the baby hippo was right up there.

Petronel Niewoudt and Ellie the hippo.
(Photo credit: Margaret Dearlove)

Our discussion with Petronel and her partner Chris was centred on sourcing some of their rhino orphans. Both seemed very keen and I subsequently sent Petronel a draft MOU on how the transaction could work. I emphasised the importance of what she was doing and that she had our full support. I confirmed that we would take as many orphan rhinos as she could provide. The basis of the agreement was that the rhinos (and their progeny) would always belong to her. I really wanted to turn this dream into reality and this was the best all round option, by far. Petronel nominated the orphans Forest, Olive and Thana to be included in our Australian plans. As we were driving away from their farm, Margie predicted that Petronel would be the next Jane Goodall or Diane Fossey.

This was in March 2015 and everything was looking exceedingly rosy. Or so I thought. Little did I know that AUSDAFF was about to scuttle my plans.

One of our best supporters, Steve Goodey, had previously worked with Lorna Davis and had mentioned the project to her. Both former South Africans, Lorna is a senior executive with a global food company and she immediately supported the project with a handsome donation. When I phoned to thank her, she increased her donation of more than $100,000 to become the largest individual donor that we ever had.

Lorna wanted to adopt orphan rhinos to ensure their safe passage to Australia and I arranged with Petronel that we would initially adopt one of her rhinos to be named Trudy, as requested by Lorna. We paid Petronel for the orphans which would "belong" to Lorna. After making her donation, Lorna wrote to her family, colleagues and friends, *"It is not often that something touches me like this. The rhino situation is really dire and there is a fabulous plan to bring rhinos to Australia to keep them safe from poachers. I have sponsored a baby orphan rhino who will be called Trojan if he is a boy and Trudy if she is a girl. He or she will be really lonely if we can't get more little ones to Oz. Please read this newsletter from Ray Dearlove and if you are inspired, donate some money and circulate this email . . . it broke my heart."*

Lorna said to me in one of her notes, *"when you are changing the world, Ray, it sometimes takes longer than you expect!"*

I made sure Lorna was kept informed of progress and, a few months later, I was able to inform her that Dr Jonathan Taylor from AUSDAFF had confirmed they would be paying for all their expenses to visit South Africa. He said that they would be likely to travel mid-year. While this promised to be a positive and a key milestone, as time marched on, I felt that "bureaucracy" was enveloping the project within the government. At the end of the day,

Lorna Davis, a great supporter

I deeply regret that I did not push for Lorna's donations to be refunded, I felt dreadful then and I still feel dreadful about this. Here was a supporter who had made a very large donation to a cause that she truly believed in. In Lorna's own words most of her commitment was due to me.

Getting back to Petronel, her communication became less frequent. This coincided with the rise in awareness of the rhino crisis. Kruger Park management struck an agreement whereby Petronel would take all their orphans. As a result, the number of orphans at Care for Wild increased significantly, as did the profiles of Care for Wild and Petronel. Prince Harry endorsed the program and became an ambassador, and we eventually became irrelevant to Petronel's needs.

When David Desilets' rhinos were poached, he moved them to Hans Kooy's farm near Thabazimbi. Hans's farm is quite spectacular, with a large paddock where the rhinos run free.

One of Hans's main lines of business is protecting rhinos. On his farm he has more than 50 rhinos, some his own, but mostly owned by others, a form of agistment. The reason for my visits to Hans were very specific – to see where Desilets' rhinos were located, to discuss quarantine facilities, and to potentially source more rhinos. My first reaction to his property was that it didn't look too secure at all as there was very little visible security. When I asked Hans about this, he agreed and added that the cost of security was crippling. Based on previous "hits", the danger was after nightfall and that was when his heavily armed guards moved in. While he appeared fairly casual, he most certainly wasn't. I asked what he did at night – he lived on his own – and he answered that he would lock up his house, have something to eat, read a book and watch television – much like the rest of us. And what if there was an incident, I asked? Oh well, I put on my bulletproof vest, grab my gun and go and investigate. He showed me his bullet-proof vest – I could barely lift it. In a chilling statement, he said, *"Ray, I know that one day the poachers will come around that corner, accompanied by their guards – all carrying AK47s and they will do just what they want to do."* No matter how much security he had, he knew (and they knew) that Hans would be outgunned.

Towards the end of 2015 I asked one of our supporters, Kirstin Scholtz, if she could take some photographs of Desilets' rhinos (hopefully soon to become ours) on Hans's farm to use as marketing collateral. Kirstin was the official photographer for the Women's Surfing League and outstanding at her job. She jumped at the chance and wrote this report after her visit.

"I was fortunate enough to visit the rhinos that have been earmarked for The Australian Rhino Project in what was supposed to be a safe haven in South Africa. Despite the electric fences, guard towers and watchdogs to protect the 50 rhinos, I quickly realized that nowhere is safe for rhino. As we skirted the inside of the large enclosure, staying close to the fence for safety, we noticed one large rhino lying under a

tree away from the others who were feeding on a pile of hay. She was waiting for them to move before she made her way to the food and it was as she got up, that we noticed something was terribly wrong. She had been shot through the fence, just above her front left leg, leaving her crippled and in obvious agony.

It is heartbreaking to think what an animal, with no natural predators and very poor eyesight, would go through during such trauma. Watching her trying to walk on only three legs was one of the most distressing sights I have ever seen. Helplessly, we watched as she tried to inch forward to the feed. With each stumbling step, the top half of her body collapsed as her leg buckled under her enormous weight. A rhino simply cannot function with three legs, and as we watched with tears rolling down our cheeks, we knew that this beautiful animal stood very little chance of survival. A few days later we learned that she had died from her injuries. She was pregnant at the time."

I just wish that the bureaucrats in their comfortable Canberra offices could have been present for Kirstin's experience. How could I instil a sense of urgency into these people before it was too late?

Veterinarian Dr Chris Brown is very well known in Australia through his television shows, *Bondi Vet* and *I'm a Celebrity, Get Me Out of Here* – the latter is filmed in South Africa, close to the town of Hoedspruit, a small farming and wildlife community at the heart of South Africa's greatest rhino population.

As the poaching war raged and word spread about the success of Petronel and Care for Wild, several other organisations were founded to rescue and rehabilitate orphaned calves. One such organisation is Rhino Revolution in Hoedspruit. Located less than 30 minutes' drive from Kruger, Rhino Revolution is positioned in the centre of the poaching war on rhinos. The organisation relies on fundraising and donations from local businesses and individuals to exist.

While filming *I'm a Celebrity* in 2015, Chris invited his father, Dr Graeme Brown, a lecturer in veterinary parasitology at Sydney University, to visit the orphanage where they met the local veterinary nurses, all UK trained. These nurses had responsibility for the rehabilitation of young rhinos and, working alongside Graeme, they confided that they really needed a microscope to perform faecal worm tests. Outsourcing such testing to local vets meant delays in processing results and was also expensive. Graeme suggested that the nurses contact me for support. Their request was for financial support, which I declined since I had a strong view that people who donated money to us wanted it to go to the project. I met with Graeme in Sydney and agreed that our best contribution was through the donation of a microscope. I was sure that the veterinarian faculty would have a few spare microscopes, and I was confident that Dean Roseanne Taylor would support this request – as she did. Through the offices of our good friend Professor David Emery, the microscope was shipped to Hoedspruit.

Dr Chris Brown. (Photo credit: YouTube)

During the Rhino Ray

Endangered Species Safari, we visited Rhino Revolution to see the orphans. While there, the nurses mentioned that the microscope donation was vital, but they could also use a centrifuge to enable the team to independently complete basic blood analyses. Up stepped a member of our safari group, Vivien Jones, who promptly wrote a cheque. The equipment has been a significant step-change for the nurses in performing tests on the orphans.

At various times in the project's life, I also had discussions about sourcing rhinos with Dave Powrie of Sabi Sands Game Reserve; Pelham Jones, President of the Private Rhino Owners Association, North West Game Parks; David Rosmarin of Investec; Dr William Fowlds; Gus van Dyk of Tswalu Game Reserve; Dr Peter Morkel, Arrie van Rensberg and the Cilliers Family. I was offered rhinos by both Miriam Wiesner of the Salzburg Zoo and Gillad Goldstein of the Tel Aviv Zoo – through Tammy Zak, a great supporter.

Contacting all of these people was one thing, persuading them to send their rhinos to Australia was another thing entirely. In most cases, the rhinos had originally been purchased, not for resale or for profit, but for the sheer enjoyment of owning an animal that had its origins more than ten million years ago. Many of these rhinos were given names like Phila, Trudy, Venus and so on and there was a strong bond between the rhino and the owner. This bond went even deeper with the orphaned rhinos. When you hear a baby rhino cry, it sounds just like an infant. Rhino owners are well aware of the risks their rhinos face, they are also keenly aware that this risk extends to them and their families and so, intuitively, they could see the benefits of sending their rhinos to a safer place, but for them to take this leap of faith, they first needed to trust me and trust is only gained with time. I worked very hard at such relationships which, I am proud to say, continue today.

So much hinged on us securing the Australian government's approval and I wasn't sure that I was winning.

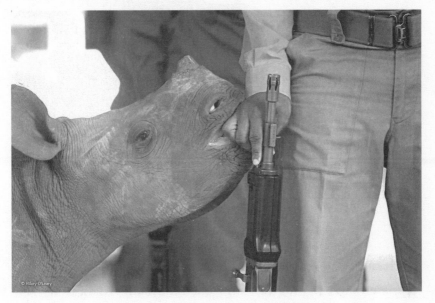

A baby rhino gives his protector a lick.
(Photo Credit: Kruger Park News)

19

THE GENERAL AND THE LOW
INTENSITY, UNDECLARED WAR

I first met Major-General Johan Jooste in 2013 while the feasibility study was in progress. I travelled to South Africa to try and get a first-hand feel for the rhino poaching situation and also to assess the possibility of sourcing rhino for our project. One of the first people I met was General Jooste and he is, without doubt, one of the most impressive men I have ever had the pleasure of meeting.

In 2012 SANParks Management decided to form a Special Projects department in an effort to implement mitigation measures to deal with the severe increase in wildlife crime and, in particular, rhino poaching in the Kruger Park. General Jooste was approached to head this group. His brief was to review current anti-poaching measures and put in place para-military strategies, structures and systems that would enable SANParks to respond to the increasing threat and constantly changing tactics of poachers. Part of this was to support and coordinate the efforts and actions of game rangers and other law enforcement agencies on the ground. It was clear that counter-poaching measures conducted within the boundaries of the national parks alone would not be sufficient, and the term' "clearing the park from the outside" was coined by the General.

Johan had retired from the army in 2006, after 35 years of active service. He had served the last part of his military career in the army's general staff in various capacities, but always involved with strategy, leadership development and knowledge management. An articulate man, he is highly qualified with an MBA in military and strategic leadership. He was appointed by CEO David Mabunda who said, *"We know that we will not be able to put a ranger behind every rhino. We need to develop innovative, modern ways of protecting the rhino in the wake of this well-organised onslaught."*

In the same statement, Jooste said, *"I am not a messiah, but I will do my best to bring acceptable results. This fight against poaching is not about an individual, and success depends on the collective collaboration and commitment from the men and women tasked with the responsibility of conserving our heritage."*

I next met the General a year later in his office in Skukuza. Every time that I met with him, he was completely open with me and I will never betray that trust. He started the discussion with the comment, *"The world has rhino fever."* We agreed that this was a good thing in that, at last, the world was sitting up and taking notice of the wildlife crime that was occurring right across the globe. Having just arrived from Sydney, I was pretty heavily jet-lagged and, as we were talking, the General mentioned the name Buffett. He must have seen the look of surprise on my face as my mind played back what he had said. Did he just say Buffett?

The author with Major-General Johan Jooste, the South African government's anti-poaching head. (Photo credit: Julia Salnicki)

"Ja, ja," he said, *"I was having dinner in Johannesburg with Mr. Howard Buffett, son of Warren"* – typical General, always so formal and respectful – *"and he asked me how much money I needed to fix the problem."*

The General responded that he thought it was about US$10 million. Buffett didn't blink and asked him to verify the amount required. The General smiled at me, *"Ray, I walked back to my hotel and my legs were shaking!"* He checked the numbers and, somewhat apologetically, said that he actually needed US$13 million. Buffett then went through the list item by item and once he had finished, he said, *"What about the helicopter, you said you needed a helicopter?"* He mumbled a response and Buffett told him to include it, adding another US$6 million. *"Now what about that eye in the sky thing that you said you needed?"* He was referring to the Tethered Aerostat Radar System used for surveillance. Again, he mumbled that they were unsure about the effectiveness of this technology in the park. *"Add it in,"* he said. That was another US$6 million. Howard Buffett smiled at the General and they shook hands on a US$25 million donation. Said the General, *"This is an absolute game changer."*

I must have looked stunned and the General said, *"Wait for Friday, it is going to be a major press release."* And so, it was.

On a slightly less positive note, the General commented that I had undertaken a *"very big and very important project"* which, ominously, he was certain, would require the South African cabinet approval. I shuddered. Additional government involvement was less than ideal. What he really liked about our project was the goal to get the rhinos to breed faster, which required good habitat and good security. This was April 2014 and he saw the tipping point as being about 24 months away. Others believed that the tipping point had already been reached.

Every time I met anyone in SANParks who was at the sharp end of the poaching onslaught, I would ask, *"How many do we have left?".* The General's view was black rhino numbers were in the high hundreds and the white rhinos about 8,000. (Noting that, in a recent discussion I had with veterinarian Dr Will Fowlds, who has dedicated his life to protecting and healing rhinos, his view is that the current KNP total rhino population is between 3,000 and 4,000 with less than 500 black rhinos.) Sobering.

After the meeting, I wrote to thank the General and he

responded, "*Thank you for making time to consult with us. I have no doubt that you are a real 'friend of rhinos' and I appreciate and respect your ambitious project. I hope you understand our explanation about the government approval, treacherous as it will be, to get rhino from KNP. I wish you well – please keep us posted. The danger of the Rhino War is 'too little too late' and I hope somewhere you get the attention you deserve.*"

I treasured this message and would often refer to it as I did with another piece of advice from my wife, Margie, "*Be careful that the emotion doesn't take over from the reality. You will have to have a steely centre to get it through the crap of the political expedience. Some people will not look beyond how it can help or hinder their careers – the ultimate outcome won't mean anything to them – they are only looking at the immediate benefit.*" My wonderful wife always keeps me grounded.

Soon after my visit, I sent the General a copy of my poem, "For the Rhino". He really liked it and a while later I sent him another poem which I called "The Game Ranger" which described how the roles of rangers had changed from conservationists to armed protectors of rhino, placing both rangers and rhinos solidly in the firing line. The General loved the poems and I was invited to attend International Rangers Day in Kruger, as the General's guest. Unfortunately, I was unable to attend, and my cousin Robbie Robertson represented me. Both of the poems featured in the official program of the day and were read out at the celebration of all South African game rangers at the Paul Kruger gate entrance to the park. One of the proudest days of my life.

There's a small sign above the General's desk at his office. It says: "Think Big, Start Small, Act Now". Here are some key points from a long discussion that I had with him in 2016.

"We are fighting a war" he said as he detailed what he and his team of rangers were doing to protect the rhinos in the vast area of Kruger. He acknowledged there were other parks at risk and other animals such as elephants in the firing line, but for now his full attention was on Kruger and the rhinos.

He said that approximately 80 per cent of poaching was done by Mozambique nationals, who infiltrated the park south of the Olifants River, usually at night, walking up to 25 kilometres to kill. Of concern, now that his teams had recently put pressure on the east, poaching from the west of Kruger, the South African side, had also increased. He said that conservatively, up to a dozen groups of three poachers were in Kruger at any one time, so about 36 to 40 poachers and three or four groups entering and exiting the park every day. A self-sufficient poaching group can spend up to four or five days in the park.

"Sometimes during the full moon period, they will concentrate in one area, knowing that the rules of engagement favour them, and this puts us on the back foot. We have to arrest them; we're not allowed to kill them. They know this, so their theory is 'let them chase us,' and they will come into the park in such numbers that we just cannot plug all the holes."

I asked him to describe a "typical" poacher and he said that they are young men, usually in their 20s, recruited from poverty, uneducated with very little hope of getting a job. The shooters however, are specifically selected, because the .458 and .375 rifles are high-value assets. The navigator is important because he's the guy who knows the park, has been in before, and can guide them at night – he will typically carry a GPS device and a couple of mobile phones. The third guy carries the knives and axe, food and water. *"As much as I despise them, the poachers can survive well in the bush, and their bush-craft is remarkable. They walk extraordinary distances at night to find their target and be back in Mozambique before daybreak. Their tracking is good, and they are a formidable opponent. With no rules. If you've grown up in destitute poverty, one successful poaching expedition changes your life. The communities adjacent to the game reserves don't have any ownership, so they ask: 'What do I get from that park? A few of my community work there, but most of us, what do we get?' The growth in poaching is slowing, but poaching is not decreasing. To bring the numbers down will require a national, regional and global solution, of which demand reduction is critical."*

Technology is critical to the success of any anti-poaching efforts and his plan was to use an array of sensors that would allow early detection of the poachers. I asked if, by default, the rhinos outside of the IPZ would be "written off"? The General bristled at the question saying that they were not neglecting the rest of the park's rhinos, but, given their resources, they just had to prioritise. This must have been an extremely difficult decision for him to take.

"We have to create a safe haven, a bastion, a fortress to make sure that we safeguard this core rhino population. If poachers get in here in numbers, they will kill as many as they can. If we lose Kruger, it is all over for the rhinos."

The General is placing a great deal of emphasis on dogs for anti-poaching. *"We've expanded the dog teams – known as K9 units – and we're aiming to place dogs at all the gates. One of the dogs is an explosive detector, so he can pick up ammunition or weaponry, while the other is a natural asset detector, trained to pick up animal products, specifically rhino horn."* (In 2018, all 102 contacts with poachers involving dogs resulted in arrests.)

On the shoot-to-kill policy, he said: *"Shooting to kill will improve our success rate, and it will be a deterrent, but it won't stop the poaching. In this park, which is 20,000 square kilometers of thick bushveld, it is too difficult to detect people, so the risk is low, and poachers know this."*

It reminded me of an incident that was related to me a year or two later. A poacher had been killed whilst he was on a mission inside the Kruger Park and his funeral was taking place in a bordering Mozambican village. After the funeral, as the mourners moved away, a man who had been watching the funeral from a distance approached the distraught widow at the grave. He commiserated with her, offered his condolences and then pulled an envelope from his pocket saying to her that her husband had been a good man and here was a bonus. As he walked away and through her tears, she called out to him asking him to wait since she wished to introduce him to her son, who wanted to take his father's place as a poacher. A truly desperate situation.

I asked the General if he could wave a magic wand what would he ask for. He responded, "We *need more men. The standard protection ratio is one ranger for every 10 square kilometres. In Kruger we have one ranger per 50 square kilometres. Ideally, we could have 2,000 rangers, and a fortified boundary of 1,000 kms around the park, with helicopters and technology. We have 400 rangers at the moment, we probably need five times that."* The dilemma for him is that the park is an international tourist destination, not an army base and he questions whether they really want that number of enforcement staff within the park. As he points out, with all those extra people comes additional risk, because there will be far more people entering and leaving the park.

His strong belief is that he must clear the park from the outside. Chasing poachers is one thing but, sadly, this is usually after a rhino has been killed and the horn removed.

"We know many of the 'level 2' poaching bosses live just across the Mozambique border in Massingir and, in truth, 80 per cent of the solution probably lies in taking these guys out. Trust me, Ray, it's enormously tempting for my teams to go across the border and bring them back here, but we can't do that. It's politically unacceptable so these middlemen see themselves as untouchable. We are fighting a war. Mozambicans are making armed, illegal incursions into my country, plundering and exiting with our resources. We have armed incursions by poachers every day, about one hundred and fifty per month. To me, that's an act of war. To win this war, there are only two long-term solutions. Giving ownership of Africa's parks to surrounding communities, so they take responsibility for their wildlife and feel a strong sense of ownership in the wellbeing of their wildlife. And second, we have to reduce demand in Vietnam, Thailand and China."

The world will watch and wait and hope.

THE FOUR PILLARS

As we moved into what I hoped would be the execution or implementation phase of the project, we constantly spoke about the four pillars, the first of which was "governance". Without exception, our board was determined to get this right and avoid scandals such as the one that engulfed the Shane Warne Foundation. Mark Stanbridge and the team from Ashurst did a marvellous job in ensuring that we complied with everything and when lawyer David Humphreys came on board, we had another pair of eyes on the subject. Our governance was impeccable.

I had always known that the project would fail unless we were able to secure tax deductibility for donations and, as a result, I spent a lot of time getting this approval. In Australia, this is called a deductible gift recipient (DGR), which is an entity or fund that can receive tax deductible gifts. This highly prized DGR status is granted by the Australian Tax Office.

Cynics told me we would never get the status: *"Why would the Australian government permit a tax deduction for a non-Australian species for an issue taking place 16,000 kilometres away?"* A fair point but I took a completely different view: rhino poaching is a global issue and Australia could (and should) play a key role in saving the species. I chased and chased our application, which we lodged in May 2014. The "experts" told me that it would take two years to obtain the approval, if we got it at all. Game on, this man loves a challenge.

While our application was being assessed, I tried any number of avenues, none successful, whereby people could donate to us via a third-party organisation.

In September 2014 I met with the Federal Minister of the Environment, Greg Hunt, in his office in Parliament House in Canberra. I'd have to say this was one of the best meetings of my life. As we were all being introduced, Minister Hunt said to me, *"No need for an introduction, Ray, I know exactly who you are and I think that what you are doing is absolutely wonderful."* Wow, what a start to the meeting. When we sat down in his office, I launched into my "background" speech and Greg interrupted me by saying, not at all rudely, but very encouragingly, *"I'm sold on The Australian Rhino Project, Ray, what do you need from me?"*

Obviously, the briefings that I had sent through had been read. I said that our DGR application was "in his office" and that I had been told that it might be three to six months before it could be reviewed. Greg fixed his eyes on his chief of staff, the delightful Wendy Black, who coughed and said that she would check. Greg responded, "*I want that document out of our office by the end of the month*," in three weeks' time. It was.

My second request was for Greg to assist in arranging a meeting for me with the South African Minister for the Environment, Edna Molewa, at the November 2014 National Parks Congress in Sydney. He delivered on this as well. Greg Hunt is one of those rare people you find in government who knows that they can help you (or hinder you), and he takes this responsibility very seriously.

The difference between success and failure often boils down to the existence, or absence, of relationships. I carefully tracked the progress of our DGR application as it meandered through the corridors of federal government departments. Minister Josh Frydenberg was the acting federal treasurer and his was the final signature we needed. Leanne Piggott, a fellow board director, is married to Peter Wertheim, who holds a senior position in the Executive Council of Australian Jewry. I reached out to Leanne to see if Peter could help expedite the approval since he was good friends with Josh. I'm not sure if the conversation ever took place, but sure enough, two weeks later, in February 2015, we had our approval. I cannot describe the feeling of euphoria and relief that swept through me – against all odds, we had got it done. While the fundraising targets had never scared me, I was now convinced that we could fund the project. So much goodwill had been built up in the year since the launch breakfast and we were well and truly on our way. Many of our supporters (and detractors) sat up and took note – these folks are serious and the Australian government is taking them seriously.

While waiting for the DGR approval, I had not been sitting on my hands. I invited Vance Martin and Britt Peterson to the Michael Knight cocktail party during the National Parks Congress. Vance is president of the US-based WILD organisation and Britt sits on the board. Vance also sits on the Wilderness Foundation Board, established by Dr Ian Player. There are certain people one meets who you immediately click with and Vance is one of these. Vance represents many of the values and attributes of the late great Ian Player. A true gentleman. We got on extremely well and when I asked him if WILD would act as a conduit for donations from US-based supporters of the project, there was no hesitation at all. *"Let me see how we can make it work,"* were his words. And he did. WILD took a modest fee of 7.5 per cent for handling the donations and sent us the balance. With strong support from donors such as Michael Nugent and Pete Drummond in the US, this was a very good financial arrangement for us.

I also contacted Jo Roberts, CEO of the Wilderness Foundation UK, and signed a similar agreement with her organisation. My cousin, Dr Oliver Dearlove, was a generous donor to the cause. Similarly, Dr Andrew Muir, CEO of Wilderness Foundation Africa, was very happy to support us by accepting donations made in South Africa. I now had donations from the United States, the United Kingdom, South Africa and Australia covered. Everyone in these countries would receive a tax deduction when they donated to TARP. A mighty step forward.

The second of the four pillars was securing the approval from the Australian government for the importation of the rhinos. At one point, AUSDAFF's Jonathan Taylor gave me an inkling that our project had international political implications and advised that they were seeking assurances from *"high levels within the South African Government'* that our plan would be acceptable to them. DFAT specifically asked the Australian High Commission in Pretoria to review the situation with the departments of Agriculture and Environment. I was thankful that I had covered off with all of the key influencers and decision-makers in both departments.

If ever there was any doubt that my plan was politically a big deal it was put to rest in May 2015 after a discussion with the Australian High Commissioner to South Africa, His Excellency Adam McCarthy, who asked me for detailed information about the plan and a list of my South African government contacts. I was obviously very happy to provide these since the High Commission team of Adam, Edward Jackson and Ben Playle had already been enormously supportive. To cover myself, I reminded Adam that the rhinos were all privately sourced and it was not illegal to export rhinos from South Africa. I also reaffirmed that we had done everything according to the protocols of both countries.

I had also established a very good relationship with Alastair McKenzie, the Assistant Director for the Southern Africa and Indian Ocean Division of DFAT in Canberra. Alastair had a good understanding of the complexities of the politics of South Africa and was as discreet a man as you could meet but also a great ally. He kept me informed of progress and pitfalls as best he could. At one point, he ventured that sometimes he wished that bureaucrats would just get out of the way. Amen to that.

I received a note from Ben Playle, *"As you know from Adam, we're seeking to discuss the practicalities of relocating the rhinos to Australia with both DEA and DAFF here. While we've been work-ing our contacts, getting appointments has not been straightforward. Accordingly, it's difficult to put a timeframe on when we'll be able to report to Canberra, but rest assured that we're pursuing this matter as quickly as possible.*" Ben's Canberra colleagues could learn a great deal from him in terms of responsiveness and overall communication. In particular, certain officials in AUSDAFF should pay attention.

I subsequently received a note from Adam saying, "*The South African national authorities have said they have no in-principle objection to granting export permits and our respective biosecurity experts are now discussing the technical details.*" Adam continued, "*Ray, your plan is working because the South African authorities (rightly) see this very much as a private entity to private entity transaction. If I start getting involved in the substance of the project it risks being seen by the South African authorities as an official Australian government project – which won't be helpful to our prospects of success for all the reasons we have discussed previously.*"

As I have said elsewhere, I have met some extraordinary people during this journey, including some wonderfully professional folk in government. The DFAT people I met are among the best. People like Adam have a tough job and, in my experience, perform exceptionally well.

By July 2014 I was able to inform the board that following a discussion with Dr Jill Millan, we had received "in-principle" agreement from both the AUSDAFF and AUSDEA for the importation of rhinos from South Africa. Considering that this was just eight months after the launch of the project, gaining in-principle agreement from both the Australian and South African governments was quite some achievement.

I moved quickly and asked Deputy Prime Minister and Minister of Agriculture, Barnaby Joyce, and Minister for the Environment,

Greg Hunt, to write letters of support for our project. Both were happy to oblige and Greg's letter stated, *"I am writing this letter in support of Ray Dearlove, the founder of the Australian Rhino Project. The Department of the Environment has been well briefed as to the aims, objectives and plans of the project and we are, in-principle, fully supportive of these strategies. We are deeply concerned about the ongoing poaching of wildlife and we are determined to assist wherever we can. We are fully supportive of the efforts of the South African Government to combat the poaching threat and we look forward to working with you in the future to prevent the risk of extermination of the species in the wild."*

I nearly wept when I read Greg's letter, and Barnaby Joyce's letter of support was also a key contributor to our credibility with all stakeholders.

With the approvals in-principle from both governments in place in less than a year, we were ideally positioned to move rapidly to getting the rhinos into quarantine in South Africa as soon as possible. Three of the four pillars had been addressed but not yet resolved. I knew that the fourth pillar of fundraising was a whole different world but I also knew that we had the cause and that I had the passion, experience and determination to raise the required money.

SHOW ME THE MONEY

If we were to deliver the 80 rhinos to Australia, how were we going to raise approximately A$8 million over the next four years? What might be surprising to some is that this did not faze me at all.

For years, I had been involved with fundraising for a variety of causes. When our sons were at The King's School in Sydney, cricket was under threat from basketball as a preferred sport. It was the Michael Jordan era and his extraordinary athleticism was converting young cricketers to basketball at a rapid rate. Why would you spend hour after hour on a cricket field, with the real possibility of no result – a draw – when you could play a high energy game of basketball that was over in an hour and then go and enjoy the beach? The late Rick Symons and I started the Captains Lunch as a fundraiser which, over time, became extremely popular and raised significant funds for The King's School Cricket Club.

Later, when both sons were playing rugby with University of Sydney, I was asked to assist with fundraising for the club and so the Finals Lunch was born. This annual lunch became a permanent fixture with the Sydney business community. Over the ten years that I organised the lunch, it is estimated that A$1.8 million was raised – not bad for an amateur rugby club. I'd also arranged fundraisers for the Australian Rugby Union, the South Sydney Rugby League Club and the Lifestart and Black Dog charities.

The second reason for my confidence was a little more esoteric. According to the latest census there are approximately 200,000 South Africans and 30,000 Zimbabweans living in Australia. Many of these people still have strong ties to their homeland and, in truth, if it were not for the deteriorating political climate and the unacceptably high crime rates, many of these people would still be in Southern Africa. I had a strong view that if we could clearly articulate the rhino crisis and demonstrate that our plan was viable, we would attract strong support from this community. I don't know any Southern Africans who don't love (and miss) African wildlife.

Finally, Australians are an extremely generous people. I was certain that if we could create sufficient awareness of this issue, Australians would be supportive.

I would never suggest that our cause was in any way superior to or more important than any other charities. How can one compare curing breast cancer with saving an animal species from extinction? You can't. But there has to be a balance. Different people care about different things. I was convinced that we would garner strong support to turn this dream into reality.

Not surprisingly, we had no money when I started the project. Our first fundraiser took place in September 2014 at the Athenian Restaurant and was entirely due to the initiative and efforts of Shaun Smith and Dee Williamson. Shaun and Dee had been stalwarts with Nicholas Duncan's Save the African Rhino Foundation before joining our team. Shaun was on our board and Dee on our Advisory Board. When Shaun offered to arrange a dinner to raise some money for us, we gratefully accepted.

The dinner was a sell-out, with 260 people cramming into the restaurant. Simon Reeve did an outstanding job as MC and auctioneer. John Mitchell-Adams of Destinations Africa donated a terrific safari to South Africa, which gave the auction a good kick along. We made a lot of new friends that night and there was much energy in the room.

When the final amounts were tallied, Shaun was able to donate $35,000 to the project; this was money that was sorely needed. It was a milestone event in so many ways.

The second fundraiser was the Sydney dinner, which we hoped would be a big one. We could not have got off to a worse start. I had set the date as 22 September, World Rhino Day, so it was perfect from a relevance point of view.

To organise successful fundraising events, I work to a simple formula.

1. Select a date that is relevant (World Rhino Day was perfect).
2. Select a venue which is convenient and suits the style of the event. I chose the Westin Hotel in Sydney for most

of the events I had organised and GM Mark Burns and Karyn Primmer and their teams provide outstanding service.

3. Have the best speakers you can find. It is these individuals who make the event that much easier to sell. People who attend such events want to laugh or learn, or ideally both – a successful combination.

4. Sell the tables. This is often the most difficult task of all, but if the first three are sorted, it does become easier.

5. During the event, raise as much money as you possibly can.

We were up and running when I happened to be "selling" the event to a Jewish friend. He consulted his mobile and said, "*Mate, that date won't work for us, it's Yom Kippur.*" My heart sank. The Day of Atonement – the holiest day of the year in Judaism. Sydney has a very large expat South African Jewish population and I knew that not having this group of people at the dinner would have a seriously negative impact on our fundraising goal. We moved the date to Wednesday, 16 September.

So, two of the five key criteria – date and venue – were confirmed, now I had to find the best possible "talent". As much as I dislike that word/expression, it is the standard term for the entertainment industry.

Channel Seven's Simon Reeve was my first choice as MC, but extraneous issues counted him out and I never had the opportunity to invite him. A quality MC is so important, he is the "glue" that pulls and holds the event together. Although I had not met Dr Chris Brown, I had always been very impressed with him. His personality, his profile and being a veterinary surgeon put him way ahead of any other candidates. The problem with Chris is that he is one of the busiest people on the planet and is also very difficult to contact. I eventually tracked him down and once I was able to brief him about our goals, he was in, and I knew that we had just lifted the bar.

To give the event credibility and authenticity, I felt we also needed someone who was right in the middle of the poaching action in Africa. As far as I am aware, the top wildlife vets in Africa include Dr Will Fowlds, Dr Pete Rogers, Dr Markus Hofmeyr and Dr Pete Morkel. Pete Morkel particularly interested me because of his closeness to Prince Harry. Whenever I read about Prince Harry being on a rhino conservation trip in Africa, Pete always seemed to be at his side. I phoned Pete in South Africa and invited him to be our guest speaker at the inaugural dinner. Pete has to be amongst the driest people I've met. Had this been me, I would have been jumping for joy but for Pete it was just another day at the office. He said he would need to check with his wife which he did and, a few days later, he was in. We agreed on dates and I asked him to also visit Perth, Melbourne and Canberra and speak to our supporters there.

Then there was the small matter of Pete's visa for Australia. Fortunately, my good relationship with High Commissioner, Adam McCarthy, came to the fore. I'm not quite sure why but Pete's visa application was slow out of the blocks; I appealed to Adam and, lo and behold, the visa was granted in just one day! The power of relationships. Thanks again, Adam.

My sense was that we also needed to have something "different" on the podium and I invited Tim Jarvis to join the speaking team. Tim is an environmental explorer, adventurer, author and documentary filmmaker, with Masters qualifications in environmental science and law. I had met Tim and thought that he would be a very good fit. If one talks about mental and physical toughness, about excruciating attention to detail and leadership ability, Tim Jarvis is your man. His book *Epic*, about Shackleton's voyage, is a masterclass in all of these human characteristics.

Vince Sorrenti has the extraordinary ability to get and hold any audience's attention. Vince does a very good imitation of the South African accent and uses Saffa expressions such as "I'm *telling* you, man" and ". . . so where do you live, what car do you drive, which school are the kids at, etc, etc" and "let's do lunch (your shout)". I was delighted when Vince agreed to speak at our dinner.

We now had the speakers lined up and the big question was how many people could be persuaded to part with $220 per ticket. My initial reservation at the Westin was for 200 people, a quarter of the capacity of the ballroom. Now we had to start selling tables. Most members of the board stepped up and we eventually closed bookings with 650 people confirmed. This was huge by any measure.

I had met Dame Jane Goodall on several occasions and I asked if she would record a message to be played at the dinner and she graciously agreed – another emotional highlight. This was part of her message: "*I think it is desperately necessary to have a population of rhinos in a country that is safer than living in Africa, it might end up being the only population of rhinos . . . What will future generations think of us when they look back and the rhinos are only in a picture book? We don't want that to happen. I don't want my great, great grandchildren to say, "Why did they let it happen?" because by then it will be too late.*"

Prime Minister Tony Abbott had also kindly agreed to send us a message for the dinner, but that week he was ousted by Malcolm Turnbull. I wasn't game to ask the Prime Minister of a few days to do the same!

On the night, 650 people enjoyed a terrific evening and, to everyone's surprise and joy, we raised almost $350,000. This was far more than our wildest dreams but the urgency of the rhino poaching situation was not lost on the attendees who were extremely generous in terms of donations, pledges and buying auction items. We were touched by the number of well-known artists who donated their works. Dr Chris Brown did a masterful job as MC with young and old queuing up for selfies with the Bondi Vet. There was a hush when Dr Pete Morkel spoke about the cruelty of the poaching and how sophisticated the poaching syndicates had become. Human beings do not deserve animals in their lives.

All in all, it was a wonderful evening, with an unbelievably positive vibe in the room. People understood the issue, bought into the plan and wanted to help. Once again, I wished that the bureaucrats from the federal Department of Agriculture could have stepped out of their offices in Canberra to feel and touch the raw emotion and commitment in the room. Emotions that included anger, frustration, pain, sorrow, helplessness and desperation. I think we also gave them a glimmer of hope.

Pete Morkel is something of a legend in Southern Africa and famous in rhino circles for having pioneered the technique of moving rhinos from locations inaccessible to vehicles, by helicopter, tied by four ankles and suspended upside-down to the transport vehicle or to a new location. He is considered to be one of the best in his field. As part of Pete's trip, I had arranged receptions in

Perth and in Melbourne for people to hear firsthand about what was happening on the front-line with the rhinos. The response was extraordinary in both cities. Phil Loader of Woodside Energy kindly hosted the highly successful event in Perth. I was in hospital so missed both the Perth and Melbourne events and, once again, Pod stepped into the breach. Pod, a great communicator, more than anyone else grasped the seriousness and urgency of the rhino poaching situation. He was also an absolute believer in our vision and had the sense of urgency, which was often lacking in others.

The Melbourne cocktail party event was hosted by Graham Craig of Wilson HTM Investment Group who was extremely generous given that the number of attendees far exceeded what we had originally planned. Steve Goodey once again demonstrated his passion and organisational skills. I had contacted the Dean of the Faculty of Veterinary Medicine at Melbourne University and invited his students to the talk. Well, they turned out in droves. Almost certainly, Pete's presentation swelled the numbers of vet students wanting to work in a wildlife environment. We raised good money, which went a long way to covering Pete's expenses.

The visit to Canberra was interesting. Andrew Cupit of AUSDAFF kindly agreed to host Pete's presentation to the various government departments. By this time, I was allowed to fly and Pete and I duly showed up in Canberra. This was no fundraising event but what I saw as a critical opportunity for the bureaucrats, who held all the aces, to step out of their roles and hear, firsthand, why this project was so different and so important. Pete did not disappoint, he absolutely gave it to the group, which included representatives from the departments of Agriculture,

Environment and Foreign Affairs. As I'd come to expect, it was Dr Allan Sheridan who managed to throw a curveball when he asked about bovine tuberculosis (TB). In his reply, Pete mentioned Dr Roy Bengis' name as an excellent reference point for TB. Pete strongly recommended that I get Roy onto my team. He said of Roy, "*There is no one in SA with his knowledge and reputation and everyone wants to use him . . . he has the experience of moving white rhino to Australia and he knows all the challenges and issues.*"

In all the discussions over the four years, I found the Australian Departments of Environment and Foreign Affairs always willing to help and to go the extra mile, and I was always deeply appreciative of their support. I wish I could say the same of AUSDAFF.

When it comes to fundraising, everyone is an expert and our board was no exception. Whereas I had spent the past 25 years of my life raising money for different organisations, charities and causes, each director had a different view on how to raise the required funds. We had several think-tanks, workshops and meetings and lots of minutes were taken with action plans. Allan Davies made a number of vital, very welcome and significant donations through his family foundation, but while some of the directors talked a good game, there was little to show for it in the bank.

Fundraising is hard – there are no shortcuts. Most members of the board attended a presentation by Taronga's head of fundraising. It was well structured and they work to a solid strategy that is proven and very successful. I was continually reminded of this presentation by members of our board. If I said it once, I said it one hundred times: Taronga has existed for 100 years, and is a globally recognised brand in the conservation space. Taronga is part funded by the government and is fully resourced to raise funds. In our case, we were "newbies" just finding our feet and I was the one leading the fundraising drive. Apart from the Davies family foundation's regular donations, without which the project would have faltered, I estimate I was responsible for more than 75 per cent of funds raised. No medals required, I wanted to do it and, by and large, I enjoyed it.

I organised a similar fundraising dinner in Melbourne in June 2016. The board was a little nervous about having the dinner, saying that perhaps it was inappropriate or premature since we still had not imported any rhinos. I convinced them that the project was a long and convoluted process and that our supporters understood this. All then agreed and, sticking to my five basic steps, we booked the Grand Hyatt Hotel and I managed to secure Mick Molloy as MC. Mick has an almost religious following in Melbourne. He is an extremely funny man with a heart the size of Africa and he did a phenomenal job. He is wonderful person – always so positive and also extremely kind and generous.

Mick Molloy in full flight. (Photo credit: Phil Hines)

I invited Jacques Brits to join the speaking team. Jacques is a recent immigrant to Australia, having left his job as warden of the Timbavati Nature Reserve. Jacques is a good friend and I knew that he was emotionally deeply connected with the rhino crisis. Once again, I invited Tim Jarvis to be the keynote speaker. I could listen to Tim for hours and the Melbourne audience felt the same way.

Selling tables was tough. We soldiered on and eventually had an audience of almost 300 people. While it was not on the scale of the Sydney dinner, it was a success. We raised $60,000 and it was certainly worth all of the effort that went into it. Paul Gardner, Angie Bradbury and their team from Dig and Fish were strong supporters of the dinner and once again, a number of artists kindly donated their works. I just shake my head at the generosity of Australians.

As sports go, and being South African born, rugby is in my

blood. I approached the CEO of NSW Rugby and long-time friend, Greg Harris, and asked if it were possible for one of the Waratahs home games to be a project fundraiser. Greg soon confirmed we had been included as one of the Waratahs charities for the season. I chose the South African Blue Bulls match for a couple of reasons: they have a strong following in Australia and their home ground is in Pretoria, the closest city to where most of the poaching takes place. I had a great ally in Phillip van Schalkwyk, Waratahs Chief Financial Officer, and himself a passionate Bulls supporter (after the Waratahs!) as well as Stu Rutherford, the Chief Commercial Officer. They were an absolute pleasure to work with and they went out of their way to maximise our success at the match. I termed the campaign "Ruck for Rhinos", which was catchy and very well received.

We developed a short video clip we could play on the big screen and I approached George Gregan, former captain of the Wallabies, and Rachel Ward to see if they could spend a morning with us doing the filming. Throughout my time at the project both George and Rachel were towers of strength and they readily agreed. The Business School stepped in and loaned us the use of their state-of-the-art recording facilities at their new campus. The clips were outstanding and a real hit at the match.

Rachel Ward AM, the author, George Gregan AM

The Young Rhinos turned out in force, including my heavily pregnant daughter, Hayley, who certainly wasn't going to miss this one. They all wore their rhino hats – very welcome on a cold Sydney night. Our mascot, Reginald the rhino, also made an appearance and Jonty Gill of Stanley Street Butchery donated lekker biltong.

I was given the opportunity to address the crowd of approximately 20,000 before the match – certainly another highlight for me – despite looking like a bit of a goose in my rhino hat. We raised good money and significantly broadened the base of our supporters.

I came up with the concept of "Rhino Guardians" as a general fundraiser. If we could sign up a minimum of one hundred Rhino Guardians donating $1,000 per annum, we would have a steady income of $100,000 each year which would easily cover all of our annual costs. The donors received a personalised Rhino Guardian certificate, 15 per cent discount on the ticket price for the annual dinner with priority table seating, an invitation to an annual exclusive event, pride of place on the Rhino Guardian Honour Roll on the website, two special rhino pins and a specially framed ten Rand note featuring Nelson Mandela and a rhino. The program was an immediate success and I soon realised that many of the donors just wanted to help and were less concerned about what they received. People like the ever generous Bruce Corlett signed up each of his and Annie's grandchildren as Guardians. All donations were tax deductible and I made a point of personally thanking every single donor.

We had one particular donation that still touches my heart. I received this note from a young lady, Lucille Moore, "*My name is Lucille and I am 14 years old. I have been saving up by making and selling crafts at markets and on my website and by receiving donations from family, friends, people in my school community and neighbours for running the 14 km City to Surf. I have finally reached my goal of $1,000 to become a Rhino Guardian!! I really hope this donation will be life changing for the rhino that I'll be safe-guarding.*" I arranged to meet Lucille and her delightful family and we lined up some well-deserved publicity for Lucille and her school in the *Manly Daily*.

In May 2016, I was contacted by the internationally famous artists Gillie and Marc Schattner, complimenting me on the "incredible initiative" of The Australian Rhino Project. They said they were thinking about creating a rhino sculpture at the annual Sculpture by the Sea exhibition to boost awareness of the rhino poaching crisis. The exhibition takes place along the Tamarama and Bondi Beach shoreline and attracts more than three million visitors each year.

Gillie and Marc had created a concept sculpture and asked if we would like to be involved. Would we what! There was one glitch, however, they needed $40,000 to make it happen. We explored a number of funding options and finally agreed that Gillie and Marc would create a limited edition of fifteen unique sculptures of "The rhino's flight to freedom" at $5,000 each. We came to an arrangement whereby Gillie and Marc would take $4,000 and we would get $1,000 to $2,250 of each sale. We easily sold the fifteen sculptures and the manufacturing of the sculpture commenced. Gillie and Marc created the world's largest rhino sculpture, which they named Shandu, meaning "change" in the South African Venda language. Shandu was five metres tall and lying upside down, buried in the sand, as a poignant reminder that rhinos are going belly up and if we don't change things they will be buried forever. In terms of awareness, the imagery of this sculpture is very powerful and received worldwide acclaim.

Gillie and Marc won the People's Award and also the Children's Award for Shandu. I received a congratulatory note from Milly Palmer, who did all the PR for Sculpture by the Sea: "*The articles that specifically mentioned TARP equated to over $400,000 worth of media value.*" The amount of positive publicity we received was quite extraordinary.

In a wonderful gesture, Gillie and Marc donated Shandu to Monarto Safari Park.

Sculptures by the Sea – Shandu on Tamarama Beach.
(Photo Credit: Marc and Gillie Schattner)

Good friend Patrick Forth attended the Sydney fundraising dinner and brought along an American associate who misheard Patrick's invitation and thought he was attending a Wino function. Patrick's wife Jules is a highly accomplished artist who asked if she could do a portrait of me to submit for the Archibald and Moran art prizes. Now that was a world first. I was embarrassed, flattered, honoured, the lot. Jules submitted it for the Moran Prize and while we didn't win, I humbly think that it is absolutely fantastic. My only request was for Jules to include a tear rolling down the rhino's face, which she did.

It is fair to say that every not-for-profit would love to have Sir Richard Branson as a benefactor. We were no different and I first contacted him through the CEO of Virgin Unite, Jean Oelwang. Virgin Unite is the giving arm of Branson's empire and while Jean was unable to direct any funding to us, she was very keen to remain in contact, particularly since Branson's Ulusaba lodge in Sabi Sands had been hit by poachers. I even designed a rhino "skin" for a Virgin plane. This was way before Emirates' Big Five campaign.

Portrait of the author by award winning artist, Jules Forth

Virgin Atlantic demonstrating the commitment to conservation

After the 2015 Sydney dinner, I was contacted by Jonnie Schaffer who was sufficiently moved by the presentations and speeches to want to become directly involved. Both former South Africans, he and Di had built a highly successful international toy business with their company Plum Products. I felt that this was going to be a special partnership and so it has turned out. Both are passionate about endangered species in general and rhinos in particular. From a personal point of view, the relationship blossomed; their support for the project never wavered and we have become firm friends. Their advice is always valuable and considered.

The various fundraising campaigns resulted in us having more than $1 million in the bank. Many people played their part, some more than others, but the consistent theme was one of an engaged support base who craved information and wanted to play their part in safeguarding the world's dwindling rhino population. Working with these people was a rich and exhilarating experience.

Two dehorned rhinos. (Photo Credit: Shannon Wild)

MEDIA AND MARKETING

Dealing with the media was one of my steepest learning curves. Over time in my role as founder, I gained more experience and confidence and managed to make most interviews current and relevant. Certainly, understanding our value proposition helped.

In late 2013 after I read that she had recently visited Africa and the visit had made a lasting impact on her, I wrote to former Australian of the Year, Ita Buttrose. She was unable to make it to our breakfast launch, but wrote back saying that she knew about the dangers facing rhinos and would like to do something for my project on her Channel Ten Studio 10 show. And so, in late February 2014, I did my first TV interview.

The Studio 10 panel of Sarah Harris, Joe Hildebrand, Jessica Rowe and Ita was very gentle with me. They showed some haunting rhino images which really brought the poaching issue into people's homes. I enjoyed the interview but must confess to being terrified beforehand.

Soon afterwards I was approached by Tony Carnie, an environmental journalist in Durban, who was very close to Ian Player. Ian had told Tony about my plan and being the very good journalist that he is, Tony jumped all over the lead and sent emails to me and to Cameron Kerr, Taronga CEO, requesting an interview. I was more than happy to have a chat with Tony, but Taronga laid down their rules of engagement for any interviews. If ever there was an organisation that craved publicity, but was equally hypersensitive about what was said or written it was Taronga. From the outset, I felt strongly that there should only be one spokesperson for the project and that I was the person best qualified. Everyone agreed, although some through gritted teeth. I was later described as being "publicity aware" in Taronga's monthly status report to the NSW government by Taronga's Director of Communications. I wasn't sure if I should be proud or insulted.

I stressed to Tony Carnie that it was early days and definitely premature in terms of publicity. He was undeterred and wrote an article which hit the front pages of the leading daily newspapers in South Africa – the *Johannesburg Star*, the *Cape Argus*, the *Pretoria News* and the *Durban Daily News*. The article was headlined, "Australia part of a plan to save SA rhinos". Tony wrote:

"Rhino conservation veteran Ian Player has thrown his weight behind a bold plan to move dozens of South African rhinos to Australia as part of a global 'insurance policy' against their extinction. The Australian Rhino Project, spearheaded by a

former South African businessman now living in Australia, as well as Taronga Zoo, could lead to the establishment of breeding populations in Australia. The proposal reflects the increasing sense of anxiety and desperation among wildlife conservationists as rhinos continue to be slaughtered at the rate of three a day. It coincides with a separate plan by local safari operators to move 100 South African rhinos to Botswana next year.

South Africa has been the target of a ferocious assault by poachers and organised syndicates for five years. Poaching levels have soared since the start of the 'rhino war' in 2008, when 80 rhinos were butchered for their horns, reaching record levels of more than 1,000 killings last year. The plan to move a limited number to Australia is based on the rationale that they would be less vulnerable to poaching and corruption, and possibly serve as a genetic seed bank.

'We are not naive enough to believe that poaching of rhinos is not a possibility in Australia, we simply believe that the risks are dramatically lower than anywhere in Africa,' says Project Founder Ray Dearlove."

Each of the articles was accompanied by this graphic, drawn by Wilson Mgobhozi which I absolutely loved.

I contacted Wilson to ask if I could use the image. Wilson was covering the Oscar Pistorius murder trial and was doing all the graphics for the media since photographs were not permitted in the courtroom. Wilson was very chuffed to be contacted and sent me the graphic commenting, *"I'm delighted to learn you liked my graphic. You surely have made my day!"*

Striking graphic by South African cartoonist Wilson Mgobhozi

The only part of the graphic I would change would be to have a dotted line returning the rhinos from Australia to South Africa.

It was around this time that Allan Davies recommended that Paul White join the board, describing him as being highly experienced in media, marketing and communications and referring to him as "a top media bloke".

In early discussions with Paul, I said that one of my goals was for TARP to become the go-to organisation for the media for all things rhino. I wanted us to be the first people that the Australian media – and everyone else – turned to as the source of information about rhinos. When I recall the number of organisations and individuals that I interviewed or spoke to, I believe that this was a goal achieved.

There were several "milestone" events in terms of media and marketing that really added momentum to our project. All of these events resulted in a significant spike in donations. One of these was the article by Sue Williams of the Fairfax Group, who wrote an outstanding article after our trip to South Africa with Simon Reeve in February 2015. The late Shaun Smith, one of the finest men you would ever meet and a founding director of the board, had introduced me to Simon a couple of years before. Simon is a TV presenter at Channel Seven. He and Shaun were close friends and had been on safari to Africa together.

Sue's article was published in the Good Weekend magazine in the *Sydney Morning Herald* and the *Age*. Sue writes from the heart and I could tell that she was deeply emotionally touched during our visits to the rhino orphanage and the darting of the rhino. Her empathy for the rhinos and anger at the poachers and the inherent cruelty of the killing was palpable. This was reflected in Sue's writing style which captured the issues so well. She titled the article *"Rhino Ray's War"*. In her article, Sue referred to my relationship with General Jooste: *"He has befriended the man everyone calls 'the General'. While some fete the General with money – philanthropist Howard G. Buffett, the son of billionaire Warren, recently presented Jooste with a US$25 million cheque to help fund his work – Dearlove wooed him, in part, with a poem he wrote about him fighting the poachers."*

Sue's article generated an enormous amount of interest and also resulted in a surge in donations. As I wrote to her manager, Ben Whithouse, at Fairfax Media, *"We have had an avalanche of response to Sue's article and we are deeply grateful for giving us such a positive story."*

During the four years with the project, I was fortunate enough to meet some wonderful media people. One of these was Paul Gardner who contacted me in early 2016 requesting an interview on the segment of his 2GB radio show, Media, Marketing and

Advertising. The interview went very well and Paul then introduced me to Angie Bradbury, CEO and Founder of the Dig +
Fish creative agency in Melbourne. Paul was also instrumental
in introducing me to Mick Molloy and Eddie McGuire, both of
whom are legends in Australia in their particular fields. Paul did a
masterful job as auctioneer at our Melbourne fundraising dinner.

Early in 2016, the Classic Safari Company built a tour to South
Africa which we called the Rhino Ray Endangered Species Safari.
We had a couple from Hong Kong and four more couples from
Australia, all from very diverse backgrounds. At my suggestion,
TARP sponsored Sarah Dennis' trip where she learned an awful
lot about rhinos and poaching. We spent four days in Madikwe
Game Lodge and then another four days at Simbavati Reserve in
the east of the country. It was an eye-opener for all involved and
they were a great deal of fun to spend time with. We saw a lot of
game, including rhinos, and everyone loved it.

As we were making the final preparations for the Safari,
Kirstin Scholtz contacted me saying that Stephanie Gilmore, six-
time professional surfing world champion was keen to be involved.
This was another wonderful opportunity to be associated with a
world-class athlete with an impeccable reputation.

We pondered on how we could get Steph to join the upcoming
safari since I was very much aware that the participants had paid
significant amounts of money and I did not want to upset them
in any way or make Steph the focal point. I approached the ever-
generous Mark Hutchinson to cover Steph's airfare. He agreed

and we were away. Steph joined us for the Madikwe sector of the safari and she was warmly welcomed by the whole group. This was a credit to Steph's genial and friendly personality. A sensitive and articulate young woman, Steph quickly demonstrated her awareness of the poaching crisis. Her visit to Madikwe coincided with the darting of a rhino which had lost its horn, presumably in a fight with another rhino. The darting was a highly emotional experience and had an obvious effect on Steph.

I have known Paul Sheehan for a long time. He is a keen rugby man and was a regular at Sydney University watching the students play. I dropped him a line congratulating him on an excellent article that he had written and also took the liberty of sending him a copy of our latest newsletter. Paul responded by return with an *"I am interested, tell me more."* He immediately "got it" and undertook to write an article in his weekly *SMH* column. After several conversations, he was certainly fired up. Fired up to the point that I was nervous it would be a negative story that pointed the finger at a number of parties that were blocking the progress of the project. There were several organisations, governments and individuals who could be targets, but primarily AUSDAFF. I stressed to him that it was really important that the article be a positive one, that there is always hope with projects such as ours, our project being one strand in a deeply complex problem. I reminded him that there were many sensitivities around this issue – some from the most unexpected sources. *"The South African government is extremely sensitive and the Australian government is*

extremely sensitive about the South African government's sensitivities, if that makes sense," I wrote.

Paul's article was published on Valentine's Day in 2016. The article was a game-changer for us. The reach of the *Sydney Morning Herald*, both in print and online, is massive and adding to that the personal following that Paul Sheehan had built over many years of journalism made for a wonderful boost for the project, both in awareness and funding.

I was constantly on the lookout for how I could increase AUSDAFF's awareness of the poaching issue and somehow "influence" them to get some urgency into their responses and responsibilities. Finally, in early 2016, I connected with James Vyver of ABC Radio in Canberra through friend Bronwyn Fagan. James conducted a very good interview and I tried to shape the conversation so that listeners would be left in no doubt that the ball was very much in Canberra's court. Immediately after the radio interview, I was contacted by Penny Travers, the ABC's online news producer, requesting more detail and photos for an online version for their website. Penny and Adam Shirley wrote a terrific article for ABC Digital. In the next few days, I just could not believe how many enquiries and messages of support we had from, literally, all over the world. The global influence of the Australian Broadcasting Corporation is extraordinary. The Facebook reach was more than 600,000 – it was the most shared and talked about story on ABC Digital in the week following the article. The article focused attention all over the world, if only for a short time, on the challenges of protecting the rhinos and it resulted in a significant increase in funding for our, and probably other similar, projects.

The article drove home that 5,000 rhino had been killed since 2010 with a record 1,400 killed in 2015, highlighting that the gestation period for a rhinoceros is sixteen months and they only produce one calf. They also pointed out a little-known fact that the horn is made of keratin, the same material that makes up human fingernails. The article concluded with a quote from me. *"If you or I don't do anything about it, who's going to do something about it and when they're gone, who will they blame?"*

Some of the best-known names in radio and TV were kind enough to give me air time about the rhino poaching catastrophe. These included Ben Fordham, Steve Price and Paul Gardner of 2GB; Mick Molloy and Eddie McGuire of Triple M; Jon Faine, James Vyver and Robbie Buck of ABC Radio; Elsa McKee, Jon Donnison and Mary Melville and Oisin Tymon of the BBC and John Laws of 2SM.

There is a saying, "You can't sell a secret", which could well have been my motto. I told our story at every possible opportunity.

WORKING, AND PLAYING,

WITH RHINOS

During Simon Reeves' and my travels across South Africa building the documentary of the TARP journey, we covered a lot of ground which would enable Simon to create a compelling story.

One of the visits to which he was really looking forward was the visit to the Care for Wild rhino orphanage. I had told him all about Petronel Niewoudt's amazing initiative of taking in orphan rhinos and rehabilitating them. At the last minute, we were joined by journalist Sue Williams and photographer Julia Salnicki. When we met Petronel, there was a cage, covered by blanket, on the table between us. As we chatted, she reached into the cage and casually took out something and slipped it down the front of her blouse. I could see the expression on Simon's face asking *"What the hell was that?"* Petronel calmly explained that it was just a ferret that wasn't too well and needed some human warmth. An interesting introduction.

We toured the orphanage with Simon filming all the while until Petronel asked, *"Would you like to see the nursery?"* Absolutely, we said. The four of us, Petronel and the keeper landed up in this small enclosure for feeding time. Julia and I were each given a large bottle containing milk and a formula mix. Each bottle had a large teat. I fed Manji, one of the babies, and Julia fed Venus while Simon did the filming and commentary. Manji seemed satisfied after drinking her bottle but Venus definitely wasn't. This poor animal had been hacked by poachers after they killed her mother and she had a plaster cast on her foot; she must have been in agony. Venus approached Simon, whose camera had a furry microphone attached to it – perhaps Venus thought the mic was another feeding bottle. As Simon coo-cooed while filming, this little rhino became more intent on sucking on the mic and approached Simon even more aggressively. You must understand that Venus's horn was about the same height as Simon's crotch and as she approached, so Simon retreated. No more coo-cooing, Simon hurdled the one metre high steel gate to get away from this pesky, hungry little orphan. Everyone collapsed in laughter.

We had a wonderful day with Petronel and that evening, as always, Simon reviewed the footage from the day. We all gathered around as he said *"Oh, here is the feeding in the nursery."* As we watched this beautiful scene, with Simon saying lovely things about the little rhino, the camera suddenly shook and filmed the ground, the sky, the wall and anything else as Simon took off, pursued by the rhino and all you could hear as he ran and jumped the gate was *"Fuck off, fuck off, you little bugger."* That cameo definitely landed up on the cutting room floor.

Simon Reeve hiding from Venus with the plaster
cast on her foot. (Photo credit: Julia Salnicki)

In recent years there has been a drive to tag rhinos and to take their DNA so as to match a dead rhino with a poached rhino horn. I had arranged for the group to experience such an exercise, which was termed rhino notching. It is a necessary task, but by allowing onlookers like us also an opportunity to raise funds for protecting the rhinos. We were due to meet vet, Dr Pete Rogers, at 5.30am in the Klaserie Game Reserve for the notching and good friend Nic Griffin, CEO of the Thornybush Collection gave us mates' rates at the beautiful Chapungu Bush Lodge.

We had been told that we must be on time for the rhino notching because of the increased stress on the rhino in hot weather so we agreed to leave the lodge at 4.15am, and 4.15am it was as we excitedly departed the lodge. We had hired a Kombi vehicle and I had received exact instructions from the lodge on how to get to the reserve gate. It was pitch dark, no moon and there are no lights in a game reserve. Within minutes I knew we were lost. We had been instructed to turn right as we drove out of the lodge and I managed to get this simple task wrong by turning too soon. We travelled along, all the while getting plenty of advice from Sue and Julia in the back seat about what I could have done, should have done and what I should now do.

One of the better suggestions from the back seat was to travel along the fence line and surely, we would eventually come to a gate. This seemed like a good idea so off we went with the electrified fence on my right. The track got progressively worse and as it started to get light, I could see that there were potholes and large rocks ahead. I stopped and asked Simon if he would mind hopping out and having a look to see if we should continue or not.

Always obliging, Simon jumped out of the car and walked down the road in the headlights and, stopping about 20 metres away he turned and gave me the thumbs down sign. I in turn beckoned him back to the car. He had taken just two steps when we suddenly heard him say *Fuck me, there's a lion.* As one, the three of us turned to our left and sure enough there was a crouching lioness about 15 metres away, between us and Simon. She sat there watching Simon intently. Visitors to game parks are always told not to run if they come across a lion, but this was like a slow-motion movie as Simon covered the ground like Usain Bolt and landed up on my lap, eyes wide, heart rate off the chart. The lioness had followed his unexpected movements and sat watching us watching her. The atmosphere was electric. Not a word was spoken. All I could think about was what I would say to Simon's dear wife Linda if the worst had happened. It goes something like this *"Well Linda, you might find this hard to believe but we were travelling along in a private game reserve. Simon had hopped out of the car to have a look at the state of the road and then the lion pounced. . ."* We finally found the gate and by this time all the chatter had stopped as we digested what might have happened.

We met up with the rhino notching team, including Dr Pete Rogers and Colin Rowles, Head Ranger for the Klaserie Game Reserve. The large group included the state vet and two heavily armed rangers for our protection. We could have used them earlier that morning.

Ear-notching is one of several different methods used to identify individual rhinos. In combination with micro-chipping, numbered ID tags and distinct physical markings, these tools help biologists and rangers monitor the movements, interactions, health and safety of all individuals within key populations.

Pete is not only a world-class wildlife vet, he is also a very funny man. As part of the briefing, he gave each of us a task. Simon would be in the helicopter with the pilot and Pete with the gun to dart the rhino, Julia was to cover the tranquilised rhino's eyes with a blanket, and Sue was given a special job. Sue is of English descent and has beautiful "English Rose" skin. *"Sue, your job will be to apply the ointment to the rhino's ear after it has been notched to stop the bleeding, prevent infection and so on."* I looked at Sue and if it were possible, she was even paler than usual and also fairly unsteady on her feet. By this time the helicopter had arrived, picked up Pete and Simon and taken off to find a rhino. The rest of us were ready in the two Land Rovers with all the gear and the support team, our hearts in our mouths.

We received the radio call that they had found a rhino and we took off at speed. The helicopter hovered above the rhino as Pete hung from the side with his tranquilliser gun ready to dart. We had vertigo just watching. The helicopter then plunged down, swooping between the thorny branches of the acacia trees, as the pilot coolly pointed into the quarry and a fully-grown white rhino with a pristine horn. The chopper kept pace with the running rhino as Pete took careful aim and darted her in the rump.

It was immediately clear that the members of this team were the ultimate professionals. When the rhino finally staggered to a halt, the team raced to the 2,000-kilogram animal and rolled it onto its tummy, inserted ear plugs and a blindfold to reduce stress so the vet could take blood samples and start the notching and micro-chip implanting processes. The rangers circled us, guns at the ready, making certain everyone was safe. It was like watching a highly sophisticated cardiac operation. Pete inserted a chip into the rhino's horn for future identification and then notched her ear, saying that this was the 227th rhino he had notched to prevent the animals from being poached.

Our team then swung into action with Simon doing the filming and commentary, Julia helping wherever she could as Sue was given the ointment to apply to the rhino's now heavily bleeding ear. She was ashen. I am not sure if her eyes were open as she applied the ointment but she was definitely swaying in the wind with tears streaming down her face.

Pete then turned to me, *"I forgot to tell you that your job is to apply the antidote to bring the rhino back into full consciousness."* I gave him an incredulous look and said, "*Pete, you can see that I have some issues with my legs and can't run particularly well. How far away will the truck be?*"

His response was an airily, "*Oh, over there*".

I said, "*OK, well then I am going to apply the antidote as rapidly as I can.*"

To which he responded, "*You can't do that, you'll kill her.*"

As I inserted the syringe, I noticed the truck was moving further away for "safety". I applied the antidote as Pete wandered off and as I removed the syringe he said, "*OK, let's go*" and sauntered off. He must have had a lead of about 10 metres but I broke Simon's sprint record from the morning, flew past Pete and was on the truck as this giant animal awoke, snorted and headed for us with a perfectly executed sidestep.

It was certainly another highlight of my life, a life-changing experience, with Sue and Julia quietly weeping in the background.

About six months later, I phoned Pete from Australia. He didn't sound his usual self as I asked him if he was okay and he mumbled, "*No, not really. I am in traction for three months.*" He told me that he had been dehorning a black rhino and had just finished when the rhino woke. Pete took off as the rhino pursued him and ran right over him. Had he not removed the horn, there is no doubt in anyone's mind that Pete would not have survived the charge. "*I suppose I didn't give the rhino enough juice,*" he said quietly. Still smarting from the antidote experience, I wished him well and said to myself, "There is a God!"

CHANNEL SEVEN VERSUS
CHANNEL NINE

An ongoing goal was to have the TARP journey documented. Many people likened the project to Noah's Ark and the highly visible nature of the animals we were trying to protect could make this project even more relevant and important from a conservation point of view. The murderous and callous methods used by the poachers were another dimension in terms of dangers to humans and animals alike.

Simon Reeve is arguably one of the most positive people on the planet. I never heard him say a bad word about anyone. He was a rock in my world. He would offer help, make suggestions and always, always be positive. Even when I was approached by Ita Buttrose on behalf of TV Channel Ten to appear on her program, in competition to Simon's Seven network, he was gracious in saying that Ten were obviously well organised and wished me luck.

Soon after we met, Simon prepared a gut-wrenching presentation on the rhino crisis for the senior executives of his network, including Chair Kerry Stokes and CEO Tim Worner, recommending that Seven be the broadcast partner of TARP. Simon knew these men personally, and he thought his relationships might help but to his disappointment, this initiative came to nothing. This did not deter him at all – he was on a mission. When I was given the opportunity to meet Jane Goodall, I asked Simon if he could arrange for the session to be filmed. No worries, he arranged for the cameraman to meet me early on a Sunday morning at Jane's hotel.

Shortly after meeting with Jane, I received a note from Jo Townsend, producer of Channel Nine's *60 Minutes* program, asking if we could meet. *60 Minutes* is the arch competitor of Channel Seven's *Sunday Night* and these programs are considered the flagships of each organisation. My first action was to advise Simon, since I felt strongly about the relationship I had built with him and thought it was the right thing to do – to let him know that his biggest competitor was interested in our story. Well, this certainly got things moving. Simon informed the Channel Seven executive producer, Mark Llewellyn, of the approach and Mark's exact words were, "T*ell* 60 Minutes *to fuck off and we will sit down and talk.*"

I let Jo know that it was early days in the project and we had an existing strong relationship with Channel Seven. She was fine with this and asked me to let her know once we had the necessary government approvals. Between June and December 2014 there was no contact from *60 Minutes,* which suited me since I was very pleased with what Simon and Iman Muldoon, producer of the *Sunday Night* program were doing for and with us. As an example, Simon and I were interviewed live in the Channel Seven studios by Andrew O'Keefe and Monique Wright on their *Weekend Sunrise* program. We had excellent feedback from the interview and reached a whole lot more people in terms of awareness. Even Paul White was sufficiently impressed to comment, *"Beautifully done, Ray".*

For no apparent reason, progress with Channel Seven seemed to stall. Sure, there was a lot happening with Simon and also Iman, but we were no closer to having anything approaching a deal. I kept Simon abreast of every contact I had with *60 Minutes* and I know he was working really hard internally, but there was nothing concrete to report back to my board. By this time Simon and I knew each other very well and I think he sensed my frustration that we were not locking anything down with Seven because he then introduced Lyndal Marks, the executive producer. In his introduction, Simon said, *"There is a long, long way to go down this road, but I do feel that my team will be capable of moving heaven and earth with the resources and the reach we have."* I met with Lyndal and was blown away by her passion, energy and dynamism.

For six months, Simon and I had been trying to craft a trip to South Africa which would form the backbone of the documentary Simon wanted to produce. Our plans included taking a celebrity like George Gregan to be the "face" of the film, but we just couldn't make the dates work. So, in late February 2015, as described above, Simon and I headed off on our long-planned trip and when we returned, Simon worked to whittle down the hours of footage into what the industry terms the "sizzle" – a short slice of video which is used to sell the product or the cause.

The Channel Seven model in making a documentary was new to me. Once they had agreed a concept and the sizzle, their sales teams worked to find a potential buyer who was sufficiently motivated to become the partner or sponsor for the planned film – Seven did not commit any money to the project. As expected, Simon produced a stunning short video that perfectly captured the poaching crisis and the project's plans to assist in preventing the catastrophe of rhinos becoming extinct in the wild.

At the time we were reviewing the sizzle, I had a call from Jo Townsend requesting an update and possible meeting. I advised Lyndal and she showed her fighting spirit by responding, *"I can assure you that* 60 Minutes *are NOT going to do anything faster than we can, I have worked for them. Also, with Channel 9 you potentially lose Simon as he's very associated with Seven."*

Jo Townsend was an excellent ambassador for *60 Minutes*. She followed up regularly and I kept her informed, but at a distance. I warned Seven that *60 Minutes* were chasing hard and, not unreasonably, I was told by the board that we had to give *60 Minutes* a chance to assess if they were really interested in partnering with us, so I met with Jo. I was beginning to get a feel for how competitive this television industry actually is. Within hours of our meeting, Jo wrote saying that she would be happy to meet with our board so that they could do their own due diligence before making a choice between channels. Her belief that the viewer figures, budget, stick-with-it story production and vast network promotion of *60 Minutes* would surely make it an obvious fit for a story as intricate and as long in the making as this one. She upped the ante by saying that anything less than a prime-time feature-length story would simply not do our story justice. Jo demonstrated just how good a sales-person she is, by concluding, "*On a personal note, I am just so impressed that you are about to pull off such a major coup. How great that my son will get to see these rhinos breeding happily in Australia in years to come. Just wonderful.*"

So, after just one meeting, we were meeting the Channel Nine management hierarchy whereas Simon had fought a long, lonely crusade at Seven and our contact with their executive was limited.

Within days a meeting had been arranged by Jo with Tom Malone, the executive producer of *60 Minutes*, which Pod and I attended. The meeting was positive and 24 hours later, we received a media partnership proposal from *60 Minutes*. An impressive start.

The issue of *60 Minutes* versus Channel Seven was debated at length by the board – of course we were flattered by the interest from the two dominant Australian TV channels, but it ran deeper than that. I spoke passionately about the strong relationships we had built at Channel Seven, in particularly with Simon Reeve, but the board voted to go with *60 Minutes*. While there was a financial consideration with *60 Minutes* of $10,000, not a lot of money, what really swayed the discussion was their reach – they kept talking about a "million-plus eyeballs". I was most unhappy that we were about to jettison Channel Seven, but could not argue with the reach potential of *60 Minutes*.

All of this meant that Channel Seven had to be informed, in particular Simon and Lyndal. There were no volunteers from the board to make the call, I was well and truly on my own. I took a few deep breaths and called Simon, got his voicemail and asked him to call me as soon as he possibly could. I then called Lyndal, who did not hold back – she blasted me from here to next week. The language of the media industry can be quite colourful. While that was a difficult discussion, I knew the conversation with Simon would be awful. And it was. There was no way this could be sugar-coated. I had spent most of my working life in IT sales and had my share of losses. I absolutely hated losing – as did Simon. His reaction was one of surprise and then anger. Clearly, he had not seen anything like this coming. For that I took complete responsibility. Simon was Channel Seven's go-to man and I was the same for the project. I felt sick to my stomach.

Simon followed up our conversation with a lengthy, emotionally charged note. It came as something of a surprise when he also had a full go at our board, saying, "*To me, this Project needs less lawyers, accountants and company directors and a lot more people genuinely concerned about rhinos rather than their own reputations.*"

Simon is a genuine and caring person and this was evident in his words, "*What I care about deeply is the future of this species, about the future of Africa, its wilderness and its people. Having poured so much personally into this since we met Ray, this leaves a gaping hole, because I desperately wanted to carry this through. I've had this image of Ray, Shaun Smith and me watching those first animals come out of a cargo hold in Sydney. I'm just plain and simply sad, desperately sad, that that isn't going to happen now.*"

Independently, Pod responded to Simon saying how much he regretted that the situation had come to this; that everyone was trying to do the right thing for the rhinos and that this story was meant to have a happy ending. He said that *60 Minutes* had presented a compelling proposal. Pod never shirks from telling it how it is, irrespective of how painful it may seem. He confirmed that I held Simon in the highest regard and that our conversation had left me *"feeling completely sick and deflated."* He went on, *"I know that Ray would dearly love to try and straighten this out. He has taken on a very significant and noble crusade and needs people like you [who are] emotionally and physically supportive. I just hope that we can reconcile and refocus the energy to fight another day for the rhinos who can't fight for themselves."*

I will regret this episode until the day I die. Simon did not deserve this and, not surprisingly, our relationship was shattered.

Driven by Pod, contractual discussions commenced with *60 Minutes* who proved to be tough negotiators, and matters were complicated by Taronga's apparent hesitance to participate and agree to what seemed to be trivial requests from *60 Minutes*. This created delay after delay. It got to a point where my frustration boiled over and I went out on a limb saying that the positions Taronga were taking reinforced my long-held view that they saw us as something of a burden and I offered a solution by suggesting that we should focus our efforts on Monarto.

Allan's more balanced view was that Taronga was understandably risk averse and he was quite correct.

Pod wryly commented, *"I agree with 'needing Taronga on the inside of the tent pissing out' rather than the other way around. For my two bob's worth I do think they could be a little more proactive."*

Over time I believe I was proved correct and TARP landed up dealing almost exclusively with Monarto, with Taronga moving into the background.

An issue which I'm sure all not-for-profits face is the dependence on people offering their services pro-bono. We cannot do without them, but we have no influence or leverage in terms of how long it will take for them to complete a task. Mark Stanbridge provided gratis legal services to our project where we would otherwise have paid tens of thousands of dollars. The reality was that, as a partner, Mark was a very busy man and he was giving us a large chunk of his personal time. If he was asked to draft or review a contract for us, we would never quite know how long it would take to get done and, in truth, this was quite understandable, we were not paying a cent for this advice. We were completely in his hands and in the meantime, it was up to Pod and me to try and keep our partners motivated. We needed them much more than they needed us.

In my view, the *60 Minutes* contract was unnecessarily limiting. Paul White reported that they were increasingly concerned about the growing profile of the project and the number of media interviews being done (by me). I was the focus of the *60 Minutes* contract and they wanted full and exclusive access to me in terms of interviews and availability before, during and after the rhinos were moved from South Africa to Australia. In the meantime, I was permitted to do interviews so long as they did not compete with Channel Nine. This obviously eliminated any contact with Channel Seven. Being the board's marketing and communications director, Paul was the contact man for *60 Minutes* and he delegated much of this to part-time contractor Sarah Dennis. I was sidelined despite being the person *60 Minutes* most wanted involved. Jo Townsend continued to take checkpoints with me on a regular basis until early April 2016, when *60 Minutes* journalist Tara Brown and her crew were arrested in Beirut during the kidnapping saga, which escalated into an international incident and, for *60 Minutes*, our project dropped off the map.

As I sensed the tide was moving against me, AUSDAFF placed more obstacles in our way and it became increasingly that the rhino move was not going to happen in 2016. The love had gone out of the *60 Minutes* marriage and in late 2016, Paul White advised them that we would not be looking to renew or extend the contract.

Sometime after the contract was terminated, I spoke to Jo and asked how she and the *60 Minutes* team felt about the ending of the relationship. She quoted the *60 Minutes* mantra, *"Don't do a story about the floods, do a story about Noah."* They felt that I was being pushed into the shadows and offering others to be the front person which was not at all what they wanted or had contracted. Jo said that the reason she had worked so hard to get the contract signed with us was because of my dream. *"Without peeing in your pocket, Ray, it was your crazy dream that excited us."*

From my point of view, it was a sad end to a long, always exciting, often painful saga. I made mistakes on the way through, but I also learned an immense amount about the television industry in Australia and how extraordinarily competitive it is. These people live for the day. Yesterday's news is exactly that. Any edge on their rivals is exploited and aggressively driven home. They work incredibly hard and despite the immediacy requirement of their jobs, they are capable of building strong relationships.

If only.

THE INVESTEC PARTNERSHIP

We had an impressive group of partners. Taronga Zoo and the University of Sydney gave TARP international credibility and gravitas and having their names on our livery set us apart and strengthened the perception that we were an organisation to be taken seriously. Nevertheless, the cold, hard fact was that these partnerships didn't pay the bills.

I had long felt that Investec would be an ideal partner for us. There were so many synergies; it is a global organisation with its roots in South Africa, with a proud and growing tradition of conservation, in particular with rhinos, and in 2015 good friend Bob Tucker offered to introduce me to Hein Vogel, another former South African and a senior executive at Investec Australia.

Pod, his daughter Kelly and I duly met with Bob and Hein. It was an excellent introductory meeting, Hein was as passionate as we were and promised to help us in whichever way he could, noting that a few years before, he had founded an organisation called Southern Crossings, a networking group, sponsored by Investec, which meets three or four times a year to assist South African businesspeople to establish themselves in Australia. Over the years, Southern Crossings has developed an excellent reputation amongst expatriates and Hein invited me to discuss rhinos at their upcoming event. If successful, it could be a good start to any relationship with Investec.

Hein put together a panel with Cliff Rosenberg, LinkedIn CEO, Mark Stanbridge, fellow board director and partner in Ashurst, and myself. Hein facilitated the discussion with almost one hundred people in attendance. The evening went really well and I could feel the momentum building..

Hein then organised a meeting with Investec Australia CEO, Milton Samios; Greg Joubert, Marketing; Jacqui Marshall, Corporate Social Responsibility and Ben Smith, Managing Director. All the key decision-makers were there. Pod and I presented our proposal to the group. It was a great session and Milton subsequently wrote that the project was a nice fit for Investec and that he could see many mutual benefits and hoped we could do something together.

As we got into the detail of the proposed contract, the negotiations started in earnest and Pod did an enormous amount of work in preparing a draft. At all times the board were kept informed by Pod and then, out of the blue, when a close to final draft was circulated, Allan seemed to be nervous about committing to the relationship. Pod has the patience of Job and calmly worked through the detail and Ashurst kindly put the meat on the bone of the contract but Pod was alarmed at some of the comments about the agreement and sent a note to the board – it was a key communication at a critical moment in the project's history. Pod said that he had been surprised about the negative reaction to the Investec deal and wished to table a few thoughts in the hope that we could keep things in perspective.

He explained that he had offered his services to the project not only because he was horrified by the global plight of the rhino but also because he respected me for my *"indefatigable efforts to turn a vision into a reality"*, and he admired my passion. He had watched and helped as I worked tirelessly from 7am to 9pm on most days including weekends to try and give this project the required momentum. He said that I had achieved, against many odds, more than many thought I would. He then reflected on what had happened over the last few months, saying that as a board and as a team, we had a lot to be proud of including:

- Sourcing six rhinos from David Desilets and a pipeline of potential sources for the next batch.
- Readying South African quarantine facilities; awaiting the AUSDAFF inspection which had been facilitated with involvement of the highest levels of government.
- Raising nearly two thirds of the funding required.
- Lining up two competing TV channels to record the first translocation.
- Building a growing database of people and companies who want to help.
- Snaring a corporate sponsor willing to work with us with a true partnership approach.

Pod warned of the risk if we pulled out of the deal. Investec would walk and our credibility in the wider market would be irreparably damaged.

One of the board's main gripes had been that the sponsorship of $100k per annum offered by Investec was too "light" given our financial challenges, but the stark reality was that we didn't have alternative sponsors queuing up to fund the project. Pod said, "*If we were to be brutally honest, the progress on contacting and engaging high net worth individuals and other sponsors has been slow – the large donors at the table now have come largely through Ray's efforts*". He pointed out that the Investec deal did not preclude other industry vertical sponsors like transport, beverages or leisure. "*We must stop comparing ourselves to some of the established and mature charities – we simply do not carry that clout or appeal.*"

I really could not believe we were in this situation. To me, signing up with Investec was an absolute no-brainer. A coup. We had rapidly built a strong relationship to the point that they were willing to sign a sponsorship deal with us committing $400,000 over four years. Investec is a fifty-year-old $4 billion international specialist banking and asset management group, providing a range of financial products and services in three principal geographies: the UK and Europe, Southern Africa and Asia-Pacific. It is listed on both the London and Johannesburg stock exchanges. By contrast, we were a fledgling organisation with a grand vision and not much more.

Pod's summary was on the money. He recommended that the proposed deal be discussed as soon as possible at a special board meeting. It was so hard to fathom why Pod and I had such difficulty in gaining the agreement of the board. Neither of us had anything personal to gain – what we did, we did for the rhinos.

At one point Pod and I thought that Investec would walk away because of what they saw as our intransigence and dilly-dallying, but finally the goodwill Pod and I had established with CEO Milton Samios and his team paid off and the contract was signed. Pod and I were elated, but there was still some grumbling that we had "squandered" the naming rights for a pittance and that these rights had significantly more value. This may have been true, but the reality was that Investec were the only game in town – we did not have anyone, let alone a global financial services organisation, lining up to partner with us.

For the next year or so, we cemented our relationship with Investec. They were wonderful allies and while we were always equal partners, I often felt that we had been taken under the Investec wing, a very comforting and comfortable place to be. As CEO, Milton Samios was not directly involved but was always there if we needed anything escalated. I admired him greatly.

In order to secure the funding, we were required to meet certain goals and very specific milestones which would trigger the sponsorship payments. The key milestone was the rhinos moving into quarantine in South Africa. I knew that this was absolutely critical to the success of the project since this event would also activate the *60 Minutes* sponsorship. A great deal was at stake.

In August 2016, I received a request from Greg Joubert, our primary interface with Investec, to meet to discuss the expiring contract on 9 September. We discussed the status of the project and, in recognition of the goodwill between both parties, and in order to keep things simple and continue the partnership, he suggested drafting a short extension, with existing terms, which he sent through to me two days before the contract was due to expire. I forwarded the agreement to the board the next day. Mark undertook to have a look at it and revert the following day. On the 9th, Greg called me saying that we really should get it signed that day. I immediately phoned Mark, leaving him a voicemail asking him to call Greg. I followed this up with an email to which Mark responded, "*I have read the amendment agreement. It is fine to sign*". I forwarded his note to Greg asking how to proceed and he said to sign it and scan it to Investec, which I did, by close of business that day. Deadline met, job well done, everyone happy.

How wrong can one person be? Over the next few weeks there was plenty of coming and going between us and Investec and through a series of misunderstandings and miscommunication, to my dismay, the agreement was allowed to lapse but not before Investec CEO, Milton Samios, sent me a note: "*I understand that our contract has lapsed and we need to decide the best way forward. Can I suggest that we have a meeting at the Investec office and talk it through? I do think it's important for Investec to understand what are the impediments and delays as well as the revised arrival date for the rhinos. Happy for you to bring members of your board or executive who are relevant to the discussion.*" As always, Milton was polite, professional and courteous.

The meeting took place at the beginning of November 2016, two months after the contract had expired. It was a very uncomfortable meeting and by May 2017 the entire relationship just fell away and Investec withdrew their sponsorship. Consequences are never obvious at the time, but the withdrawal of Investec raised a number of questions from other partners and also our supporters. Investec's prominent logo was removed from all of TARP's documentation and the vitally needed financial contribution was gone.

Milton called me after the meeting and had some very complimentary things to say: *"You are the project, the passion and the driving force."* It was welcome praise, but I felt that I had failed.

I felt sick. Despite Leanne Piggott having resigned from the board, we had remained in close contact and I told her what was going on. Leanne said, *"I'm so, so sorry about this. It's just awful. I'm glad I'm no longer on the board as it would have gutted me to see what is happening. This only strengthens my belief that you need to take a sabbatical from TARP."*

THE QUARANTINE SAGA

At that very first meeting with Dr Andrew Cupit of AUSDAFF in mid-2014, he made it clear that the quarantine issue would be a major hurdle for us to overcome and that we would not be permitted to bring the rhinos directly into Australia – they had to be quarantined offshore for at least one year. Over time, AUSDAFF softened this requirement and agreed to direct importation under strict quarantine conditions. A major win for us.

In the initial planning meetings in 2014, I was advised that it was probable that an AUSDAFF officer would need to undertake a site visit to South Africa to inspect the pre-export quarantine facilities. Since their resources were limited, costs associated with this visit would be met by us. I agreed to this requirement since I was confident that we could raise the required funding and I was equally confident that the South Africans would pass the test. They export wild animals all around the world every week.

My plan was always for the rhinos to be quarantined in South Africa under the care of their state vet, guided by AUSDAFF. Once given the all clear, the rhinos would be flown to Sydney and be transported to the quarantine facility at Western Plains Zoo, which had previously been certified by AUSDAFF and the Environment Department (AUSDEA), the key gatekeepers. The rhinos would remain in quarantine until these departments and the resident veterinarians were satisfied there was no risk to the fauna and flora of Australia. This process, as required by CITES and Australian law, would be followed for all rhinos subsequently imported under the auspices of the project. This plan was logical, practical and agreed to by all parties. It was also in line with Ian Player's recommendation and the foundation stone of his support.

From the outset, in my meeting with Taronga CEO Cam Kerr, I had committed to the first batch of rhinos being available to zoos who wanted to join the rhino breeding program, but only if they had the wherewithal to house and care for the rhinos. I believed that this commitment acknowledged the support of Taronga and ZAA, representing the collective voice of the zoos, aquariums, sanctuaries and wildlife parks across Australasia.

Over time the Australian destination was modified so that post quarantine, the first rhinos would be split into two groups, one joining the existing herd at Western Plains and the other being moved to Monarto Safari Park to build that breeding herd – we believed it was critical to spread any form of risk, be it security or be it disease.

In the early days, I had an excellent working relationship with

AUSDAFF's Dr Andrew Cupit and Dr Jill Millan, Director Animal Biosecurity. Jill is an outstanding professional and seemed able to eliminate or at least limit the amount of bureaucracy required in seeking an outcome. In July 2014, she drafted what turned out to be a pivotal letter to her South African counterpart, Dr Mike Modisane, saying that AUSDAFF and AUSDEA had met with me about the proposal to import rhino. She said that, in principle, they supported the proposal. Jill advised that her department was responsible for engaging with other authorities to develop biosecurity measures under which live animals could be imported into Australia and stipulated that the rhinos must be resident in an approved or registered zoo or wildlife park in the exporting country since birth or for at least twelve months immediately before export. Australia also required biosecurity risk management measures for a number of diseases including anthrax, bovine tuberculosis (TB), foot and mouth (FMD), Johne's disease, rabies and Rift Valley fever.

The first step in this process was for AUSDAFF to undertake an assessment of South Africa's animal health status and official inspection and certification arrangements. She mentioned again that "*officers from my branch will visit South Africa to verify its inspection and certification systems, and the Kruger Park facilities for the holding and isolation of rhinoceros.*"

There were a number of key statements in this letter including, "*We support in principle the import proposal.*" There it was, in writing, that the department supported our proposal in-principle. Secondly, the approval was limited to rhinos from the Kruger Park. Given previous imports, I was quite happy with this.

Thirdly the statement "*Officers from my branch will visit South*

Africa to verify its inspection and certification systems." Again, I was quite happy with this requirement since Dr Markus Hofmeyr, Chief Scientist for SANParks ran a tight ship.

It had become clear that the officials from AUSDAFF were very concerned about the general state of veterinary management practices and protocols in South Africa and questioned whether there had been any deterioration in these standards. This was a reasonable position to take given the changes in government and professional personnel in South Africa.

Getting information from the South African authorities was difficult, especially from Dr Modisane, Jill's equivalent, who seemed to take little interest in the questions asked of him by AUSDAFF. It was either that or he belonged to the school of thought, *"if you ignore them for long enough, they will go away."* After numerous follow-ups, he responded with a half-baked reply that was never going to suffice.

Unfortunately, at this crucial moment, in June 2014, Jill was transferred to another department and was replaced by Dr Jonathan Taylor. Although very sorry to see Jill go, I held high hopes for building a relationship with Jonathan since he is South African born and obtained his veterinary science degree from the University of Pretoria, the world's leading wildlife management veterinary school, universally known as Onderstepoort.

At the same time Dr Allan Sheridan came on to the scene. Allan's title was Principal Veterinarian, Animal Biosecurity. While Sheridan reported to Jonathan, he seemed to have complete authority over our destiny and from day one, it looked like he wanted to make his mark.

To this day, I am uncertain about Jonathan's true feelings or opinion about our project. He said all the right things but would never try and find a way, a compromise or an agreed position. Perhaps Jonathan thought he should have an arms-length relationship because he was a Saffa. Or perhaps that is the way of government.

Sheridan was completely risk averse and, from the get-go, the level of bureaucracy increased dramatically. His first communication to me set the scene for the next eighteen months, saying that from the material provided there was no easy way to meet the existing requirements for imports from RSA, however, I should be aware that the US and many EU countries were approved for the export of rhinos to Australia.

He referred to the timeline requirements for disease freedom on farms of origin, which would be an area SADAFF would need to work on to establish some form of equivalence of animal health status for the diseases of concern to Australia. Despite everyone else having agreed that twelve months was more than adequate, he said that, given Australia's animal health requirements, "it could be sensible" to have at least a two-year record of where the animals had been held to help establish, to Australia's satisfaction, the sourcing of those animals in relation to disease risk areas. Without any apparent justification, they had just doubled the quarantine period that, just a few months before, according to his predecessor Jill Millan, was twelve months. With a wave of a wand, this one year and then two-year requirement would later stretch out to five years. Considering that all of the rhinos we were pursuing were wild caught, how on earth could this information be provided? Logic just flew out of the window.

Sheridan said that they were planning to meet with AUSDEA

to understand their timelines for providing the required CITES information. Then the kick in the guts: *"We will establish whether there is a way forward."* My heart sank. Up until that point there had never been a "whether", only a "when".

Sheridan also seemed to be side-lining DFAT, saying that they were *"an observer rather than a key participant."* In my view, DFAT was an absolutely key decision-maker. He said that AUSDAFF appreciated the pressure that we must be under and apologised if it all seemed slow and overly bureaucratic and that I should be mindful that the beef, sheep, wool and dairy industries in Australia are worth more than A$15 billion and that this industry *"must be protected."* All of us at TARP agreed absolutely with this but to me it seemed a patronising comment.

He concluded by saying that diseases like TB and FMD had the potential *"to cause human misery on an almost unimaginable scale in rural Australia should they get in and destroy our access to export markets"* and that AUSDAFF's job was to ensure that certification for imported animals included proper animal health controls. Obviously choosing to ignore that rhinos (and other animals) had previously been imported from South Africa, he concluded that they were *"working to develop certification from scratch."* This was not what we had agreed with his predecessor.

He then dangled the carrot saying that it would all be different if we were to import the animals from the US. A pre-export visit could occur with very little delay once animals were flagged for shipment as AUSDAFF knew that the US could assure them that the animals met acceptable animal health conditions. Our board had previously rejected this option. It was enough to make a grown man cry. We had been working with Andrew Cupit and his team for a year and making progress, and now here was yet another set of what looked like insurmountable requirements.

One of the major issues that I encountered with AUSDAFF was the absence of any management hierarchy. In business, if you have an issue which can't be resolved at one level, you can escalate the matter up the line. Here, the bureaucrats held all the aces and they knew it.

The next twelve months were spent trying to gather the information that AUSDAFF had specified. One of the main reasons for setting up the Scientific Advisory Board was to assist in situations such as these and Professors Roseanne Tayler and David Emery never wavered in their support of me and the project.

The folk from Taronga Zoo and ZAA really stepped up and did their best to help us respond to all of the AUSDAFF questions/concerns, as we certainly did not have the expertise on our board. Drs Andrea Reiss and Benn Bryant from ZAA were particularly supportive. Looking back at the correspondence, it is staggering how much time was spent on trying to get some resolution or at least direction on what was required to come to an agreed position for both governments.

The complexity of this venture is indicated by the multiplicity of stakeholders which included Taronga, Monarto, the Australian departments of Agriculture, Environment and Foreign Affairs, ZAA, the South African departments of Agriculture and Environment as well as a number of South African provincial authorities.

Dr Charles van Niekerk provided extraordinary support. I was introduced to Charles by Dr Markus Hofmeyr of SANParks as being, by far and away, the best operator when it came to exporting wild animals and managing quarantine facilities. Our need for Charles' facility – Wildlife Assignments International – came about because we were unable to use the previously used quarantine facility at Skukuza.

I first met Charles at his facility near Hammanskraal an hour or so from Pretoria. It is an impressive set-up. He is geared for transporting every conceivable animal around the world, from giraffes to small antelope.

Charles was always responsive to the many requests I put to him. In early 2015, when, not for the first or last time, we thought we were close to getting the rhinos into quarantine, Charles provided us with a comprehensive quote for darting, capturing, transporting and quarantining the rhinos. This quote formed the backbone of all of our budgets.

A lot of this was highly complicated stuff. As an example, the size of the doors of the aircraft that was to transport the rhinos was critical. Charles offered the following advice on this seemingly simple but potentially limiting factor for using a passenger aircraft:

"We refer to 'lower deck' height. 161cm is the door size. We are therefore limited to animals that are a maximum of two and a half years old. This severely limits the source of the rhino. There are other potential complications with regard to socialisation and future breeding from this young age-group. Lower deck would also probably mean the animals are in the 'belly' of a passenger flight which gives us vets no access to them in flight. Not a good idea when one looks at the length of potential flights."

Detail that we would never have thought of and Charles made sound so simple.

Charles' partner, Martin Krog, has responsibility for building the crates for each individual animal and has a fully equipped workshop. It is a slick operation that filled me with confidence that we could satisfy all of AUSDAFF's ever more stringent (and changing) requirements.

By August 2015, the SADAFF had still not responded to the letter from Allan Sheridan who seemed reluctant to follow up. I intervened and called Dr Jyotika Rajput in Pretoria. Dr Rajput's title was State Veterinarian, Import/Export Policy Unit at SADAFF and she was a vital cog in the decision-making process. Over the next eighteen months, I had several dealings with Dr Rajput and met her on a number of occasions. I found her to be a smart, dedicated professional who had trained as a veterinary surgeon. We understood each other's roles and we got on very well.

Contacting Dr Rajput directly did not go down well with Sheridan. I reported back to him as to the content of our conversation and asked him to reach out to her. He didn't like that one bit and came back to me, *"With respect, we are doing our jobs appropriately."*

In October 2015, once again, I thought that we were getting closer – certainly on the South African side. Dr Rajput convened a meeting with all the people who were crucial to the success of our project, including Charles, the state vet for Limpopo Province, and Hans Kooy.

This meeting was convened as a direct result of my earlier discussion with Dr Rajput. It was a critically important meeting. For the first time, all the South African stakeholders sat around a table to agree what was required to approve the export of rhinos to Australia. Dr Roy Bengis attended the meeting representing me and commented that in all of his thirty years of working with and for the government this was a unique experience – sitting around a table with all of those who could make it happen.

The meeting went very well and roles were defined and responsibilities assigned. In Roy's words, *"The general feeling was that most of the requirements regarding pre-export quarantine, location, facilities, the operation and disease certification are attainable and we can comply."* This was massive, the South African Government was cooperating.

To try and obtain more concrete information about the bovine tuberculosis (TB) issue which loomed large in Allan Sheridan's mind, I arranged a three-way conversation with Roy and Pete Morkel and reported back to AUSDAFF that Roy had said that rhinos were *"very unimportant"* in terms of diseases, specifically TB; that rhinos live with buffalo, kudu and warthogs all of which carry TB with no effect on the rhinos. He was unaware of any cases involving TB in rhinos and said there was no validated test on live rhinos for TB, and that the key issue was to ensure that the rhinos were de-ticked.

Jonathan Taylor responded to me, *"That is really interesting information."* I went for the gap, saying that I was acutely aware that our success or failure was in his hands and that I wished and prayed every day for an approach from his team that *"we are going to do this thing, now how can we make it happen."*

I wasn't expecting a response and I didn't get one, but I thought what the hell, this guy is human, just like me, he is South African born, just like me and he loves animals, just like me!

Jonathan advised that it was imperative that we got Roy Bengis into our team. Roy was clearly considered a guru by AUSDAFF and what he says goes. With the approval of the board, I signed Roy up as our consultant in South Africa. This turned out to be money extremely well spent, particularly when Jonathan Taylor commented to me that it was really useful *"to have Roy Bengis' expertise, credibility and experience to assist in providing the information which they required."*

The rest of 2015 was spent by the South Africans collecting and collating the information that had been requested by Canberra. Drs Rajput and Bengis did a mammoth job pulling together the volumes of information that had been requested. Finally, I received a notification from Dr Rajput, *"The communication was sent on the 15th of December to Dr Sheridan. A covering letter, draft health certificate and the response to the questionnaire was sent."*

I cannot describe how excited I was. Australia had requested an incredibly detailed and complex set of questions from the South Africans and they had delivered on every single point.

Not very much happens in Australia from mid-December until Australia Day on 26th January. As in Europe in August, most Australians take their summer holidays in January. Government pretty much closes down, so I did not expect much feedback until February.

Both Dr Rajput and Roy followed up with me in January seeking a reaction or response from AUSDAFF from their submission. I chased and I chased.

Early in February, Allan Sheridan returned from leave and told me it would take four to six months for him and his department to respond to the South African submission. Once again, I was speechless and within our board I questioned Sheridan's commitment. By this time, we had identified an airplane that could transport the rhinos from South Africa to Australia. It was scheduled for 1st August, 2016. We now had a target date. Now let's get this done.

Despite Sheridan's six-month predicted timeline, Jonathan Taylor, Sheridan's boss, had separately been in touch with Roy Bengis and, once again, raised the question of TB. This had been raised so many times that it did not come as a huge surprise to me. Taylor wrote, *"We are keen to access survey data and information drawn from field investigations to verify the prevalence and incidence of those diseases of biosecurity concern to Australia, specifically Bovine Tuberculosis TB. After that process is finalised, we will finalise the draft Health Certificate."*

Ever the professional, Roy responded to Taylor saying, somewhat pointedly, *"I certainly understand the need for thorough investigation and assessment of any potential risk of animal disease introduction. I also appreciate the importance of animal-based agriculture to the Australian economy. Please remember that I was also a DAFF State Veterinarian (Disease Control) for 34 years."*

Roy went on to say, *"The whole issue of TB in rhino is complex, and I would like to highlight some reasons why I believe that rhinos are an extremely low-risk species for carrying or transmitting TB."* He went into minute detail supporting his position, essentially that there are few reports of TB in rhinos in any literature; that South Africa had the largest white rhino population in the world; that they are relatively free-range animals and have high financial value, so disease or mortality is usually thoroughly investigated. In addition, probably the only positive aspect of the horrendous rhino poaching saga is that many rhino carcasses underwent necropsy examination in order to locate bullets for forensic matching to firearms. This afforded veterinarians the opportunity to examine the victims, and to date, there was not one report of any tuberculosis lesions. *"This is especially significant in the Kruger Park where the majority of white rhino occur in regions of the Park with the highest TB prevalence in African buffalo. Almost all poached rhinos have been thoroughly necropsied in Kruger. To date there have been no reports of bovine TB in white rhinos in South Africa, and should it occur we would consider it an unusual event."*

Roy referred to a confidential recent research project in Kruger, where the objective was to evaluate and improve on diagnostic testing for bovine TB in white rhino. Three surplus young white rhino bulls were artificially infected with the TB virus. The diagnostic tests were monitored over the next six months, after which these animals were euthanised. At necropsy, only a few very small nodules could be detected, and these were histologically inactive and culture negative. This research would be published shortly. *"In closing, it would appear that although rhino can be infected with bovine tuberculosis, this is a rare event and they appear fairly resistant to infection and progression of disease."*

This was an extremely important piece of work in the context of my project. I forwarded Roy's note to the board, noting the significance of Roy's work and comments.

Seemingly not satisfied, Jonathan Taylor requested more information from Roy who responded with a detailed analysis and assessment of TB in rhinos in South Africa which included a survey by seven highly regarded South African wildlife veterinarians, all of whom confirmed Roy's findings.

I chased Sheridan to ensure that he had received Roy's additional submission. In March he replied that he had and that

AUSDAFF now had to assess the response before locking in a date for the verification visit to South Africa. He covered all the bases by adding that he could not give an accurate estimate of the likely timeframe, but his best guesstimate was around three months for the full assessment and the visit a few weeks later. A further six months to finalise the report of the assessment and finalise development of an agreed health certificate. He concluded by saying that it would be an absolute minimum of five months before we could apply for an import permit for the first consignment with confidence.

I consider myself to be as positive a person as anyone, but this estimate troubled me, there was no commitment despite us giving them every single piece of information that they had requested, and often more. Once again, we had no control over AUSDAFF's timelines. Stalemate. So near and yet so far.

EVERYONE LOVES TARONGA

TARP's relationship with Taronga Zoo was complicated. Unnecessarily complicated. Taronga had a full deck of cards, everyone loved them. They had a 100-year legacy and most Sydney-siders had visited the zoo at some stage of their lives. That they jealously guard their position was recently evidenced when Jake Burgess and his family had the temerity to build a zoo in Sydney's West and named it the Sydney Zoo. Taronga fought them tooth and nail.

I think they saw their relationship with us as a challenge. We had a cause that nobody could dispute and a leader who had passion and the ability to communicate a vision. There was also a large body of people, not only in Australia but across the globe, who could see that this was a viable alternative to preventing extinction and really wanted to become involved and to make a difference to ensure its success.

In the early days, Taronga seemed to be testing us by insisting that we pay full freight for any support they provided. Thanks to Allan Davies' generosity, we passed that test. Then Simon Duffy joined our board, which was a true coup for us. Every time I did a press interview or spoke at an event, I showered Taronga with praise. Their agreeing to our request to use their logo was epic and gave us an enormous amount of credibility. But this also became a lever for them. When they thought that we were getting too big for our boots, they pulled their logo.

As the public interest in our project increased, so did media interviews, seemingly to Taronga's chagrin. Inexplicably, I was instructed by them not to mention Taronga in any interviews. Shortly thereafter, I did a live radio interview at 2SM with well-known Australian host John Laws. It went well and I sent all concerned a transcript of the interview. Simon Duffy's reaction was to request an email prior to media interviews when I might mention Taronga. I pointed out that I was unable to predict the questions that I might be asked. He wouldn't let it rest and retorted that Taronga took brand reputation and risk to their brand very seriously, *"In future please do not mention Taronga unless you notify us prior to the media event."*

Let's play out this nonsensical scenario. John Laws asks me how we managed to bring Taronga on as a partner. Should I then either ignore his question or say that I am unable to discuss Taronga at all? Or phone a friend? What a nonsense. Simon Duffy is a smart young man and has a great career ahead of him and I could never fathom why he sent such a silly note.

In 2015, we received a letter from Cam Kerr which according to Allan, was a result of their frustration with TARP about a range of issues – lack of a project plan and timeline, lack of structure, expectations that Taronga would be required to provide a range of services for TARP which it could not afford, plus the extra work that it was doing to support TARP and so on. Cam gave notice that Simon would resign as a director of the board and would be replaced by Matt Fuller, GM of Western Plains Zoo.

Allan said, *"My conclusion is that there is NO imminent danger of TARP losing Taronga as a partner. These are normal growing pains for an organisation like TARP which is transitioning from an idea about an ideal to something quite tangible."*

I was disappointed Simon had been asked to resign since he had contributed much to our project. A fairly earnest young man, his conservation knowledge is deep and his passion for animal welfare strong. We would miss him. Matt Fuller was a very different person – a personable man who politically, was very astute. Cam Kerr was very fortunate to have two very good lieutenants of this calibre in his team.

Shortly after the 2015 Sydney dinner, whilst negotiations were peaking with *60 Minutes*, we really needed Taronga to decide who, from their side, would be available for interviews. They seemed hesitant and I wrote to the board that this action, or lack of action, reinforced my view that Taronga saw us as something of a burden and a challenge to their own rhino fundraising efforts. Pod said the day was soon coming when we would need to assert our independence. We were *not* a division of either Taronga or ZAA. Both needed to understand and respect this.

A few short weeks later, we received a letter from Taronga that effectively terminated the partnership. The key components of the letter were the withdrawal of their "Partner" status, wanting their role to be one of "Technical Advisor"; the removal of the Taronga logo from all TARP livery; and the resignation of Matt Fuller as director. They confirmed that they were prepared to negotiate a new MOU and that they would provide a technical advisor to the project but that was all.

Members of the board implied that I was the problem and the probable reason for the withdrawal. Pod had a different view by saying , *"Taronga have been 'in the tent' for their benefit without adding any real value. They are good at 'no' and 'caution' but not so good at pulling their weight."*

I believe Taronga saw us as a nuisance from three points of view: our ability to capture the hearts and minds of the general population, the media's captivation with our story, and our success in raising money. While they saw us as eating into their sponsorship and donations pie, I saw the situation completely differently – we were actually increasing the size of that pie – a really important distinction.

I felt somewhat vindicated in my opinion when, within days of breaking our relationship, Taronga announced the establishment of a new rhino foundation with a full-page advertisement in Sydney's *Daily Telegraph* newspaper and an ABC interview with Cam Kerr. Slow-moving bureaucracies like Taronga are unable to react with such speed – this had been a long time coming. I was convinced Taronga had thought we would fail, just as others had in the past.

On the positive side, I believe that several of our achievements during the Taronga partnership will stand the test of time. We valued and respected their brand; we persisted and stayed the distance; we built an excellent conservation network in Australia, South Africa and internationally; we had a world-class social media program; we signed up with *60 Minutes*; against all odds, we had the support of federal and state politicians; we held a highly professional fundraising dinner which raised a stunning amount of money; we secured an internationally known banking institution as a sponsor, joining other world-class partners – the Veterinary Faculty and Business School of the University of Sydney. Probably controversially, I also hold the view that our program stimulated Taronga to restart their rhino breeding programs.

What is good for the rhino is good for me.

Interestingly, during this saga, I had a note from Maurice Newman AC, Chairman of the Taronga Foundation and doyen of Australian business: *"Thanks to people like you and people at Taronga, the future of wildlife now has a chance for the next 100 years."*

I had never heard of Monarto Safari Park before I started this project but over time it has become the favoured destination for our rhinos. It is part of Zoos South Australia (ZSA) and is situated some two hours east of Adelaide, where the city zoo campus is located. In 2009, Monarto sought private investors to develop a wildlife experience similar to those provided by large African game parks. The 1,000-hectare zoo had acquired an additional 500 hectares of land and hoped to develop a *"world standard eco-tourism resort boasting both African and Australian wildlife, 4x4 tours, fine dining and overnight stays."* Conservationist and philanthropist Heather Caddick, President of ZSA at the time, was the brains behind the idea. Luxury accommodation would provide overnight stays in a new "Wild Africa" precinct with a quality restaurant and swimming pool.

In September 2014, Heather invited Margie and me to Monarto for a lunch with some potential sponsors of our project. She and her husband Alfie are dedicated conservationists and in Heather I found a kindred spirit. Her passion and concern for rhinos matched mine. She has written a number of immensely readable books about rhinos. Over the next couple of years, Heather was to become a firm friend and ally. We also met the newly appointed CEO Elaine Bensted and the Director of Health Sciences, Peter Clark. It was clear that ZSA was in excellent hands.

After lunch, we were shown the site of the planned Wild Africa development. I reported back to our board saying that Monarto, the biggest open plains zoo in the world, had very specific plans for expansion, most of it centred on rhino. They had two black rhino bulls and wanted more, and they had prepared costings for quarantining "our" rhinos. As a private zoo, not funded by government, I concluded that they would make an ideal partner. With the benefit of hindsight, this was a very important meeting as the relationship with Monarto constantly strengthened – much of this due to Heather's and my efforts.

In January 2015, I floated the idea of a partnership with Monarto with Heather and with our board. Heather really liked the idea and undertook to raise it with Elaine or EB as she prefers to be called. EB was a pleasure to deal with and very efficient while Peter Clark was always willing to share his considerable experience and expertise. He loved the African bush.

Everything worked really well and Allan visited Monarto and returned circulating a proposal he had crafted. The proposal was to have TARP fund a supervisor at $90,000 over twelve months to facilitate the fast construction of the Wild Africa area at Monarto which would supposedly house up to 30 rhinos. Said Allan, *"I feel it's a very elegant way to contribute to the development of facilities which will allow us to house our rhinos."*

I'm not sure what was meant by "elegant". Our immediate and critical need was for quarantine facilities. $90,000 was a fortune to shell out when we did not have any assurances of success from either the South African or Australian governments.

This was raised at the next board meeting as a firm proposal and despite Mark and I being against it, it was eventually passed; he and I were of the same view that, if at all, the payments to Monarto should only commence once the rhinos were in quarantine in South Africa – the trigger date for several milestones.

The money we had raised was specifically designated for bringing the rhinos to Australia. There was always going to be a need for a quarantine facility and Taronga had committed to provide this. I think that our donors and sponsors would be aghast that their donations were being applied to building a facility at a zoo where rhinos would be amongst other "display" animals.

Apropos of nothing, one of the cleverer quotes that I came across during the zoo negotiations was, *"A man walks into a zoo. The only animal in the entire zoo is a dog. It's a shitzu."*

INCREASING AWARENESS AND
SEARCHING FOR SPONSORS

There were so many disparate aspects to this project. Bringing the project to fruition was paramount and while the four pillars provided the strategy, I also took every opportunity to chase down anyone who might be able to provide funding or increase awareness of our project through their profiles or connections and, consequently, I met some interesting people. Without exception, each one committed to assisting us in whichever way they could.

Several years ago, our family visited Johannesburg and Margie and I decided to show the children the house where we had lived more than 30 years ago. As we left, our son Kevin excitedly asked me if I had seen the photos of the band on the walls of the house. I hadn't and asked which band – the Dave Matthews Band, he replied, rolling his eyes. Only when I did some research did I realise how big a global superstar Dave is. I thought he would make an ideal ambassador (and possible donor).

From my experience in organising major events with high-profile artists and entertainers, I know that the most difficult task is actually getting to talk to, and, if necessary, negotiate, directly with these famous people. There are always several layers of gate-keepers whose job seems to be to protect their clients from speaking directly to the wider population. Undeterred, I tracked Dave down in the US and wrote to him, inviting him to become a patron.

After several preliminary discussions with his management company, I was eventually permitted to speak to Dave. He was intrigued. Like most South Africans, he was deeply concerned about the onslaught on South African wildlife. He was about to visit Sydney for a concert and suggested that we meet. He provided me with two tickets and Margie and I sat in this jam-packed theatre not knowing even one of the band's songs – we were really embarrassed by this since every other person in the audience seemed to know every word of every song. After the concert ended, we were escorted back-stage to meet Dave who was in his dressing room, winding down with his two young daughters. He is a delightful man and you would never know that he is a superstar. He was very much aware of the plight of the rhino and, as we left, asked me to give some thought as to how he might help.

We remained in contact and Dave was always supportive. At his request, I sent him my poem, "For the Rhino", for consideration of putting it to music. He was fiercely moved by the poem but said it was not "ideal" as a song.

This was yet another situation where through ever more Australian government delays, nothing concrete was achieved. Having said that, I know for certain that if the opportunity arose again, Dave would make a sizeable financial contribution to the cause. He said as much.

After my 2016 TED talk, I was contacted by Stefani Chinn, who heads up the marketing division of Optus, one of Australia's two major telecommunications companies. Optus is a major sponsor of the Australian domestic version of the cricket T20 competition known as the Big Bash League (BBL). One of the superstars of this competition is Kevin Pietersen MBE, the former England cricket captain who is sponsored by Optus and played for the Melbourne Stars franchise. KP, as he is universally known, was born in South Africa and is a passionate conservationist. He had previously supported Mark Boucher's rhino organisation In Safe Hands and was keen to assist our project. We had a number of conversations on how best to achieve this – he is a generous man who puts his money where his mouth is. In 2017, he batted at the famous Melbourne Cricket Ground (MCG) with Save the Rhino stickers all over his cricket bat and also generously donated a signed Melbourne Stars shirt to auction at our 2016 Melbourne dinner. In late 2017, Melbourne Stars CEO, Clint Cooper, con- tacted me to say that KP had nominated a match at the MCG as a fundraiser for the rhinos and wanted us to be the beneficiary. He asked if there was another "rhino" organisation that he could support. After I assured him that TARP's governance was solid, the benefit match was held and more than $30,000 was donated to the project – a nice injection of funds for little effort.

The great Roger Federer's mother is South African born and knowing this, I reached out to him to enlist his support – if only I could get a soft endorsement from him. Craig Tiley, born in Durban, had an illustrious tennis career as a player before being appointed CEO of Tennis Australia. Craig supported me with "money can't buy" auction prizes for every event I organised and is a good friend. I asked him to put me in touch with Roger and he obliged by giving me the contact details of Janine Handel, CEO of the Roger Federer Foundation. I called Janine in Zurich, only to be told that she was in Australia with Roger preparing for the Australian Open. When I called, she answered, speaking very quietly. It turned out that she was on the Centre Court in Brisbane waiting for Roger to play a charity exhibition match against Jo-Wilfried Tsonga. She was happy to talk as long as I understood that as soon as Roger appeared on court, she would hang up. I launched into my pitch and Janine listened intently. She said that Roger was very much aware of the poaching issue since he tried to visit South Africa every year, but he wouldn't be able to help because his foundation is very specific in its fundraising goals being focused on the education of South African children aged between three and twelve years. One can only applaud the generosity of people like Roger Federer. From my point of view, I was satisfied that Janine undertook to brief Roger about TARP.

The film Invictus made Francois Pienaar's name famous all over the world. As captain of the victorious rugby Springboks in the 1995 Rugby World Cup, he is a legend in South Africa. Through yet another introduction by Bob Tucker, I spoke to Francois asking him if he would consider becoming an ambassador and also if he could assist me in getting access to certain South African politicians. A very gracious and humble man, he said that he would try but wasn't confident. As it turned out, he was unable to contact the minister but he committed to help us wherever he could.

Marc Player, son of Gary and nephew of Ian, has been incredibly supportive of me and TARP. The love of wildlife runs deep in his and his family's veins. He sent me a message from his dad, a global legend: *"My brother Ian and his colleagues are rightfully credited with saving the white rhino from extinction. This was a monumental effort which took persistence and determination, two characteristics that Ian instilled in me as a young boy. It caused Ian great sadness before his passing that the rhinos were, once again, under threat from the scourge of poaching. Ian believed strongly that a key element of saving the species was spreading the risk and, for this reason, he supported moving a group to Australia as envisioned by Ray Dearlove and TARP."*

Phil Liggett MBE and his wife Trish are as inspirational a couple as you will find. Phil is known internationally as the "voice of cycling" and Trish is an olympian, having competed as a speed skater at Grenoble. I met Phil when he was covering the Tour Down Under in Adelaide. He and Trish are wonderful company and Margie and I had a delightful dinner with them in Adelaide. Phil tells the entertaining story of when he was broadcasting at the Salt Lake City Olympics and in a joyful accident, speed skater Steven Bradbury sailed over the line as every one of his opponents toppled onto each other on the final corner of the race. As Phil said, it was probably the most unexpected gold medal in history and Bradbury was the hero for finding joy in merely taking part. A "Bradbury" has become a part of Australian vernacular.

He and Trish are fierce conservationists and they have created the Helping Rhinos charity in the United Kingdom. I spent a morning with them at their enchanting home on the banks of the Olifants River in Balule with Trish's homemade muffins for breakfast. Our goals are distinctly similar and I was very pleased to sign up with their Rhino Alliance – an important initiative that attempts to streamline a number of rhino support organisations' goals and focus. They are a formidable team and I was proud to be associated with them.

I first met Natalie Houghton at the World Parks Congress, she was CEO of the Jane Goodall Institute in Australia and we got on like a house on fire. It was entirely due to Natalie that I had a private meeting with Jane during her visit to Sydney. While Jane is tiny, that big heart beats strongly and the eyes flash as she warms to her subject. It is said that you know when you are in the presence of greatness and that was exactly my feeling when I met her. She is so quiet, so calm, so personable that, initially, I was quite unsettled. I'm sure that she noticed my nervousness and immediately put me at ease.

While chimps are Jane's first love, she has a deep knowledge of and concern for all endangered species. She is a passionate believer in the need for and power of education and she founded the wildly successful Roots and Shoots program to educate the young.

Jane has an exhausting travel schedule but when you meet her, you would never guess that she is in her eighties. Margie and I have been fortunate enough to meet Jane on a number of occasions and she is always the same – interested and interesting. And inspirational.

Margie Dearlove, Dr Jane Goodall and the author.

Patron of the Wilderness
Foundation Adrian Gardiner

Adrian Gardiner is what one would call the ultimate entrepreneur. He created the famous Shamwari Game Reserve and is the founder of the Mantis Group, a mini-empire of over 40 game reserves and luxury boutique hotels around the world. The late Dr Ian Player started the Wilderness Foundation and Adrian replaced him as chairman and took it global. Adrian is a bit like that Energizer battery, he just goes and goes with the drive and stamina of someone in his thirties. Adrian was a steadfast and vocal supporter of our project and wrote this wonderful tribute to Ian when he passed away: *"One smile can start a friendship. One word can end a fight. One look can save a relationship. One person can change your life. For me that person was Ian Player, a legend, my elder brother and a true hero."*

Adrian and his son Paul introduced me to the international superstar Bear Grylls. The plan was for Bear to do a series of events in Australia, including the Survival Academy concept with live shows and they wanted me to manage it. Unfortunately, we just couldn't get the dates to work for everyone and we postponed the tour. Despite that, Bear has been a wonderful supporter of the project. Every time we had a significant milestone, such as

World Rhino Day, I'd ask him to tweet or post something on his Facebook page, mentioning the project and he never let us down.

I had never heard of Pete Bethune until a mutual friend said he wanted to meet me. I was flying into Hoedspruit Airport and Pete was flying out. Friend Ron Hopkins said to me, *"You will love this guy. Nothing gets in his way, just like you."* I was immediately struck by the power of the man. A few scattered tattoos and a serious visage seemed somehow menacing, but Pete is well educated with an MBA from Waikato University. As soon as he mentioned Sea Shepherd, I placed him. He told me his story, no bravado, just matter of factly. In February 2010 in the middle of the night, he attempted to board the Japanese whaler Shōnan Maru from a jet-ski, planning a citizen's arrest on her captain, Hiroyuki Komiya, alleging attempted murder. He also intended to present a claim for $3 million for the ramming of his vessel, the *Sea Shepherd*.

Pete managed to climb between the anti-boarding spikes and onto the side of the hull, where he then cut through the protective netting and clambered aboard. He tells a delightful story of him knocking at the locked bridge door where the crew were hiding from this one man "invasion". He was quickly detained and taken to Tokyo, where he was arrested for trespassing. He was later indicted on a number of charges, facing up to 15 years in prison and held in the maximum-security Tokyo Detention Centre for six months. In his final statement to the court, he said: *"I took action because I wanted to stop Japan's illegal whaling."* Pete was convicted of disruption of business, destruction of property, illegally boarding a vessel, assault, possession of a knife and given a two-year suspended sentence. Two days later, he was deported to New Zealand.

Pete finished his story with a wry smile: *"A man has to do what he's got to do, now let's talk about you."* I told him what I was trying achieve and it sounded really tame as compared to what Pete had done. He didn't see it that way at all; he has dedicated his life to conservation and environmental campaigns and is involved in anti-poaching and stopping wildlife smuggling. All he wanted from me was to film the journey. In his words, *"This could go down as one of the greatest conservation success stories of all time."*

I would have loved to work with Pete Bethune, I think that he would have given the story an edge which few other operators could have done. Unfortunately, we were locked in negotiations with *60 Minutes* at the time, so it came to nothing.

Gail Kelly is probably the most recognisable executive in Australian business. Born and educated in South Africa, Gail moved with her family to Australia and became CEO of Westpac Bank. In 2015, she retired from this position but remains a highly visible and popular individual.

I tried on several occasions to get Gail to be the guest speaker at various fundraisers, without success, but she regularly sent messages of support for my work with rhinos. A few years ago, I was at Pick n Pay supermarket in Hoedspruit buying supplies for a holiday at our house in Ingwelala. I was walking behind this woman who I was sure was Gail – at that time still head of Westpac – and said, "What is my bank manager doing in Hoedspruit?". She turned and laughed out loud – I'm not sure that, as CEO, she had ever been called a bank manager. It turned out she was doing the exact same thing – picking up supplies for a week in the bush. We talked rhinos for a while and then headed off to buy our biltong and boerewors.

In 2015, I was invited by Kyia Clayton to speak at the inaugural Tasmanian eco Film Fest (TeFF). TeFF is an initiative of the Tasmanian Conservation Trust, Tasmania's oldest environmental protection organisation. I was privileged to be part of an auspicious panel discussion along with Dr Richard Kirby, Plankton Scientist UK; Todd Houstein, Director of Sustainable Living in Tasmania; Chris Darwin, conservationist and great-great-grandson of Charles Darwin; Ginger Mauney, international wildlife filmmaker and board member of the Save the Rhino in Namibia; Peter McGlone, Director of Tasmanian Conservation; and David Ritter, CEO of Greenpeace Australia. It was a fascinating discussion around the topic "All roads lead to the environment". I have never seen myself as an activist, but there were certainly a few of those on this particular panel.

After the panel concluded, I was approached by Kyia who said that Rachel Ward wanted to meet and have a chat. My heart skipped a beat, I had always thought that Rachel was a marvellous actress. Rachel was at the festival supporting her and Bryan Brown's daughter Matilda, an actress, writer and filmmaker. Rachel was interested in finding out more about the rhino issue and wanted to get involved so we met in Sydney a few weeks later and she graciously agreed to become an ambassador for TARP. Rachel was a wonderful ally; she knows a vast number of people and was always willing to introduce me to potential donors, sponsors or influencers including Mark Carnegie and Erica Gregan. Rachel and Bryan also attended a rhino threat awareness dinner, hosted by JB Were in Sydney for some of their clients, and, in truth, they were the stars of the show.

I'm not sure our board ever really bought into the "ambassador" concept I created and promoted. Not once in the four years did anyone recommend anyone for the role.

I had the privilege of meeting Tony Park on a number of occasions. Tony is a prolific author and is seen by many as Wilbur Smith's natural successor – a compliment to both men. Tony is a major in the Australian Army Reserve and served six months in Afghanistan. He and his wife Nicola were active supporters of the project with Tony always donating some of his books for raffle prizes. They live an idyllic life, six months in Sydney and six months at their home in the bush bordering the Kruger Park, where Tony does most of his writing.

Professor John Shields is the Deputy Dean of the Business School and his support for me never wavered while I was at the helm of the project. If we had a problem, I'd call John and he was ever happy to help, both materially and with advice and counsel. In Dr Kristine Dery and Professor Leanne Piggott, he also identified two outstanding Business School representatives to serve on our board.

The University of Sydney Business School is one of the most prestigious in the world and to have them as a partner was a huge coup. It gave us true international credibility. After one of our events, John wrote to me: *"You do not walk alone, my friend. Yours is an utterly inspirational cause and it is a privilege to have the opportunity to be involved. I am proud of our students' contribution and proud of our association with you."* I deeply treasured this comment and quoted it on several occasions in the talks I gave.

The World Parks Congress took place in late 2014 in Sydney and I invited Dr Michael Knight to be the guest speaker at a cocktail party I planned to host during the congress. Mike has been involved in rhino conservation for the past twenty years and there are very few people who can match him in his knowledge of the highly complex rhino issues. He is a man of conviction and strong opinions and I knew that we would have an entertaining discussion.

I approached fellow director Leanne Piggott requesting that the Business School host the event at their Sydney City Campus. Leanne took it up with John and away we went. Almost sixty people accepted the invitation including some key South African decision-makers such as Thea Carroll, Director, SA DEA; Bandile Mkhize, CEO Kwa-Zulu Natal Parks; Vance Martin, President of WILD; Mvusy Songelwa, Acting CEO SANParks; Michael t'Sas-Rolfes; well-known conservation economist; and Barbara Thomson, Deputy Minister of Environment.

There was an amusing incident just before the event started. I was setting up, when one of our helpers rushed in saying that there were three South African ladies out the front who said they were leaving unless *"Mr Dearlove comes to meet us right now."* Well Mr Dearlove hightailed it out to reception and met the ladies. I'm not sure if they were hungry, thirsty or weary but I warmly welcomed them and was rescued by Maurice Mackenzie, Board Member of Kwa-Zulu Natal Parks, who charmed the three of them with his impeccable Zulu. The ladies must have been very important.

Mike gave a riveting presentation from someone right at the front-line of the war on poachers and to round things out, I had invited George Gregan and Tony Park to participate in a panel discussion, which was light and very well received. I was very proud of our association with the University of Sydney Business School. They are a world-class organisation.

THE EMOTIONAL

SUBJECT OF HUNTING

I cannot abide the hunting of wildlife. It is such a complex and divisive subject and volumes have been written on the subject so I will limit myself to a personal experience, some statistics out of the United States, a short comment on Botswana's brave but controversial stand against hunting and the ongoing debate about hunting black rhino in Namibia.

Many years ago, Margie and I travelled with a group from Johannesburg to a friend's property in what was then Rhodesia. Our visit coincided with the annual culling of wild animals on the farm. One evening, we were invited to join the Professional Hunter – known universally as the PH – on the hunt. Not quite knowing what to expect, we hopped on the Land Rover. The

PH drove with his three rifles lined up on the windscreen/bonnet alongside him. The fellow with the spotlight was on the back of the vehicle with us. The first animal we saw was a magnificent kudu bull standing on an anthill. Blinded by the spotlight, this beautiful beast did not move as the PH shot it. Only one bullet was required and this regal animal became just a lump of meat. Margie was sick on the spot.

A more recent experience took place on one of my trips to South Africa to source rhinos. I was introduced to Philip Mostert by Dave Weidner. Philip owns the Hunting Legends group of lodges. We met him at his palatial Valley of the Kings Lodge at Thabazimbi, a few hours north of Johannesburg. I have been fortunate enough to travel extensively and I can honestly say that this six-star lodge is one of the finest I have ever seen. It caters for the extremely wealthy and from all over the world they come to Hunting Legends to kill animals. Through a permit system, it is legal to hunt in South Africa and there is a strong body of opinion that says the income from hunting sustains the conservation of endangered species. What is made absolutely clear is that, if you have sufficiently deep pockets, and the licence to kill, you can hunt pretty much any animal, including the Big Five, at Hunting Legends. Mostert's clients include President Trump's sons Eric and Don as well as actor Tom Selleck.

Philip Mostert is a charming man and a gracious host and knowing that my interest was anti-poaching, not hunting, he related an interesting story. At another of his lodges most of the hunting was for so-called plains game, mainly antelope or zebra. Almost without exception, the hunters, be they American or from the Middle East, only wanted the "trophies" – the head and/or horns and also possibly the hide of the animals. The hunters were always asked if they wanted the meat and the answer was almost always no.

There are four primary schools on the boundaries of the lodge and all of the pupils are from the lowest socio-economic groups. There is high unemployment and significant poverty. Mostert had established a small meat processing plant at the lodge and his staff vacuum packed the meat into two-kilogram packs. Once a week they delivered the packs to the schools. The principal of the school had two options, he could either sell the packs to the parents for a nominal R20 ($2) so that the proceeds flowed back to the school or the school conducted a weekly braai (barbecue) so that the children got at least one substantial meal a week.

Said Mostert, *"And you know Ray, as a result of giving them the meat, we have not had one poaching incident at the game farm for three years. As soon as a stranger, who could be a poacher, appears in town, the locals inform the authorities."* Simple but effective. Give the surrounding communities an interest in the enterprise and everything changes.

In 2014, Botswana President Ian Khama took the courageous but contentious decision to ban all hunting in his country. The ban covered all species. He justified the ban by stating ecotourism had become increasingly important for Botswana and contributed more than 12 per cent of the overall GDP. Furthermore, he said that hunting had fuelled poaching and the resulting "catastrophic" declines in wildlife, while preventing sustained growth in the tourism industry.

In 2011, Dr Mike Chase of Elephants Without Borders had released results from aerial surveys over the Okavango Delta that demonstrated that the populations of certain species had been decimated by hunting and poaching over the previous decade. The research found that eleven species had declined by 61 per cent since the 1996 survey. As an example, Dr Chase said, "*The numbers of wildebeest have fallen below the minimum of 500 breeding pairs to be sustainable. They are on the verge of local extinction.*"

Botswana's visionary policy choices are an example to other African countries that depend on revenue from ecotourism, but the law changes have been strongly opposed by conservation groups in Botswana, which argue that hunting quotas issued to local communities near wildlife management areas are a heritage right and actually empower these villages. There is no doubt that wildlife hunting has a role to play in local economies and in the funding of private conservation efforts.

This move by Botswana will no doubt garner a strong reaction from hunters. Professional hunters and their clients will simply go elsewhere, and that means focusing on the last remaining unprotected wilderness areas in Africa such as Tanzania, Mozambique, and Zambia. North and West Africa have no wildlife to speak of anymore, while South Africa is saturated with game farms to meet demand for hunting. Sport and trophy hunting have no doubt played a significant role in the decimation of African wildlife populations, but wars, famine, fire and land conversion have killed even more wildlife and represent more of an extinction threat than modern-day trophy hunting. Times are changing and the wilderness areas are becoming exponentially smaller every year. In South Africa, most hunting happens on private game farms which add value to wildlife, trade in the best stock, and manage the farms for maximum productivity. Game farms now protect millions of hectares of land in South Africa and hunting drives the rural economies.

Recently, Tshekedi Khama, Botswana's Minister of Natural Resources and Environment, and brother of the president, said that his country is under unprecedented pressure from the pro-hunting lobby in the European Union and regional neighbours to lift the hunting ban. He accused neighbours of failing to fulfil their obligations in the development of the Kavango–Zambezi Trans-Frontier Park, which is a regional initiative created to promote the free cross-border movement and conservation of wildlife. He attributed the influx of elephants into Botswana from Zimbabwe, Zambia, Namibia and Angola to a failure by those countries to provide basic water and security infrastructure for the animals.

Hunting is not a cheap pastime. Apart from all of the logistics of travel, accommodation, the cost of weapons, ammunition and the like, according to a recent report compiled by the US Democrats Natural Resources Committee, the costs of Big Five "scalps" was as follows:

- Lion – up to $50,000
- Elephant – up to $60,000
- White rhino – $125,000+
- Leopard – up to $35,000
- Buffalo – up to $17,000

Clearly cost is not a consideration for the hunters.

In January 2014, all hell broke loose in the media when it was revealed that a licence to shoot a black rhino in Namibia had been bought by an American hunter for $390,000 at an auction run by the Dallas Safari Club (DSC). The animal rights movement jumped all over the announcement, denouncing it as "immoral".

The licence permitted the killing of a single, post-breeding bull, with Namibian wildlife officials on hand to make sure an appropriate animal was selected – the Namibian Government officials fully supported the auction. The hunt would help in managing the rhino population and provide an underfunded Namibian government with hard cash in the expensive battle to thwart poachers. Each year, the government allows for a few, carefully regulated hunts under internationally approved guidelines with proceeds going to fund conservation.

I read the articles with mixed emotions. I detest hunting, but I also understand that countries like Namibia, with a sparse population of 2.5 million living in an area of 820,000 square kilometres, do not have the resources to protect their wildlife against the international crime syndicates.

The DSC was being hammered in the global media and I saw an opportunity by trying to contact Ben Carter, Executive Director of the DSC, who was also getting plenty of stick. The internet is a wonderful thing, but do you know how many Ben Carters there are in Dallas, let alone the US? I persisted and after several false starts, I finally got through to a Dallas number. The conversation went something like this:

"Hello."

"Is this Ben Carter?"

"Who wants to know?" Clearly Ben had been receiving a number of unwanted calls.

I explained who I was and why I was calling. He then said, *"How the hell did you find me? What do you want from me?"*

As gently as I could, I put it to him that he and the DSC clearly had a worldwide major image problem. He reluctantly agreed. We, the Australian Rhino Project, also had a problem – we had no money. I suggested that, if the DSC were to donate to a conservation project such as ours, the world might see them in a different light, certainly in a more positive light. There was silence. I thought, he hasn't put the phone down. Maybe, just maybe, I have a chance.

This was right at the beginning of our journey; we literally had no money at all. No sponsors in sight, and I really believed this could be a win/win – their reputation, our finances.

Ben wanted to make sure that I knew exactly what had actually happened and that he was very upset at the way the media and animal rights had interpreted and reported the auction. The Namibian Minister for the Environment had been in the room in support of the auction and, if it had not been for the negative publicity, the auction could have yielded up to US$1 million. *"Imagine what a difference 13 million Namibian dollars could have made to conservation in that country."* He was bewildered that his critics could not see it that way. He honestly believed he was assisting a poor country to fight off, at least for a while, the international crime syndicates decimating the country's wildlife.

After a lengthy pause, Ben said he thought my suggestion had merit and asked me to drop him a line detailing what I was proposing.

To his credit, he moved quickly and by mid-March, he had approved a donation of US$5,000, with a commitment of more to come. I was elated.

And then came the bad news. With some excitement, I raised this donation at the next board meeting, hoping for at least a muted cheer, only for Simon Duffy to vehemently oppose the proposal saying that they could not support anything to do with the DSC or the hunting of the black rhino.

The call to Ben Carter declining the donation was excruciatingly difficult.

Adam Cruise wrote an excellent article for the Nikela website, about the Safari Club International (SCI), America's most powerful hunting group's plans to auction 280 African animals to raise funds to lobby the Trump Administration *against* measures protecting threatened species such as the Big Five. In the auction, American hunters would be offered the chance to kill all of South Africa's iconic species. Successful bidders would be able to shoot giraffe, hippo, zebra, baboon, wildebeest, sable antelope, warthog, kudu, impala, springbok, blesbok, caracal, African wildcat, with 119 other animals proffered as "upgrades" for an additional cost. And the Big Five. The hunts were valued at US$1 million and all profits from the trophy hunts would go solely towards funding SCI to lobby the US government towards a pro-hunting stance. The group hoped to wield considerable influence on the Trump administration. It is estimated that there are approximately fourteen million hunters in the US.

As part of the online auction, there were two hunts valued at US$16,500 each that offered hunting wildlife with dogs, a controversial practice known as "hounding", where an animal is chased until exhausted, trapped, and easily shot.

Am I missing something? These people were planning to kill animals, many of which were endangered, 17,000 kilometres away from their cosy homes and offices to further their political ambitions? A bloody disgrace.

SCI also promotes prestigious awards for its members, one of which is the African Big Five Grand Slam, where the hunter has to kill an elephant, a rhino, a lion, a leopard and a buffalo while the African 29 award requires a minimum of 29 African wildlife kills.

Finally, there is an extremely wealthy fellow in the US, his name is Jimmy John Liautaud, who made his money through Jimmy John's Sandwich chain. He counts amongst his trophies an elephant, a rhino, a brown bear and a leopard.

Why would a man who has everything choose to shoot elephants and rhinos? Maybe because he can. A part of me wanted the elephant to wake and stick his tusk where the sun doesn't shine.

The death of Cecil the lion at the hands of American dentist Walter Palmer in 2015 sparked worldwide outrage and just two years later, one of Cecil's cubs was shot dead by a yet another big-game trophy hunter. The six-year-old lion named Xanda, who was in his prime, was killed just outside the Hwange National Park in north-west Zimbabwe, not far from where Cecil was killed. He was wearing an electronic collar, fitted to monitor his movements.

Of course hunting is not solely to blame for the world's wildlife crisis. Poaching and human encroachment do more damage but, given such catastrophic levels of biological collapse, can the world really permit rich men and women to kill iconic wild animals and deplete the gene pool for what they see as sport?

THE ELEPHANTS AND THE LIONS
(AND GIRAFFE AND HIPPOS)

Consider this: If there was no demand for rhino horn, tiger bones, pangolin scales and ivory, the poaching would stop. The three components of the extinction crisis are demand, greed and corruption. At the heart of this crisis, which is driving more and more animals, birds and reptiles to extinction, is the mighty dollar or yuan or whatever currency you use. The annual wildlife trade is estimated at US$23 billion. Putting it bluntly, all demand roads lead to Asia, more specifically China and the Southeast Asian countries of Laos, Vietnam, Cambodia and Thailand – with a total population of 1.6 billion people, or 20 per cent of the global population. In many of these countries there has been a rapid increase in standards of living and the consumption of many of these products is associated with increased wealth. At $65,000 per kilo using rhino horn is an expensive pastime. There is no demand of note for these products in Japan, Korea, India or Indonesia, or the West.

A five-kilo rhino horn can fetch about $300,000 on the black market. (Photo credit: Brent Stirton, Getty Images)

Ivory trafficking has largely flown beneath the radar in South Africa yet customs officials have seized more than 1,000 kilograms of ivory destined for Asia in the last five years. The seizures are the tip of an iceberg of what likely has slipped through unchecked. As confirmed by the WWF, tens of thousands of African elephants are killed every year for their ivory tusks. The ivory is often carved into ornaments and jewellery – China is the biggest consumer market for such products. The rapid growth of human population and the extension of agriculture into rangelands and forests formerly considered unsuitable for farming mean that elephant habitat is continuing to be lost. It is the age-old humans versus wildlife conflict.

An example of what was once a strong elephant population is the Niassa Reserve in Mozambique, where elephants are now at risk of extinction. The reserve covers a total area of 42,300 square kilometres, twice the size of the Kruger National Park. In 2009, there were 20,118 elephants in the reserve, but by 2016 there were only 3,675 left. In seven years, 16,360 elephants were killed in the largest concentration of conserved animals in Mozambique.

Vietnam has been listed by CITES as being of "primary concern" both as a source and transit country for illegal ivory. Vietnam has been implicated in over 42,000 kilograms of seized ivory since 2005; crudely put, this equates to about 1,000 elephants. A public hearing in The Hague recently revealed that 579 products of rhino horn, 220 tiger parts, and almost 1,000 pieces of ivory were sold openly in just one small village in Vietnam. Vietnamese nationals are the most commonly arrested Asian nationals related to wildlife trafficking in Mozambique and South Africa, while Laos has been one of the worst offenders in the context of ivory and everything else for more than a decade. Laos shares a border with Vietnam and has been subject to several CITES non-compliance processes, but little decisive action from CITES, beyond veiled threats of a wildlife trade ban, has so far occurred. At least eleven tonnes of ivory with links to Laos have been seized globally since

2010. Eleven tonnes is a lot of elephants. Laos is now the fastest growing ivory market in the world, according to an investigation by Kenya-based group Save the Elephants. Investigators visited a Chinese casino resort on the Mekong River and described a hub of gambling and prostitution, where ivory sales are booming among Chinese visitors who make up more than 80 percent of sales. The researchers found dozens of shops openly selling thousands of items: carved tusks, ivory bangles, pendants and bracelets. The prices are cheaper in Laos than on the Chinese mainland, and law and order is lacking, meaning the illegal cross-border trade is not policed. International criminal syndicates are involved, which encourages, and is encouraged by, corruption across Africa.

A WWF Living Planet report, first published in 2014, states that Earth has lost 50 per cent of its wildlife in the past forty years. Some examples quoted include 90 per cent of lions, 60 per cent of forest elephants and 95 per cent of leatherback turtles. Said Anthony Barnosky, Executive Director, Jasper Ridge Biological Preserve at Stanford University: *"When you realise that we've wiped out 50 per cent of the Earth's wildlife in the last 40 years, if we keep cutting by half every 40 years, pretty soon there's going to be nothing left."*

Entire populations of plants and animals are crashing, even if they're not yet on the brink of extinction. An example is the African elephant which could be extinct in the wild by 2040 – an unbearable thought.

In a recent interview with the former UN climate chief Christiana Figueres, Sir David Attenborough was asked about the world his great-grandchildren will live in. He said: *"I don't spend time thinking about that because I can't bear it."*

There is little disagreement among scientists that humans are driving an unprecedented ecological crisis. And the causes are well known. People are burning fossil fuels and they're chopping down forests and other habitat for agriculture. The global population of people continues to rise, along with the thirst for land and consumption. Poachers are driving numbers of elephants, pangolins, rhinos, giraffes and other creatures with body parts valuable on the black market to worryingly low levels.

If I hadn't started the campaign for rhinos, I would have tried to shine the spotlight on the crisis that elephants are facing. I have been visiting game parks for more than sixty years, and my heart still lifts when I see elephants. Their family structures are so like ours – they can be loving, they can be caring, they can be angry, they discipline their young ones and the females do not put up with any nonsense from the males. I can and do watch them for hours.

The slaughter of these innocent animals is heartbreaking. Fifty years ago, there were 2.5 million elephants in the wild, now there are less than 300,000.

The South African authorities have some very odd practices. Firstly, there was a clampdown on rhino poaching statistics, now the same is happening with information on elephant poaching, with SANParks refusing to provide statistics on a regular basis of how many elephants have been poached in the Kruger Park. The problem with this approach is that everyone then makes up their own numbers. There is worldwide sympathy for the plight of rhino and elephants, and while some argue that the South African government should do more to stop the poaching, there is universal support for any and all action that is taken against the poachers.

Available statistics show that 24 elephants were poached in

South Africa in 2015. This doubled in 2016 while 2018 numbers exceed 100. The latest figures are the highest recorded in decades. Dr Michelle Henley, CEO of the Elephants Alive research group, said that she was deeply concerned about the apparent refusal to release statistics on elephant poaching. *"I can't see that releasing the number of poaching deaths will put elephants in jeopardy and I think it is important for the public to realise that ivory poaching in Africa is moving southwards. I don't think it's a good thing that these figures are not released."*

I don't think that any "normal" human being can fathom the depths of cruelty that poachers will plumb when it comes to killing their quarry. The world was shocked when poachers in Zimbabwe killed more than 300 elephants and countless other animals by seeping cyanide into waterholes and salt licks. Photos revealed horrific scenes. From the air, Hwange National Park could be seen to be littered with the deflated corpses of elephants, often with their young calves dead beside them, tusks ripped out. There is deep concern that the use of cyanide represents a new and particularly damaging weapon in the already soaring poaching trade. After the elephants died, often collapsing just a few yards from the water, lions, hyenas and vultures which fed on their carcasses were also struck down, as were other animals such as kudu and buffalo that shared the same waterholes. The circle of life. Or death.

Zimbabwe's authorities say the cyanide had been planted by villagers who sell the elephants' tusks for around US$400 each to cross-border traders. They can be resold in South Africa for up to US$15,000 a pair, often re-emerging as carved artefacts such as bangles in Cape Town's craft markets. Ivory is highly prized as a "white gold" in Asian countries where a growing middle class is seeking safe investments.

In another hotspot, Luanda in Angola, more than 10,000 trinkets made from illegally poached elephant ivory are on sale as souvenirs. Researchers found twenty stalls covered with ivory beads, bangles, necklaces and name-stamps at the market. Once again, China is involved. The traders catered almost exclusively to Chinese expatriates who numbered at least 260,000 in the 2017 census, compared with fewer than 500 in 2002. In a repeat of the early 1900s, another "Scramble for Africa", this time spearheaded by China.

In 2016, the Kenyan authorities held a huge bonfire of all the elephant tusks they had collected from poachers and also those from elephants that died a natural death. The fire received global publicity, and was hailed as one of the most momentous events in the battle against poaching. In my view, it was largely symbolic and certainly has not stopped the poaching.

Only a third of Chinese polled by WildAid knew that ivory might have come from poached elephants. Many believed that tusks simply fell out like baby teeth, or that they grew back after being cut off without harming the animals. As consumer attitudes changed, so did the policies of key governments. The US and China jointly pledged to close their domestic ivory markets. China began a phased process of closing all carving factories and retail stores by the end of 2018 and, in February 2018, Hong Kong politicians decided to ban the sale of ivory. The ban would be implemented in steps, with all sales prohibited from 2021 onwards. But it's like squeezing a balloon: affluent Chinese will continue to buy ivory from countries like Laos and Vietnam, where laws are less strict.

The good news is that since the announcement of China's ban, prices have dropped sharply with a March 2017 report finding that the wholesale price of ivory tusks had fallen by 65 per cent to $730 per kilogram on the mainland. The combination of better elephant protection on the ground, stiffer penalties, improved law enforcement efforts, and reduced demand has made the illegal ivory trade riskier and less profitable. But as long as consumers are willing to buy ivory, whether the trade is legal or illegal, elephants will be killed to meet that demand. In places of weak governance and low economic development, illicit returns from poaching and trafficking will continue to outweigh the risks. And the killing continues at the dizzying pace of about 30,000 elephants a year.

And what about lions – the so-called kings of the jungle? In a fair fight I would back a lion every time, but the hunters and poachers never ever engage in a fair fight. In just twenty-one years Africa has lost 42 per cent of its wild lions. It is estimated that in 1960 there were 500,000 lions in the wild, today there are between 20,000 and 23,000. A reduction of well over 400,000 in just fifty years. From CITES records, lion trophies were exported from South Africa to Laos for the first time in 2009, even though there were no records of Laotian clients ever having hunted lions in South Africa. Laos now dominates the lion bone export market. They are sold as tiger bones, which have become rare in Asia thanks to the demand for wild tiger products.

Following a study, the National Geographic's Big Cats Initiative found that almost 700 lion trophies were legally exported from Zimbabwe between 2001 and 2012, and yet the wild population was estimated at only 850. This suggests that, at the current rate and if lion numbers don't increase, in another decade trophy hunters alone will have wiped out nearly all remaining lions in Zimbabwe. Certain South African canned hunting operators sell lion bones, generally disregarded by trophy hunters, to Laotian importers for US$1,500 per skeleton. After arrival in Laos, the bones are illegally transported to Vietnam. There they are boiled down, compacted into a cake bar and sold at a price of around US$1,000 to consumers who add it to rice wine. Such wine is traditionally consumed in Asia for its perceived enhancement of virility and strength.

In 2017, the tracks of three poachers were detected in the Limpopo National Park in Mozambique. Rangers followed the tracks as it became clear that the poachers were tracking a lion. The rangers found a camp and nearby snare line with bait laced with poison to attract lion. Unfortunately, the poachers beat the rangers to it and the carcasses of three lions and one hyena were discovered. It was strongly suspected that the lion carcass and bait were poisoned with Temic, a substance more lethal than arsenic.

Peter Leitner from Peace Parks Foundation, voiced his concern: *"It is clear that there is a definite escalation in poaching lions for the lion bone trade. This is simply a diversification of business of the wildlife crime syndicates that are uncovering another lucrative trade. Lion are as threatened as rhino, with current worldwide estimates indicating that there are only 20,000 wild lions remaining."*

This ongoing Asian demand for lion bones led to another horrific wildlife poisoning just inside the Mozambican border from the Kruger Park, where a research team came across the carcasses of two nyala, a warthog and an impala laced with what they describe as a black granular poison. Lying nearby were two lions, 51 vultures, three fish eagles, a yellow-billed kite and a giant eagle owl. Hold onto your hats, folks. The lions had been dismembered, their bones removed, and 22 vultures had been decapitated, their heads presumably to be used for Muthi. All the lion bones had been removed and meat had been cut into strips, dried and mostly removed. What possesses a human being to do that?

And it doesn't end there. Hippos too are under threat as are pangolins and turtles. Hippo teeth contain ivory, and carvings made from the teeth are cheaper than elephant ivory. Hippos are described as vulnerable on the IUCN's list of threatened species, which estimates the global population is between 115,000 and 130,000, and that their conservation should be a "priority" in countries where they exist. According to experts, hippo populations are threatened by poaching, disease, loss of habitat, deforestation, and pollution. They are hunted by poachers who export their long canine teeth from African countries to places such as Hong Kong and the US, where they serve as substitutes for elephant tusks. The hippo's teeth may grow as long as 50 centimetres and the significant decline in hippo population has brought to light the trade in hippo teeth. An article published in the *African Journal of Ecology* states that since 1975, Hong Kong has processed 90 per cent of the 770,000 kilograms of hippo teeth that have been traded internationally, representing more than 150,000 hippos. Tanzania and Uganda stand out as jointly providing 75 per cent of hippo ivory into Hong Kong.

The IUCN predicts that over the next 30 years the hippo population will decrease by 30 per cent and at that rate, hippos could be extinct within the next 100 years. One hundred years, you say, oh well, that's not really a problem. Well, actually, it is. It means that your grandchildren will likely only see hippos in a zoo.

Hippo teeth products for sale in an ivory shop in Hong Kong. (Photo credit: Alexandra Andersson/HKU)

With attention fixated on elephants, rhinos and gorillas, there was widespread shock across Africa, as populations of the world's tallest mammals quietly, yet sharply, declined. Giraffe numbers across the continent fell 40 per cent between 1985 and 2015, to just under 100,000 animals, and they are now also vulnerable to extinction. The giraffes are hunted for their tails; apparently some African men use the tail as a dowry to the bride's father while the long black hairs are often turned into fly whisks.

When will this slaughter end? Sadly, CITES seems to have become a regulatory body with no teeth. Hopefully, the next CITES convention will demonstrate that the organisation has a backbone.

THE BEGINNING OF THE END?

After about a year or so into the project, Allan recommended appointing me as CEO. From inception, I had not been paid a cent and I was quite fine with that since, in many ways, this was "my" cause and I would do whatever was necessary to make it succeed. At the launch breakfast, he had compared me with Campbell "Can Do" Newman, the then Premier of Queensland. *"No challenge is too great for Ray,"* he said.

I thought his CEO proposal was reasonable and after considerable discussion, Allan referred the matter to a recruitment agency. They responded saying that they thought an annual salary of $200,000 was appropriate. Allan and I agreed this was way too high and I suggested $120,000 per annum. My reasoning was very simple: I was doing this work because I believed in it and wanted it to succeed. I was also very conscious of the fact that every cent spent would need to be raised through donations. Allan subsequently took the proposal to the board, saying that finding a CEO with my "knowledge, commitment and dynamism" would be very difficult. Everyone agreed that once we had received the tax deductibility status, I should be appointed to the CEO role. I was thrilled with this, as was my family, who were the only ones who knew the amount of time I had been devoting to this project. This was in December 2014.

Around May of the following year, I underwent what was supposed to be fairly routine surgery but got an infection and also a pulmonary embolism. I was not in good shape and once I had recovered, I sat down with Allan and suggested that he take on the role of chairman, since I just could not do the job of chairman and also that of a CEO (even an unpaid one!). Pod contributed strongly to the new structure and it was soon implemented.

Inexplicably, this was the last mention of me (or anyone else) becoming CEO. We secured the DGR tax deductibility status but not a word was said. There were occasional murmurings that we really needed a CEO – and Pod pushed hard on this, not out of sympathy for me, but because he believed it. But it all came to nothing and in my almost four years on the project, only two people were paid for their time: Sarah Dennis and Shaun Aisen.

I raised the issue a couple of times but to no avail. To this day, I have not been able to fathom why there was resistance to me being paid any form of compensation since everyone knew I was working at least twelve hours a day, every day. Because of the time zones, when Australia closed for business, South Africa opened for business. How did they know? He knew because people like Pod told them.

I would regularly represent our organisation at not-for-profit meetings and look around at these CEOs and managing directors with more than a little degree of envy, and also embarrassment, knowing that I was the only tosser in the room who was not being rewarded for my efforts.

There was another strange intervention when, in June, I called Allan to brief him about a contentious article in *Nature* magazine that had some implications for us. Once I finished, he asked me if I had spoken to Susan Hunt, the CEO of WAZA. I said yes and that, at her request, I had arranged for her to meet Adam McCarthy, Australian High Commissioner to South Africa during her upcoming visit to that country and Susan had said that we should have a chat when she got back. I asked him why the question. He said he had had a call from Taronga saying that I had told Susan that AUSDAFF was being unreasonable. Biting my lip, I said that was incorrect and I had simply given her an update of the situation. Mischief was in the air.

Shaun Aisen was engaged at the beginning of 2016; Shaun's speciality is the transportation of animals and other cargo and he refers to himself as an aviation consultant. He has a very successful track record in this field and his TARP responsibilities were project management, strategic planning, ground handling operations, regulatory planning and support, load control, and planning air and ground logistics support for the transfer of rhino shipments from South Africa to Australia. All very straightforward and we agreed that his expertise would be useful when the time came to move the animals. The problem was that we still did not have the approval to import the animals, so why hire him at this particular point in time? As per his job responsibilities there was no need to do anything now, so why not hold him in reserve?

I was asked to brief Shaun, which I did to the best of my ability. It is not easy to condense three years of work into a few conversations; this was no ordinary move, it was complicated and, with so many disparate stakeholders and moving parts, it was highly sensitive.

In terms of the rhinos, the South Africans had provided all of the information requested by AUSDAFF. Allan Sheridan's crusade to find a TB issue had been soundly knocked on the head by Roy Bengis's research and there were now detailed discussions about AUSDAFF visiting South Africa to inspect the quarantine facilities. So much so that in late March 2016, in response to my questions, Jonathan Taylor wrote that they would arrange the visit and pay for all their expenses and would likely be ready to travel mid-year. While I was really excited about this "plan", I was becoming sufficiently hardened to realise that my urgency was not matched by many others. Nevertheless, it was progress.

Around this time, AUSDAFF started asking detailed questions about the South African quarantine facility and I happily arranged for photographs, including aerial shots, to be provided. Clearly, I wasn't the only one becoming frustrated by AUSDAFF's lethargy, since Roy Bengis wrote to me after seeing the aerial photos, "*I certainly hope that this aerial photo plus the ground level structural photos will go a long way in setting the Australian authorities' minds at rest. This is a professional quarantine facility, not a backyard holding pen.*"

Our progress with AUSDAFF was like a game of snakes and ladders; a general upwards trajectory with some major falls along the way. Off my own bat, I arranged for a meeting in April in

Canberra with all of the main government players to introduce Shaun. At my invitation, we had a full house with representatives of the departments of Foreign Affairs, Environment and Agriculture attending. At the time I reflected that we had done a very good job in building awareness and relationships with all of the Australian government stakeholders. It was a good meeting and as I reported back to the board, AUSDAFF seemed particularly pleased with the combined technical expertise of Dr Andrea Reiss, Nick Boyle and Shaun.

At this meeting, it became obvious that AUSDAFF had decided to focus their attention on the South African quarantine facility, and Jonathan Taylor requested TARP to provide "standard operating procedures" (SOP's) from Dr Charles van Niekerk's wildlife export quarantine facility for their assessment. I shuddered when I heard this, and what a saga it turned out to be.

When I phoned Charles to tell him about the latest request, he burst into laughter reminding me that I had visited him several times and I was familiar with his operation; that it was only a junior vet and himself who did all the animal work and his partner Martin, who ran the workshop building the crates for transporting the animals. The rest of the people working at the facility were bussed in each morning and bussed out each evening – for security purposes. "*They are labourers, Ray, all of them illiterate. We don't have a standard operating procedure; every shipment is different. We have no need for bloody standard operating procedures which are going to sit on a shelf, gathering dust. Jeez Ray, you should know better.*"

Charles is a taciturn person at the best of times. This was a long speech for him. He is also a very polite man and this request obviously got under his skin and who could blame him, but he undertook to see what he could do and, soon after, he sent through some documentation. I passed it on to Shaun for AUSDAFF, which had now been renamed the Department of Agriculture and Water Resources (DAWR). The documentation was deemed unacceptable by DAWR and after I had tried unsuccessfully to source examples of SOPs from various organisations, Shaun said he would personally draft a set of SOPs. I was impressed – this was really adding value.

A few weeks later, Shaun sent through his version of the SOPs, which I reviewed very carefully in the context of know-ing Charles' operations (and maybe learning something). The documents were all over the place. Shaun had cut and pasted documentation that he'd previously used for the importation of racehorses into Australia. The documents were full of references to horses, not rhinos. It was a sloppy piece of work but after much time-wasting and exchanging versions, DAWR finally accepted our submission.

As each day went by, I became more and more concerned. Shaun had little knowledge of what we had done in the previous three years and he was seriously out of his depth when discussing our requirements with the seasoned professionals from DAWR. Another example of this came up in October 2016 when he breathlessly, almost triumphantly, brought the news from Allan Sheridan at DAWR that *"rhinos recently sent from South Africa to the US West Coast had tested positive for TB."*

Clearly Shaun did not know enough about the issue to ask any probing questions at the time, instead he threw the hand gre-nade into the laps of the directors. Every way that I looked at this "news" (this was before Donald Trump's "fake news" became part of the vernacular), it was a major issue. If this was true, we now had serious problems in terms of importing rhinos from South Africa. If it was indeed fake news, we also had a problem, in that DAWR would have yet another reason to delay matters whilst this was investigated.

I immediately contacted Charles van Niekerk and Roy Bengis and asked if they had any knowledge of this story. Roy clearly understood the serious implications and he responded overnight saying that he had called two wildlife TB specialists, one of whom had just returned from a wildlife vet congress in the US, and neither knew of any TB diagnosed in rhino going to the US, commenting that this would have been headline news. Charles responded in a similar vein saying that he was not aware of such a case and that he had spoken with the US the previous day.

I went back to Shaun with their comments stressing that this was a very serious matter, saying that if true, we needed to get the details: where the animals were quarantined, where the TB was "found", and, if not true, we needed to knock it on the head as soon as possible. This was a major issue for rhino conservation, not only in Australia but the whole world.

That same day, Charles forwarded me a note from San Diego Zoo, the supposed destination of the infected rhino, which confirmed there was absolutely no truth to this story. Charles commented, *"Please get to the bottom of this . . . potentially it has very, very serious implications for us and your project. If it is an unsubstantiated rumour, we also need to deal with it and smother it before it gets out of hand."*

I wrote to my fellow directors, referring to Charles's comments and said they exactly matched my concerns and that Shaun needed to rapidly establish the source and veracity of this bombshell. I pointed out that the major exporter of rhino from South Africa, the acknowledged expert of rhinos in South Africa and the biggest importer of rhinos into the US West Coast all knew nothing about this story.

A separate note from Roy said, "*I would be interested to know the Australian source, as they seemed pretty certain about their facts quoting an "event". Ray, I feel that you need to act on this quite strongly on your side as it has a direct bearing on our credibility, the currency of our knowledge, how seriously we take a threat like TB, as well as how we react to information of this nature.*"

At this point, I was asked by the board to immediately truncate the discussion with South Africa about TB and the only issue was that we needed to get further information from DAWR before "*more rabbits are sent down burrows*" and that Shaun would deal with it "*in good time*".

This was a huge dilemma for me. Much was at stake. I understood the potential international ramifications of the reported TB in a South African-sourced rhino. Rhinos were being moved all over South Africa and to international destinations such as the US and Botswana. All to keep them safe. If the report about TB was correct, this relocation of rhinos would stop. Immediately. Seasoned veterinarians such as Roy Bengis and Charles van Niekerk are not alarmists, their concerns were firmly based. This was a potential catastrophe for the rhinos. My fellow directors and Shaun Aisen clearly did not understand the gravity and the immediacy of this "story" and seemed reluctant to engage or challenge DAWR.

Messages continued to come in from South Africa, indicating how serious an issue this actually was. Roy wrote, *"I cannot understand how the Australian authorities can quote and use such unsubstantiated hearsay in their import risk evaluation."*

Roy, being the consummate professional that he is, also checked the situation with Dr Jyotika Rajput from the South African DAFF. She came back with a categorical "no" regarding this mystery infected rhino.

I reported back to Allan, who simply told Charles that I was no longer involved and that Shaun would now be his main and only contact with TARP for logistics issues and rhino sourcing. As I swallowed my pride, I asked myself, why? This was a major issue and it was being swept under the carpet, but in truth I had to admit Shaun was the nominated logistics guy so perhaps that made sense.

By now, I was pretty sure that my time with TARP was fast coming to an end. In the eyes of the board, my knowledge, experiences and relationships counted for very little. I was hurt and I was angry. It was becoming clear to me that I was seen as an obstacle. I had spent the past three years working every day towards getting rhinos to Australia. During this time, I had built strong relationships with many entities and people. I had pressed and tried to respond to every question openly and timeously to the point of being congratulated by AUSDAFF for working to the protocols. I had an excellent relationship with the Australian High Commissioner to South Africa and had letters of support from the South African High Commissioner to Australia as well as politicians Barnaby Joyce, Greg Hunt, Mark Speakman, Troy Grant and Kevin Humphries. In terms of ZAA, I had an excellent relationship with Susan Hunt – CEO of Perth Zoo and now President of WAZA. I had solid relationships with all of the key South African stakeholders and had also briefed the South Africa Minister for the Environment, the late Edna Molewa.

I gave Allan a call and told him I was really disappointed that I was no longer in the team but, more importantly, that Shaun now had full responsibility for the execution of the project. As an aviation consultant, I had no doubt that he was good at his job, but now he had effectively been charged with the most important aspect of the project and that was getting the final approval of the Australian government. I pointed out that, in fairness, Shaun could not possibly know what had been achieved to get us to this point but, as I saw it, he was working with no real knowledge of the history of the project, much of which was critical to the project's success. I named several recent examples: confirmation that AUSDAFF would pay their own way to South Africa – this was not new news; it had been agreed with Dr Andrew Cupit a year ago. Then there was the sudden introduction of Dr Pete Rogers on the South African side despite us having an existing relationship with Dr Roy Bengis, one of the most highly regarded wildlife vets in the world. Another example was the rhino database – Rhodis – which was managed by Dr Cindy Harper in South Africa. In my discussions with Cindy she had advised that it is still very much a work in progress. It certainly did not hold information of every rhino in SA, an impossible task, but it seemed to be built up into something it wasn't by Shaun.

With regard to the Desilets rhinos, I said that we had not had an outright no from David and, as such, we should be moving ahead on the basis that we would still get them.

I said that we all wanted this project to proceed and proceed as fast as possible. A month earlier, Jonathan Taylor had given us a tentative date of "end of June/beginning of July" for visiting the quarantine facility in SA. Since then I hadn't seen an update and asked if there had been one. We could all live with this date, but it needed to be revised or firmed up. AUSDAFF had had the South African response since late December and done nothing (visible) with it.

I concluded by saying that we didn't need to be told all the reasons why our plan couldn't work – we had enough of those. I suggested that Shaun needed assistance to shortcut any potential issues and again offered to help him, otherwise any date offered by DAWR could well become a self-fulfilling prophecy.

By this time my family was asking me what the point was in continuing – I could never win. They were spot on.

In early November 2016 Shaun reported back from the most recent meeting with Allan Sheridan and Jonathan Taylor. The preamble of his feedback was laced with woolly, feel-good comments about how much Sheridan and Taylor supported the project and were committed to its success referring to it as a "noble cause". Then came the bad news. DAWR had told Shaun that they were resource constrained and they needed specific details and timelines if they were to continue their support for The Australian Rhino Project. Their primary issue was that South Africa was not approved as an exporting nation of rhino to Australia. I sat there speechless. Delivered as "new" information, we had known this from day one and had worked tirelessly with AUSDAFF/DAWR to resolve this matter.

Specifically, DAWR required exact detail about the rhinos that were to be imported. Again, this was no surprise, but what came as a shock was that they now required precise information about the previous five years, or years since birth, for each rhino. This had now become an absolute precondition of issuing any import permits for our rhinos. Five years! Before Allan Sheridan became involved, it was one year. What must be borne in mind is that the rhinos would almost certainly be wild caught so their "wild" history was unknown. I was further convinced that DAWR were stringing us along and I began to question whether they really had any intention at all of permitting rhinos entering Australia from South Africa.

For no given reason, DAWR was also highly critical of Charles' quarantine facility. Shaun then said that DAWR would also now need to consult with the South African Government to see that our plan had enough substance to allay any concerns they may have.

I tried to stay calm – I had spent months in conversation with the Australian DFAT and with the Australian High Commission in Pretoria gaining their confidence and agreement to our plan. In turn, the High Commissioner had several meetings with senior South African government officials for them to satisfy themselves and the Australian government that our plan was acceptable to the South African government and that there would be no impediments to the export.

Finally, Shaun advised that DAWR required all this information be provided by us not later than January 31, 2017 – two months away, even though Australia "closes down" for summer holidays from mid-December to the end of January.

Then came the kicker. Shaun delivered a speech as to why we would be much better off importing the rhinos from a third country, saying that the US and South Africa had existing protocols for the exportation and importation of rhino and that, in turn, Australia and the US had existing protocols for the importation of rhino. And that the rhino only had to be in the US for twelve months, and, and, and . . . I just stared at Shaun. We had been down this path two years before and discarded it as a non-viable option.

Shaun finished with the startling recommendation that the third country solution should be adopted and said that in his view, it would be the end of 2017 before we would see rhinos in Australia if we went for the direct option. (Being just a year away, I would have been delighted with that result.)

My head was spinning. Assuming we found a willing organisation/individual to take the rhinos into the US or New Zealand within the next three months, we would need to buy the rhinos, establish their whereabouts for the previous five years, quarantine them in South Africa, transport them to the US or New Zealand destination where they would need to be quarantined, be fed and kept safe and healthy. For a year. And then it was likely that they would need to be back into quarantine before transporting them to Australia, and quarantine them here for three to six months. We were talking 2019 at best, and at what financial cost and impact on the rhinos' health themselves?

In my view, the first assumption is particularly relevant: why would the US or any other country or organisation "foster" the rhinos in the first place? Surely, if you went to the trouble and cost of moving rhinos out of South Africa, wouldn't you keep them? This was why we had rejected this option several years earlier, it was too risky.

There was silence. Then Mark Stanbridge spoke. He said that, in his view, it was all over and we should look at winding up the organisation. I wouldn't want this man at my side in a fight.

At that point I became quite emotional. As far as I was concerned, it was all over for me. My opinions, knowledge and efforts were of no value to this group of people. They seemed sick and tired of it all and were prepared to throw in the towel. I left the meeting with an ache in my heart and tears in my eyes.

"If you want a fight, we're up for it." Those were Allan's words to me when I refused to resign from the board.

And yet, a short three months earlier, he had written to me full of praise referring to what had been accomplished in the previous three years as "nothing short of miraculous". He listed some examples: the awareness of the plight of the rhinos was at an all-time high both locally and internationally; we had achieved DGR status; we had raised close to $1 million and still had "*close to $700k in the tin*", we had developed an organisation that was fit for purpose and very focused; the process of obtaining approvals to import rhinos was well underway; and he asked the rhetorical question, "*What other private organisation has done this with CITES administered animals recently? None.*" He added that corporate Australia were on side and we were well advanced with explaining our case, which put us in good shape for raising more funds once we had "*proved the concept*". He went on to say, "*A large part of this progress is entirely due to your enthusiasm and drive.*"

How could things go so terribly wrong in less than three months that the board would now be demanding my resignation?

I hadn't changed my behaviour or modus operandi. I did what I had done for the past forty months and that was to work like a slave to turn this vision into reality.

I'm pretty sure that my often-voiced frustration with Shaun and the Australian government irritated the board members who did not seem to share my sense of urgency. Since I started this venture, close to four thousand rhinos had been slaughtered and my steadfast belief was that we at TARP had to play our part, if only for the rhinos.

With the benefit of hindsight, the writing had probably been on the wall for most of 2016, as I was gradually squeezed out of any meaningful role, and so the above highly complimentary (and very much appreciated) note from Allan really surprised me.

It is in my nature to push hard to achieve a desired outcome. In humility, I attribute this characteristic to my career success. Ian Player's words rang in my ears, *"All bureaucracies are a nightmare and the only way to get anywhere is to keep on hammering on the door."*

Soon after, I circulated my thoughts on a revised board structure. I was uncomfortable with the existing structure mainly because the size of the board had shrunk to three directors plus me and also there were no women on the board. My proposal had barely seen the light of day when I was summonsed to a directors-only meeting. More than a little nervously, I attended the meeting, which was focused on me only. A new structure was tabled which removed me from any decision-making role. I was to report to Mark on matters of fundraising and to Paul on all media and communication matters.

I was told that I had less than a week to accept the role or they would wind up the project. Allan knew very well that taking that action was my absolute worst nightmare. I mentioned that I was having surgery on that date, not playing a sympathy card simply stating the fact, but all he wanted to know was when I would be out of hospital.

It was at this point that I decided that I could no longer fight this battle on my own and phoned Peter Scott for advice. Peter is one of the most highly respected businessmen in Australia and we have been friends for a long time. In an illustrious career, Peter had been CEO of MLC, Chairman of Perpetual and a director of Stockland and Transurban – all listed companies. Peter also chaired a not-for-profit, Igniting Change.

Peter was a breath of fresh air. He listened intently and then commented; he made no "judgement", just assessed everything that I said and sent to him. Out of respect for Peter's position and our friendship, I will limit much of the detail of our discussions, direction and counsel he provided as the board continued to hassle me for a response, despite me being in and out of hospital.

With Peter's comments under my belt, I went back to Allan saying that I had thoroughly reviewed and considered the new structure and I was not prepared to sign it in its current form. A few minutes later I received an email saying that my response was totally unacceptable.

I sent a copy of his note to Pod. In his direct fashion, Pod responded, *"Ray it's time to throw it in. This will kill you if you continue. You so deserved a better outcome."*

I told Pod that the project had taken over my life and that I couldn't let it go and would fight on. In retrospect, probably not a very smart comment.

I was then summoned to yet another director-only meeting with Allan warning me that the future of TARP was now dependent on how my refusal to resign was resolved. Once again, he was playing the ace, knowing that I would do pretty much anything to save the project. We had come so far and I still felt that a successful result was in sight.

Given the threat to dissolve the project, I made it clear that I had no desire to resign, did not believe that it was not in the interests of the project, and looked forward to working with them to resolve any issues. As advised by Peter, I tried very hard to take a positive approach, the "high ground" as Peter put it. Despite all of the grief and hurt, I could not bear to divorce myself from the project. It felt so surreal, was this really happening to me?

The meeting was short and sharp. Without giving any specific reasons, I was told that the directors had lost confidence in me and wanted me to resign from the board forthwith. For me, it was now or never to say my piece. I questioned the practicality of Mark directing fundraising, given how busy he was.

I also questioned the feasibility of phoning Paul before I had any contact with the media by using a real-life example. Let's say that David Barr from East Coast Radio phoned me (which he regularly did) and asked me for my view on, say, the burning of the elephant tusks in Nairobi. I would normally respond to his question and he would take it further, or not. Now, I would have to say to David, *"Sorry mate, I'll just need to check with one of our directors before I get back to you."* Utter nonsense. I would never get another call and the project's very positive image with the media would soon evaporate. The meeting concluded with the formal demand that I immediately resign.

There was a short conference call during the week between the four of us. I was at home and was using Skype so the call was on speaker phone. There was some fairly strong language; my wife heard the comments and left the room in tears.

Coincidentally, in the same week, our project was recognised in a Tumblr post entitled, "Good things that have happened in 2016." Alongside some very significant events such as new chemotherapy breakthroughs that had increased the five-year survival for pancreatic cancer from 16 per cent to 27 per cent and Michael Jordan donating $2 million to try and help bridge the connection between police and the community, there was a one-liner that said, *"A retiree is launching a project to transport 80 endangered rhinos to an Australian reservation to save the animals from poaching."* I circulated this, as I always did, thinking that it was really good news and publicity for the project.

Well, I got that wrong too. A sharp email from Mark read, *"We are close to done on this project. Why are we lauding this?"* Adding, *"Seriously. Get a grip about our dire situation."*

Get a grip? We were both directors of The Australian Rhino Project. I don't talk to my dog like that.

Earlier in 2016, I wrote to Pod saying that while my family agreed that success in this venture was paramount, they were as one that the way the board was treating me was totally unacceptable. I wrote, *"Perhaps because I'm so old they are also concerned about the effect of all this on my health. I might be extinct before the rhinos."*

November 25, 2016 will go down as one of the unhappiest days of my life. The three not so wise men finally got me. The pressure the directors had put on me paid off and I tendered my resignation. My resignation letter was simple. It read, *"I am resigning from the board with immediate effect. For the sake of the rhinos, my hope is that The Australian Rhino Project goes from strength to strength."*

This was not a decision taken lightly or in isolation. Peter Scott and Pod McLoughlin, both of whom I respect greatly, advised me to get out. My family encouraged me to call it a day.

When I was planning the Sydney dinner, I had asked our three children and partners to come along since I knew it was going to be a special night. Kevin, Rebecca, Hayley and Jeremy attended but Paul refused. I was surprised and also deeply hurt as I wanted the whole family to be there. When I asked Paul why he said, *"Dad, I am not going to support something which is killing you. They will suck you dry and then spit you out."*

There was truth in this statement. I was working day in and day out and my health had suffered. I had been in and out of hospital in 2015 and 2016 and, as my physician put it, I had twice dodged a bullet. However, I want to be absolutely clear that my resignation was not due to health reasons and was not voluntary.

Now I had to let my friends, my supporters, sponsors and donors know that I had resigned. In many ways I felt I had let them down and I hated it.

I received letter after letter of support. Everyone was incredibly kind and supportive. Among the many kind messages were:

From Dr Roy Bengis, *"Your letter came as an unexpected unpleasant surprise to me. It was such a worthwhile project. It was a pleasure working with you."*

From a man who I admire immensely, General Johan Jooste, *"Thank you for the difference you have made. It may not have ended the way you envisioned, but your good work will contribute to the final solution."*

From the Australian High Commissioner to South Africa, *"We were sad to see the news of your departure from the board as we all knew how much the project meant to you."*

From Adrian Gardiner, almost like a brother to Ian Player, *"You know how grateful we all are in SA and especially myself and the late Ian for all you tried to do. A sad day indeed, however take consolation on the following words. 'I learned the truth – that the greatest hurt comes not from your enemies but from the silence of those you considered were your friends!'"*

From Phil Loader, a Vice President with Woodside Energy, *"It was your vision that established it."*

From Janine Kirk, who runs Prince Charles' charities in Australia, *"I am so very sorry to learn you have stepped down, I know how passionate you are about saving rhinos. We both shared the experience of a 'social good start-up' so I know how much of yourself – mentally, emotionally and even physically you have to put into turning a vision and passion into a reality. It is not much comfort I know, but you have earned a great deal of personal respect for your passion and dedication, and for also raising the awareness in Australia for the plight of the rhino. Your work will continue."*

From Dr Jill Millan of the Australian Department of Agriculture, who was there from day one, *"Your drive, vision and passion for the project has been truly remarkable. Your foresight to understand and appreciate the many hurdles (aka brick walls) seemed to only increase your determination."*

From Dame Jane Goodall, *"I am so sorry to hear this news. Unfortunately, our world is filled with egos. People start working together, and suddenly things go wrong. I know this only too well and can read between the lines."*

Reading them was like reading my own obituaries but I deeply treasured these comments from these and other very special people.

THE MUSCLES FROM BRUSSELS

Throughout the four years I led The Australian Rhino Project, I would always go out of my way to meet and assist anyone who was involved in the conservation of endangered species – though with, obviously a preference for rhinos. Examples included Jake Burgess of the new Sydney Zoo, Leanne Elliott of Cheetah Outreach, Margaret McBride of White Leeds, Damien Mander of the International Anti-Poaching Federation, David Ritter of Greenpeace, Dr Graeme Brown with the orphanage at Rhino Revolution. And there were more.

So, when I was approached from two different directions to assist a "very well known global personality", I was happy to oblige. The first contact was in September 2016 from Alex Fieri, a property developer from the Gold Coast, who said that this global personality wanted to create a wildlife sanctuary in

Australia, he had heard about my work with TARP and would I be prepared to talk to him? All very secretive. I responded that it would be a pleasure. At about the same time I had a call from a Yolantha Morrigan from Melbourne who asked if I could assist her in developing a plan for "someone very famous" who wanted to do something with endangered species in Australia. All very mysterious. Both Alex and Yolantha were talking about Jean Claude van Damme although neither knew that the other had contacted me. My excitement level was high, thinking that Jean Claude might be able to fund the sanctuary for the rhinos.

I had heard of him, but never having a jot of interest in martial arts, all Jean Claude was to me was a name. I didn't know what he looked like; I'd never seen any of his movies but, as I was to find out, he has one of the most recognised faces in the world and has an enormous global following.

On October 15, I had my first discussion with JC (as he prefers to be called, and referred to as JCVD). To say it was wide-ranging telephone conversation would be an understatement. It went every-where – from his friend Joseph Kabila, President of the Democratic Republic of the Congo, to his desire to buy land in Australia for the wildlife sanctuary, to an Australian Martial Arts Academy. What was glaringly clear was his passion for saving animals.

I had ongoing discussions with JC. He was set on buying some land in Australia for the sanctuary and I cautioned him that this was a step that should be considered much further down the track. I suggested potential locations such as White Leeds at Broken Hill, Yeeda in Western Australia, and Goyd Park in Queensland. I told him how tough a road it was/is to obtain the Australian gov-ernment approval to import rhinos into Australia, so buying land was premature. On November 14, at JC's request, I met with Max Markson. Again, I had heard of Max and had always thought that the name of his company, Markson Sparks, was very clever.

Ten days after I resigned, I had yet another call from JC and I decided to assist him wherever I could. I did not take this decision lightly. My heart was breaking but equally I had little confidence that the remaining directors would be able to deliver on my vision, let alone my strategy. If I could find someone with an international profile and who was wealthy, like Jean Claude van Damme, to fund the whole process and assist in getting the rhinos, or any other endangered species, into Australia as quickly as possible, I would give that person or organisation all the support I could.

I made it clear to JC and Max that I did not want to feature in any form of promotion or publicity but would happily assist in the background. I thought this was only fair to those involved with TARP. I did the same with every meeting I arranged for JC. As an example, when I wrote to Diana Hallam, Chief of Staff to the Deputy Prime Minister, Barnaby Joyce, I asked. *"Once again, Diana, please can I stress that this has absolutely nothing to do with The Australian Rhino Project."*

I suppose these things happen, but some really nasty things seem to have been said about me to people who I really cared about and considered friends. When I contacted them, one put the phone down on me and the other two did not return my phone calls. This hurt me deeply, I wondered how these people, who all knew me well, whom I really liked and for whom I had deep respect, could believe I would change into such a pariah.

By and large the media who followed JC on his whirlwind trip around the east coast of Australia honoured my request for anonymity, including James Jeffrey, the editor of *Strewth*, who wrote about JC's meeting with Senator Dastyari and other senators in *The Australian* newspaper. *"A man with a touching eagerness to not have his name in print spoke of a fenceless system of microchips and tags."* That was me.

After the heartache and stress of the past six months, the "Muscles from Brussels" caravan was a lot of fun and restored my faith in humanity. Through my contacts built over the past twenty years, I was able to arrange a number of appointments with those politicians who, in my view, could assist JC to realise his dream.

JC flew into Melbourne from Los Angeles accompanied by Irishman Jim Bennett, who had worked with JC for 25 years. An actor in his own right, Jim is built like a piece of granite and, apart from his friendship with JC, he also acts as his bodyguard, road manager, the lot. Jim was the man that you wanted at your shoulder in any type of situation.

Meeting Jean Claude van Damme for the first time was quite something. He is a lot smaller than I expected, but without an ounce of fat on his lean torso. Bright eyes with a twinkle and a ready smile. I was impressed.

The next week gave me an insight into how the rich and famous live. JC had a mountain of luggage which proved to be no challenge for the Qantas concierge assigned to assist with his passage through airport formalities. As we walked through Melbourne Airport, a surprisingly large number of people stopped JC and asked for photos or selfies. Without exception, JC obliged with a big smile on his face.

Our first Melbourne stop was to meet Raphael Geminder, universally known as Ruffy, South African by birth and married to Fiona, one of Richard Pratt's daughters. The Pratt family is one of the wealthiest in Australia and Ruffy has made his own way, being extraordinarily successful.

I had met Ruffy before and he kindly agreed to meet with JC. It was a fascinating discussion. JC apologised for not having had time to change out of his jeans and Ruffy was his usual polite and engaging self. Opening the conversation, he mentioned that he too had just flown in that morning – from Sydney. The previous night he had dinner with *"Bill and Melinda"* and *"Twiggy, his brother-in-law Anthony and Gina had all been present"*. The combined wealth at that table with Gates, Geminder, Anthony Pratt, Twiggy Forrest and Gina Rinehart would probably have exceeded the GDP of several countries. Ruffy reiterated his support for assisting us once government approvals were confirmed.

After the meeting, we left for Canberra and I prepared a brief for the politicians and bureaucrats outlining Jean Claude's plans for the wildlife sanctuary. The brief highlighted that he had strong views about protecting the world's wildlife and he had noted, with increasing concern, how the pressure of people was squeezing wildlife areas. He had now decided that it was time for action and he wanted to move fast to play his part to establish a wildlife sanctuary in Australia which would be a fortress protecting some of the world's most endangered species. He was convinced that Australia was one of the safest places on the planet for threatened and endangered wildlife. His plan was to acquire a suitable, large tract of land in Australia and, over time, introduce both native and exotic (non-Australian) species to the sanctuary. To ensure the survival of these species all feral animals would be removed from the sanctuary. The property would have sufficient water and irrigation to support the animals and would be completely fenced. Expert advice would be sought with regard to the location of animals to maximise breeding programs as well as ensuring genetic diversity. The goals included making this a world-class tourist attraction including the establishment of a lodge which would match the best in Africa.

It was a bold plan and Jean Claude fully understood that it was likely to be a long and costly campaign. It was his vision that this sanctuary would be a beacon of hope for the endangered species of the world and a model, which could be replicated, to ensure that animals, insects, reptiles and wildlife could live in peace and harmony for future generations.

The following day gave me a glimpse into some of the problems we were to face travelling with this global superstar.

JC was staying at the Jamala Wildlife Lodge in Canberra while I stayed in the CBD. As I have made clear on a number of occasions, I am not a zoo person, but Richard and Maureen Tindale have built a masterpiece in Jamala Lodge. It is as authentic an exclusive African-type lodge as you can find.

We had a full schedule at Parliament House and, as agreed, I was at Jamala bright and early to brief JC, but there was no JC. I was to learn that he is not a morning person. He goes to bed around 3am or 4am and rises at around noon. This has nothing to do with jetlag, it is his sleep pattern wherever he is in the world. By contrast, I am a stickler for punctuality. Eventually, Jim managed to get JC to breakfast – this did not take long, he doesn't eat much – and then off to Parliament House.

Our first meeting was with the, then, Minister for the Environment, Josh Frydenberg. The meeting was on the Thursday before parliament rose for the Christmas break and there were Christmas trees, party lights and streamers wherever you looked. We entered Minister Frydenberg's office which was overflowing with his staff and the media – all of whom wanted to meet Jean Claude van Damme. Josh was so excited – he is a big fan and there was much joking and teasing. The media wanted some photos and Jean Claude duly obliged. The press was satisfied and off they went.

Jean Claude van Damme sparring with Federal Minister of the Environment, Josh Frydenberg. (Photo Credit: Cole Bennetts)

After they left there was more posing and more punches "thrown". Josh then asked for a real action shot and, without warning, Jean Claude kicked. Bearing in mind that he was wearing a fairly tight-fitting suit, the kick whistled past Josh's head. There was a gasp from those present. Josh went white.

Vikki Campion, with whom I had formed a good working relationship when she was attached to NSW Minister Troy Grant's office, had kindly arranged for us to see Deputy Prime Minister Barnaby Joyce. We were due to see him next and, as we were making our way down the corridors, my phone rang – it was Josh saying that the press had heard about the kick and could we please return for another photo opportunity? After the Barnaby Joyce meeting, we returned to Josh's office and the photographers were all pretty excited. *"Ready?"* asked Jean Claude and then kicked. It was so quick that none of the photographers got the shot and JC had to repeat it, with ripples of nervous laughter. The photograph received nationwide coverage.

Our meeting with Barnaby who carried the agriculture portfolio, was a hoot. Jean Claude has a very strong French/Belgian accent and English is obviously his second language. He is the first to admit that he is not very good with names and, as an example, he calls every woman he meets *"lady"*. Always very politely; it is just easier for him.

He asked me how he should address Barnaby, I said just use "Minister", he will be fine with that. Well, we walked into the boardroom where Barnaby was lunching with his National Party colleagues. (It looked like a lovely lunch – cold meats and salads – we were all starving but weren't invited to join!)

Barnaby Joyce is a fairly gruff individual and it looked as if he didn't enjoy his lunch being interrupted. The opening conversation went something like this:

"Good afternoon Mr Barnaby."

"Joyce."

"Good afternoon Joyce."

"My name is Barnaby Joyce."

"My apologies, Mr Barnaby."

By this time, Vikki and Diana Hallam, Barnaby's Chief of Staff, and I were in stitches. Not so Barnaby Joyce. *"How can I help you, Mr van Damme?"* to which Jean Claude responded, *"Please call me Jean Claude or JC."* Diana and I looked at each other and I'm sure she was thinking what I was thinking: let's not start that again.

After a while JC's charm softened Barnaby and he committed his department to assist with the establishment of the sanctuary if all the biosecurity requirements were met. Only I knew what that meant and, inwardly, I rolled my eyes.

Jean Claude demonstrating the deadly kick with Josh Frydenberg. (Photo Credit: Cole Bennetts)

We then met several senators at a presentation arranged by Senator Sam Dastyari who seemed genuinely pleased that Jean Claude was only marginally taller than himself. Senator Sarah Hanson-Young of the Greens Party was also present, so it seemed that we had covered all political party bases.

JC then joined an unscheduled press conference with Senator Pauline Hanson, leader of the right wing One Nation Party. We had a good conversation and despite the often extremely negative comments about her in the media, we found her to be polite, articulate and very politically astute.

Our final meeting at Parliament House was with the Minister of Health, Sussan Ley, whom we met because JC was keen on setting up a martial arts academy focused on underprivileged youngsters. This was another side to the man that was somewhat unexpected. He had some personal challenges with drugs in his past, as well as a bipolar disorder, and had deep concerns that today's youth were not exposed to exercise as an outlet for their energy and frustrations.

Sussan's reaction was really positive and assured Jean Claude that the federal government would support the establishment of any such an academy. She suggested that the focus of such a venture should be widened to include the Indigenous youth in Australia who had particularly serious issues with illicit drugs and alcohol.

As we left Parliament House, everyone agreed that it had been a good, productive day.

I had carefully planned the next day. JC was fixated on buying land for the sanctuary and I was equally certain that it was premature. Consequently, I had arranged for us to fly to Broken Hill to view the White Leeds property owned by Steve Radford and his wife Margaret McBride which covers an area of approximately 25,000 acres, all of which is gazetted as a wildlife refuge.

My vision was a "hub and spoke" model where there would be species-specific sanctuaries scattered across Australia housing animals that were more suited to different habitats than what White Leeds might offer, as an example, primates in tropical North Queensland with its rainforests. I thought that White Leeds would be an ideal "hub" for JC's endangered species sanctuary.

Steve Radford had arranged for one of his planes to collect us from Canberra and fly to Broken Hill. It was all arranged and we were due to depart Canberra at 10.30am. I was getting more used to JC's odd sleeping patterns and I thought that a 10.30am start would work well. How wrong I was. Jim was still trying to wake him up at 11am! We finally left Canberra after 12pm in a very comfortable Beechcraft King Air and arrived at White Leeds to a sumptuous lunch. Apart from anything else Steve and Marg are excellent hosts. After lunch we were driven around their magnificent property. They have spent a fortune on creating an oasis in the parched Broken Hill region using recycled water. Their enthusiasm for being the pilot program for Jean Claude's plans was extraordinary. Knowing the difficulties involved, I tried very hard to steer the conversation away from rhinos and pushed them to consider all endangered species.

Steve informed JC that he was prepared to gift the land for the sanctuary – an astonishing offer. JC was deeply moved. He read Steve and Marg perfectly and clearly articulated what he was trying to achieve assuring them that, as far as he was concerned, White Leeds was, by far and away, the best possible location.

As an example of the kindness of this tough global superstar, I was really struggling with my ankle, which was later surgically fused, and I couldn't walk very well. At one point I thought I was going to pass out because of the pain and sat down. JC was first to my side, offering assistance.

Later that night, when we flew into Sydney's Bankstown airport, I was given another glimpse into this man's life. Now that we were in the city, there were bodyguards everywhere. All large, serious looking men, dressed in black and probably armed. I needed a cold beer.

On the Sunday, I had a call from Jim saying that JC wanted me to join him on the Gold Coast to attend the meetings with the Queensland politicians; apparently, he really liked my "style" with them. I think he also appreciated that I would write thank you letters, on his behalf, within twenty-four hours of the meetings.

I joined them at the five-star Marriott Hotel at Surfers Paradise. JC was happily ensconced in the Presidential Penthouse suite. It was extraordinary accommodation. I have been lucky enough to stay in some wonderful hotels around the world, but nothing could match this. Beautifully furnished with every amenity that you could hope for, a personal butler, everything available at the end of the phone line. JC is not a demanding type of person but he is clearly accustomed to such luxury and took it in his stride.

During his stay on the Gold Coast, Jean Claude did a martial arts clinic for a local academy. It immediately became clear why he is so popular. He was completely at home with the group, smiling all the while as he explained and demonstrated his moves. He then posed for any number of photographs with the youngsters. The kids (and their mums and dads) loved it.

We then travelled to Brisbane and met Minister for Tourism and Major Events, Kate Jones, and JC won yet another heart. I prepared a brief on the Jean Claude van Damme Gold Coast Martial Arts Academy proposal (quite a mouthful) which was as a result of a meeting that Jean Claude had with Gold Coast Mayor,

Tom Tate. The proposal described his passion for working with young people to give them a goal in life and, in some cases, give them hope. The envisaged target group would include Indigenous and also under-privileged children. His success in life had come about through his athleticism and his unrelenting focus on "*being the best that he can be*" and he now wanted to "*give something back*". He wanted to establish the first JCVD Martial Arts Academy in Surfers Paradise on the Gold Coast. Like many other major cities around the world, the Gold Coast has its share of crime and juvenile issues.

Jean Claude's vision was that this academy would become a beacon of hope and excellence in one of the fastest growing regions in Australia. He believed strongly in discipline and there would be strict adherence to the "rules" in the academy. Trainers would be closely vetted before being employed. Obesity – particularly amongst the young – is a global cause for concern and Jean Claude is passionate about the need to address the issue. Minister Jones was very impressed with the academy concept and offered to assist wherever possible as she could see the benefits of such an innovative venture.

We then went our separate ways with the plan to meet up on Friday with NSW members of parliament. These were important meetings for me since I had previously briefed Environment Minister Mark Speakman and his predecessor Rob Stokes about TARP and they had been extremely supportive. I had developed a strong personal relationship with Bran Black who was Mark's Chief of Staff. Mark Speakman, in particular, was out of the top drawer and it would not surprise me if he were to be seen in a leadership role in the future.

The NSW government boardroom was overflowing. Mark Speakman chaired the meeting which was different from all of the others. These people were serious about creating an endangered species sanctuary in NSW and asked some probing questions, raised some realistic issues and made some valuable observations and suggestions. It was a good meeting in that Jean Claude heard from people who weren't star-struck but knew what they were talking about and the complexities and benefits of what was involved in making his dream come true.

I had worked really hard to secure all of these meetings and used every bit of personal capital that I had built up over the years to make them happen. I considered many of these politicians and their staff as friends. I trusted them and they trusted me.

In all the time that I spent with him, JC never disappointed. In his own way, he is a deeply spiritual man. He cares deeply about the environment and the future of the planet although he may not articulate this as well as a David Attenborough.

That weekend JC and Jim left Australia for a number of appearances in Asia. JC had done an excellent job in raising awareness in Australia about the critically endangered species and the challenges that faced those who were trying to do something about it. He was very well received by all the politicians and decision makers that we had met and Max Markson had arranged some very positive publicity for him.

From my point of view, I was really pleased with what I had done to ensure that Jean Claude saw all the "right" people. I had spent an exhilarating two weeks with a global superstar, while my heart was aching. There was never a dull moment and he really is a man of action. Did we progress the chances of getting endangered species to Australia? I believe so, but only the passage of time will tell. JC makes at least one movie a year and he has his hands full with that. I pray that the fire continues to burn within him.

THERE IS HOPE

"*We must accept finite disappointment, but we must never lose infinite hope.*" *Martin Luther King Jr*

I genuinely believe there is hope for rhinos. While the lack of political will, of funding, of focused education of the communities and overwhelming corruption are exposed as undeniable causes of the rhino disaster, there are definitely some green shoots.

Organisations like the San Francisco company, Pembient, believes its plan to bioengineer fake rhino horn will curb the seemingly insatiable demand for wild rhino horn. Their plan is to create fake horn which artists could carve into lifestyle items such as jewellery, libation cups and chopsticks. The merchandise would then be sold in China and southeast Asia, where demand for rhino horn fuels rampant poaching.

Pembient hopes that synthetic horn – priced at about one-eighth of the reported $65,000 per kilogram that genuine horn commands on the black market – will flood the market. Prices for the real thing would fall, goes the argument, curbing the economic incentive for poachers, and help save rhinos.

Many conservationists have attacked Pembient's plan, asserting that fake rhino horn won't solve the poaching problem and could even make it worse, saying that rhino horn powder-infused products could open more markets for illicit horn. Pembient is now shifting its emphasis away from synthetic powder because the company has, *"Gotten a lot of pushback. The carving process and the durable goods market seems very interesting to us because it's been around for such a long time and it's something that people maybe understand a little bit better."*

The international crime syndicates reacted quickly to this perceived threat in their own ruthless fashion by insisting that the poachers prove that the rhinos were wild caught by cutting off an ear during the gory kill.

Taking a different approach is Craig Spencer, one of my favourite people, the founder of the all-female anti-poaching unit, the Black Mambas, at the Balule Game Reserve, which borders Kruger and is a hotspot for poaching. Craig is a highly excitable and passionate advocate for conservation and is applying lateral thinking to the onslaught, which has reduced the rhino population within Balule by nearly 70 per cent since 2012. Because the poachers go for the big bulls, family groups have been severely compromised and sex ratios skewed, leading to a dire situation for the natural prosperity of the rhinos.

The Mambas work long days on foot patrol, looking for animal traps and signs of poachers entering the park so they can find them before they kill any rhinos. The teams work to the "broken window" philosophy, striving to make their area of influence the most undesirable, most difficult and least profitable place to poach any species.

The objectives of the Black Mambas include being a powerful voice in their communities. They work to address the social and moral decay, a product of the rhino poaching that has brought loose morals and narcotics into their communities. These young women want their communities to understand that the benefits gained through rhino conservation are greater than poaching.

Craig has also initiated the Bush Babies Environmental Education Program, a community-based project which is driving a conservation philosophy within the communities surrounding the protected areas by targeting future leaders. As part of this program, the Mambas visit the twelve local primary schools and talk about animals, the importance of tourism in creating employment and why animals are worth more alive than dead. They also take children and the elderly into the Kruger Park, showing them wild animals that most have never seen. My wife Margie and I have spent a lot of time with Craig and the Mambas and we recently donated R85,000 from the proceeds of sales of my book of poems, *For the Rhino,* to upgrade the Bush Babies Bus.

Another project that excites me and in which I am involved is the Wildlife Protection Program (WPP), a pro-active system which utilises a breakthrough technology to alert reserve security operations well before any at-risk animals, such as rhinos, are in danger. In my view, there needs to be a change in mindset from "fighting the poachers" to "protecting the rhinos".

The WPP system uses sentinel animals, such as impala, zebra and wildebeest which are skittish by nature but are not poaching targets, fitted with sensors. The animals' movement patterns and other data are recorded and transmitted to a cognitive computing platform via a secure network. Predictive algorithms, developed by Wageningen University, analyse the sentinel-animal data and alert security operations of poacher threats. This system is based on an Internet of Things design and was developed in partnership between Welgevonden Game Reserve, the multinational Cisco, Dimension Data, enChoice, a visionary US-based software company owned by good friend Tony White, IBM and the Dutch Wageningen University. It is a powerful syndicate. It is early days, but the pilot phase has just been completed with excellent results. This system could well be a game-changer in protecting rhinos and other endangered species and I hope that I can make a contribution to its success.

When suspected poacher Joseph "Big Joe" Nyalunga was stopped by police, it appeared they were too late. Investigators found bags that they suspected had held rhino horn, but were empty – the horn had already been passed on to the next link in the poaching chain. Investigators hoped there might still be clues left in the bags, so they sent them to the Veterinary Genetics Laboratory at the University of Pretoria. *"In those bags there was only dust,"* explains Dr Cindy Harper, but Cindy and her colleagues were able to tease DNA from the dust and link it to two dead rhinos found poached in the Kruger Park in previous weeks. The "dust case" was one of more than 5,800 forensic investigations that involved the use of the Rhino DNA Index System or RhODIS, and it is this crime-fighting tool that is offering renewed hope in bringing the poachers to justice.

Since RhODIS was set up by Cindy, it has been used in more than 120 cases where rhino carcasses were linked to either recovered horn or blood-stained objects used in the commission of the crime. Evidence taken at crime scenes or seized at airports is compared to the DNA profiles of thousands of individual rhinos. There are now more than 50,000 rhino items in RhODIS and Cindy is receiving cooperation throughout Africa in keeping the database current and relevant.

My view has always been that the poaching war will not be resolved through the barrel of a gun. Without the involvement and the buy-in of the communities in and around wildlife areas, endangered species have next to no chance of survival. For this reason, I am very happy to be supporting Adrian Gardiner and Di Luden of the Community Conservation Fund Africa (CCFA) born out of the merger between the Mantis and Accor Hotel groups, since it approaches the poaching crisis from a completely different point of view. These two global hospitality groups have recognised the urgent need for community upliftment, which will benefit Africa's wild animals and wilderness at a time when both are under threat. CCFA was established to help put the spotlight on rural African communities that live among the wild animals but by and large have received few benefits from the tourist boom associated with the Big Five and other wildlife.

CCFA is both a fund-raising and a grant-giving organisation active in educating and empowering local communities to implement sustainable wildlife management systems on the ground. Such solutions are funded by CCFA whose mission is to address these inequalities and investigate ways of giving rural African communities a greater role in wildlife tourism, ownership and management. An excellent working example is Ombonde People's Park, located in Namibia, home to desert-adapted elephant, black rhino, giraffe, lion and cheetah, all vulnerable or threatened. This project builds on and enhances community ownership of wildlife and natural resources and will be a genuine partnership between communal conservancies and the government. Wherever possible, CCFA aims to be the catalyst in creating awareness and involving communities in conservation.

There has not been one day since May 2013 when my dream of establishing a breeding herd of rhinos in Australia did not occupy my mind. It was always going to be a tough and complex journey and for that reason, I assembled a world-class team of experts to make it happen, including South African vets Pete Morkel, Pete Rogers, Will Fowlds, Charles van Niekerk, Markus Hofmeyr and Roy Bengis, and in Australia we had access to Dr Benn Bryant. These men are the best in their field of wild animal care.

Dame Jane Goodall introduced me to the Wildlife Conservation Network (WCN). This is an extraordinary US-based not-for-profit. WCN protects endangered wildlife by supporting conservationists who ensure wildlife and people co-exist and thrive. Over the past decade, WCN has raised an extraordinary amount of money for endangered wildlife. Paul Thomson leads a remarkable group of people who have dedicated their lives to conservation. I was extremely proud when I was asked to be a Strategic Adviser for the WCN Rhino Recovery Fund.

There are others who made a significant contribution and where the fire of passion for such a project still burns and I owe them thanks. They too are beacons of hope.

I have the utmost admiration for His Excellency, Adam McCarthy, Australian High Commissioner to South Africa. He does a tough job with dignity and calm. He was always straight down the line with me, even when the news he was delivering was not good.

Minister Greg Hunt is one of the most professional, efficient and hard-working politicians I have ever met. He contributed greatly to the project.

In 2016, the Australian national census was an absolute disaster with the website crashing on launch night. There is now some poor civil servant in Canberra who has "CENSUS" etched on his forehead and he has probably sought an alternative career. I always felt that the AUSDAFF bureaucrats who were assigned to our project were terrified that something would go so wrong that he or she would similarly be blamed and have "RHINOS" tattooed on their foreheads. They were completely risk averse.

Mind you, AUSDAFF were not the only ones who were risk averse. Friend David Marquard, a partner at EY, the global consulting firm, offered to do a risk management review of TARP, questioning what would happen if, as an example, I was knocked over by the proverbial bus or the South African authorities terminated all exports of rhinos, or, or, or . . .

I was excited, thinking that this was timely and sorely needed in our organisation. I put it to the board more or less as a fait accompli, saying that David had briefed Heidi Riddell, who headed up EY's risk practice and, as a South African, she was keen to develop a risk management plan for us, pro bono. To my astonishment, the board said no.

The safest place in the world for a rhinoceros to roam free is

Eswatini, until recently Swaziland, an African kingdom. Anyone daring to kill a rhino for its horn in this country, or any other protected wildlife, is likely to be shot by rangers or jailed for a minimum of five years. They would also have to pay for replacing the animal, or face a further two years in prison. As a result, only three rhinos have been killed by poachers in 26 years. This is the number that are butchered in South Africa every day.

This remarkable success story is due to Ted Reilly, the farmer son of a British horse soldier in the Anglo–Boer War, with the support of King Mswati III and the approval of the Queen Mother. Between them, they have transformed a tiny country from a slaughterhouse of wildlife to a sanctuary where animals roam free of human predators and are content to share their domain with visitors; proving that with political will, the battle against poachers is winnable. But, as the great Groucho Marx said, "*Politics is the art of looking for trouble, finding it everywhere, diagnosing it incorrectly and applying the wrong remedies.*" A reasonably accurate description of most countries involved in the decimating of the rhino population.

Gary Edstein has been a friend for a long time. He is Vice President of the global logistics firm DHL. Gary is passionate about sport, but as a man with a very big heart, he is very conscious of his and DHL's role in the community. The cost of moving our rhinos from South Africa to Australia was always going to be a big-ticket item and Gary was one of the first people I spoke to when I started. I asked if DHL could move the animals and, if so, at what approximate cost. I even did a mock-up of a rhino and its baby on a DHL aircraft.

A mocked-up DHL airplane with rhinos

Gary and his deputy, Mark Foy, took a hard look at my request but unfortunately DHL do not fly direct from Johannesburg to Australia. I was fine with that since I knew that if Gary and Mark could help, they would.

About a year later, I picked up a story that DHL had moved a black rhino from the Czech Republic to Tanzania. Somewhat triumphantly, I gave Gary a call. He laughed and said, *"You never give up, do you? Send me the details."*

DHL had used a specially modified aircraft for the flight, during which Eliska the rhino was accompanied and monitored by a team of support staff, including my old mate, vet Pete Morkel. Gary related how this came to pass. DHL Express Global CEO Ken Allen was in his London office when the phone rang.

"Good morning, is that Mr Allen?"

"Yes, who is calling?"

"Mr Allen, it's Prince Harry."

"Oh really, nice try mate, pull the other leg. I'm really busy, who is it?"

"It's Prince Harry, Mr Allen. I want to talk to you about moving a rhino to Africa."

Ken, to himself, *"Oh God!"* then to Prince Harry, *"Of course, Prince Harry. How can I help?"*

Who could resist such a call from Prince Harry?

I didn't even have to ask as Gary said he would see what he could do and, a few months later, he invited me to a meeting at the Westin Hotel with some visiting senior international DHL executives. After an emotional hour discussing the catastrophic situation that Africa's rhinos found themselves in, we all shook hands with DHL agreeing to transport the rhinos from South Africa to Australia. At no cost. All we had to do was to secure the approval of both governments and it would be done.

As I left the meeting, in a highly emotional state, I faced a huge dilemma – what was I to do with this coup? By now, I had a strong feeling that my time at TARP was coming to an end. I didn't know how the board would react to this news and I feared there was a strong possibility I would not be believed and someone would call Gary to confirm, just as they had done with Susan Hunt of WAZA. This would destroy the relationship. I was not willing to take that chance and my intuition was to keep the information to myself until the time was right. That time never came. So sad and such a waste.

Shortly after this meeting with DHL, I contacted Raphael Geminder, a former South African and one of Australia's wealthiest men. Demonstrating the power of LinkedIn, I was able to arrange a meeting in Melbourne with him. As charming a man as you will ever meet, he was absolutely still as I told him of my plans to bring rhinos to Australia. Such silence can be quite disarming;

however, Ruffy was listening intently. When I was finished, he asked me what my major issues were. I said they were gaining the Australian government's approval and also fundraising. He said that he could not help with the first one, other than introducing me to certain politicians, if that would help, but surely that was purely a question of managing risk? Amen.

With regard to fundraising, his words, which I will not forget, were, *"Ray, you get the government approvals and leave the rest to me."*

I stumbled out of Ruffy's Melbourne office, tears welling in my eyes. So, here's the thing. I had now secured both funding and transport for the first batch of rhinos. At no cost.

I reported back to the board about my meeting with Ruffy, expecting, at least a drum roll or muffled cheer. Nothing. Absolutely nothing. In my IT sales days, when we won a big deal, we would ring the bell. Not here – the silence was deafening.

I left The Australian Rhino Project with a heavy heart and a hole in my soul, but was confident the building blocks were in place for the new team to deliver the rhinos to Australia's shores. Our governance was impeccable, tax deductibility for donations was in place for Australia, South Africa, the US and the UK. We had approximately $750,000 in the bank – more than sufficient financial cover for the first batch of rhinos with Allan Davies generously continuing to support the project financially. We had identified multiple sources for rhinos; a world-class quarantine facility in South Africa; the South African government had been provided with all of the required documentation and approvals; the Australian Department of Foreign Affairs and Trade were briefed and supportive; the cost of transportation of rhinos from South Africa to Australia had been covered by DHL. At no cost.

A generous donor had underwritten all costs of importation; we had a strong and vocal supporter base and active and sympathetic allies in the media. Three strong possible destinations for the rhinos were locked in. Each was quite prepared to do whatever was required to be classified as a zoo – a prerequisite for locating rhinos on their properties – all at no cost.

This last point was so important to me. Never ever did I intend to take rhinos out of the wilds of Africa and place them in a zoo – irrespective of the capacity of that zoo. The owners of each of the above properties were in complete agreement – their plans were to replicate the "free-range" environment for the rhinos. This was also critical – if we were to repatriate the rhinos to Africa in the fullness of time, they needed to be "wild", not tame.

So, when all is said and done, it will all come back to the Australian authorities and the challenges of dealing with government. I have the utmost respect for Australia's biosecurity laws and controls, and for the authorities who do their job. The foundations are in place for the TARP team to apply gentle, but sustained, pressure on the bureaucracy, who are quite content to play the waiting game. The easiest decision for government is a no decision, and they run the risk of missing being in the vanguard of one of the greatest conservation accomplishments of the century.

In the words of John F. Kennedy, *"Change is the law of life. And those who look only to the past or present are certain to miss the future."*

With time to reflect on my years with The Australian Rhino Project, it was a massive and complex endeavour. All the way through, I was driven by a number of factors – the world was running out of time to rescue the rhino species from possible extinction in the wild and I was utterly convinced we were doing the right thing by attempting the seemingly impossible. As Larry Ellison, founder of Oracle Corporation said, *"When you innovate, you have to be prepared for people telling you that you are nuts."* Very occasionally, I was told exactly that but I saw myself as a catalyst for creating a safe and secure crash of rhinos away from the danger zone.

The journey was a rollercoaster of emotion. There were times that my heart would soar and other times I would find myself in a very dark place. To the surprise of many, I am quite sensitive. Personal attacks strike deeply but the encouragement of people like my family and the inspirational, late Pod McLoughlin would always lift my spirits.

While some did, I never saw myself as an activist, in fact I thoroughly disliked the label. In my view our cause was just and as Dr Jane Goodall said, it was an idea whose time had come.

I absolutely loved what was achieved over the four years with The Australian Rhino Project. Despite some of the pain described above, each member of the board put his or her shoulder to the wheel and I do believe that we made a difference; I certainly hope so.

Until the day I die, I will believe that persistence and constant, constructive engagement will result in a crash of rhinos peacefully and safely breeding in a paddock in Australia, under the Southern Cross, far from the city lights. We owe this to the remaining rhinos on Earth.

After the crushing personal disappointment of leaving The Australian Rhino Project, I face the world with renewed hope for the rhinos and a certainty that Australia will play its part.

The author during the TED talk. (Photo Credit: Stuart Spence)

PROCEEDS FROM THIS BOOK GO TO THE BLACK MAMBA – ANTI-POACHING UNIT

Founded in 2013 to protect the Olifants West Region of Balule Nature Reserve the Black Mambas were invited to expand into other regions and now protect all boundaries of the 62,000 ha Balule Nature Reserve, part of the Greater Kruger National Park in South Africa.

The objectives of the Black Mamba project are not only the protection of rhinos through boots on the ground but also through being a role model in their communities. These 22 young women and 1 man want their communities to understand that the benefits are greater through rhino conservation rather than poaching, addressing the social and moral decay that is a product of the rhino poaching within their communities.

FOR MORE INFORMATION OR TO DONATE VISIT: WWW.BLACKMAMBAS.ORG